Natural Bodybuilding

Natural Bodybuilding

John Hansen

HUMAN KINETICS

Library of Congress Cataloging-in-Publication Data

Hansen, John.
Natural bodybuilding / John Hansen.
p. cm.
Includes index.
ISBN 0-7360-5346-8 (soft cover)
1. Bodybuilding. 2. Bodybuilding--Competitions. I. Title.
GV546.5.H37 2005
613.7'13--dc22 2004023782

ISBN: 0-7360-5346-8

The Web addresses cited in this text were current as of October 2004, unless otherwise noted.

Acquisitions Editor: Ed McNeely; **Developmental Editor:** Jennifer L. Walker; **Assistant Editors:** Mandy Maiden, Scott Hawkins; **Copyeditor:** Annette Pierce; **Proofreader:** Pam Johnson; **Indexer:** Dan Connolly; **Graphic Designer:** Robert Reuther; **Graphic Artist:** Kim McFarland; **Photo Manager:** Dan Wendt; **Photographer (interior):** Dan Wendt, unless otherwise noted. Photo on p. 13 © GMV Productions; pp. 1, 4, 7-12, 18, 113, 219 © Michael Neveux; pp. 21, 47, 60, 262, 279, 313 courtesy John Hansen; **Cover Designer:** Keith Blomberg; **Photographer (cover):** Dan Wendt; **Art Manager:** Kareema McLendon; **Printer:** United Graphics

We thank Diamond Gym in Orland Park, Illinois, for assistance in providing the location for the photo shoot for this book.

Human Kinetics books are available at special discounts for bulk purchase. Special editions or book excerpts can also be created to specification. For details, contact the Special Sales Manager at Human Kinetics.

Printed in the United States of America 10 9 8 7 6 5 4 3 2 1

Human Kinetics
Web site: www.HumanKinetics.com

United States: Human Kinetics
P.O. Box 5076
Champaign, IL 61825-5076
800-747-4457
e-mail: humank@hkusa.com

Canada: Human Kinetics
475 Devonshire Road Unit 100
Windsor, ON N8Y 2L5
800-465-7301 (in Canada only)
e-mail: orders@hkcanada.com

Europe: Human Kinetics
107 Bradford Road
Stanningley
Leeds LS28 6AT, United Kingdom
+44 (0) 113 255 5665
e-mail: hk@hkeurope.com

Australia: Human Kinetics
57A Price Avenue
Lower Mitcham, South Australia 5062
08 8277 1555
e-mail: liaw@hkaustralia.com

New Zealand: Human Kinetics
Division of Sports Distributors NZ Ltd.
P.O. Box 300 226 Albany
North Shore City
Auckland
0064 9 448 1207
e-mail: blairc@hknewz.com

This book is dedicated to my brother, Don Hansen.
Without his incredible support, encouragement, advice, and brutal honesty,
I would not have had a fraction of the success that I had in bodybuilding.
Thanks for being there for me, Don, you made the ride so much more fun
and rewarding. I share every victory in my career with you because,
without you, it would not have been possible.

Contents

Preface

I still remember that episode of *Starsky and Hutch* like it was yesterday. I was about 12 years old, and I never missed an episode about the coolest cops on TV. They had the car, the moves, the attitude, and they always, always caught the bad guys in the end.

This particular episode stuck in my mind, however. Starsky and Hutch encountered a drug dealer who was about to sic his hulking bodyguards on television's favorite supercops. The normally unshakable Starsky looked apprehensive about the impending battle with these muscular henchmen until his partner, Hutch, assured him that there was nothing to worry about. "Those guys just take pills to look like that," Hutch commented.

I was puzzled about that statement for days. What did he mean by that? How could someone develop massive muscles like the drug dealer's bodyguards by just popping pills? I finally decided to ask my father about it.

My dad knew as much about bodybuilding as I did at the time. However, displaying his proven values of common sense and experience, he had an answer for me. "I don't know much about it, but I'm sure that it takes years of hard work to look like that. You don't get muscles that big just by popping pills."

Years later, when I decided to start lifting weights and openly declared my intentions of one day becoming Mr. Universe, the issue of popping pills to build muscles raised its ugly head again. The pills were known as *steroids,* and it didn't take me long to figure out that many of the massive bodybuilders I admired in the magazines used them regularly to help attain their incredible physiques.

Fast-forward 25 years and steroid use is taken for granted in the sport of bodybuilding. Anyone with a muscular physique is immediately suspected of drug use. Anabolic steroids and other growth-enhancing drugs are believed to be as important in bodybuilding as training and nutrition are.

This perceived association of drug use with bodybuilding is an insult to the true meaning of the sport. Bodybuilding is all about the art of transforming your physique into a living, breathing piece of sculpture through intense, intelligent training and superior nutrition. The challenge of *building* your *body* naturally and without the use of illegal, and often dangerous, drugs is the genesis of the sport.

My childhood fantasy of becoming Mr. Universe and earning my living as a professional bodybuilder ended when I realized that steroids and other muscle-building drugs were an integral part of the sport. I could not and would not risk my health and my future on the chance of becoming a pro, even if it meant abandoning my dream and walking away from my passion.

Thankfully, I soon discovered natural, or drug-tested, bodybuilding competitions. These physique contests include testing specifically for steroids and other bodybuilding drugs. All participants in natural bodybuilding competitions develop their bodies exclusively through intelligent nutrition and intense training. This is the way the sport of bodybuilding was originally intended to be.

After winning the Natural Mr. Universe competition twice and capturing the first Mr. Natural Olympia title, I realized that information for bodybuilders who wished to develop their physiques and eventually compete without using drugs was sorely lacking in the marketplace. Most of the books about building the physique and competing in the sport were written by bodybuilders who used steroids and other drugs to become champions. Because these drugs give the user a definite competitive advantage over the drug-free bodybuilder, many of the training and diet programs outlined were irrelevant for those hoping to develop their physiques naturally.

This book fills that void. The information provided here is exclusively for the drug-free bodybuilder. Everything you want to know about developing the physique through training and nutrition is covered. With more than 35 competitions on my resume and 27 years of hard, consistent training behind me, I know firsthand what it takes to develop the physique naturally, and I share those secrets with you.

In addition to the information on building a winning, drug-free physique, is a section on how to successfully compete in a bodybuilding competition: details for preparing for a competition, as well as the inside story of what goes on backstage and onstage at a physique contest. If you're an aspiring bodybuilding contestant, this information is invaluable.

My passion for bodybuilding is founded in the incredible challenge of transforming your God-given body into an award-winning physique. Resorting to dangerous and illegal drugs for this purpose destroys the original concept of the sport. Build your body exclusively through the use of intelligent training and nutrition and leave the drugs to those who lack the inspiration and guts to pursue the sport the way it was intended. Let me be your guide in the pursuit of developing your own work of art.

Acknowledgments

Bodybuilding is often thought of as an individual sport. When a bodybuilder is up onstage competing, he is by himself with no equipment, no uniform and no teammates. However, the process of building the physique to successfully compete in a bodybuilding competition requires the help of others. It is the people in our lives who provide inspiration, support and love that allow us to become successful. I want to thank those individuals who helped me in my bodybuilding career and provided the background for writing this book.

I first must thank the man who provided me with so much inspiration over the last 25 years. He is known to most of the world as the Governor of California and one of the biggest movie stars in Hollywood, but I was introduced to him as the Austrian Oak. Arnold Schwarzenegger has inspired and motivated me more than any one else on the planet. His incredible physique and winning attitude gave me the hope that I could make my dream of becoming a bodybuilding champion a reality. Without Arnold's inspiration, I'm not sure I would have been able to overcome the inevitable obstacles that arose on my road to being a bodybuilder.

I also want to thank the numerous training partners I've had that have helped me throughout the years. It was your support and encouragement during the brutal training sessions in the gym that allowed me to overcome my weak points and develop a prize-winning physique. Thanks for putting up with my hard and heavy workouts all in an effort to win my next contest.

Many of my former training partners are still my best friends to this day, others have moved on in their lives. I want to thank all of you for being there for me. You all made the whole process so much more enjoyable! These training partners include Dennis Durkin, Nick Roti, Jim McGovern, Gino Loffredo, Joe Silzer, Mel Chancey, Ken Gibson, Dave North, John Gust, Bob Martin, Rich Michniak, Paul Hinderman, Tom Crain, Jason Glasch and Tim Canino as well as many others.

I also want to thank the staff at Human Kinetics for coming to me and suggesting this project. Thanks to Ed McNeely for approaching me with the idea. Thank you to Jennifer Walker and Ted Miller for guiding the project to completion and to Dan Wendt for his dedication in taking all of the training and physique pictures for the book. I want to thank Joe Silzer and Ebony Thomas for taking the time out to model for the exercise photos in the book. Thanks also to Diamond Gym in Orland Park, Illinois for providing us with the facility to take the photos for this book.

Last but not least, I want to thank my family for the loving support and encouragement they have given me over the years. Bodybuilding is a sport that often required me to bring my own food to family parties and be different than everyone else. I was lucky to have a family that not only understood this sacrifice but supported it. My parents, Don and Jeri Hansen, who have always been so loving and positive, my sister Kim, her husband Eric, my nephew Zane, Eric's brother Larry, my sister-in-law Jeni and my nephews Sam and Joe. Thanks also to Suzi and Sammy for the joy and happiness you have brought to my life.

Key to Muscles

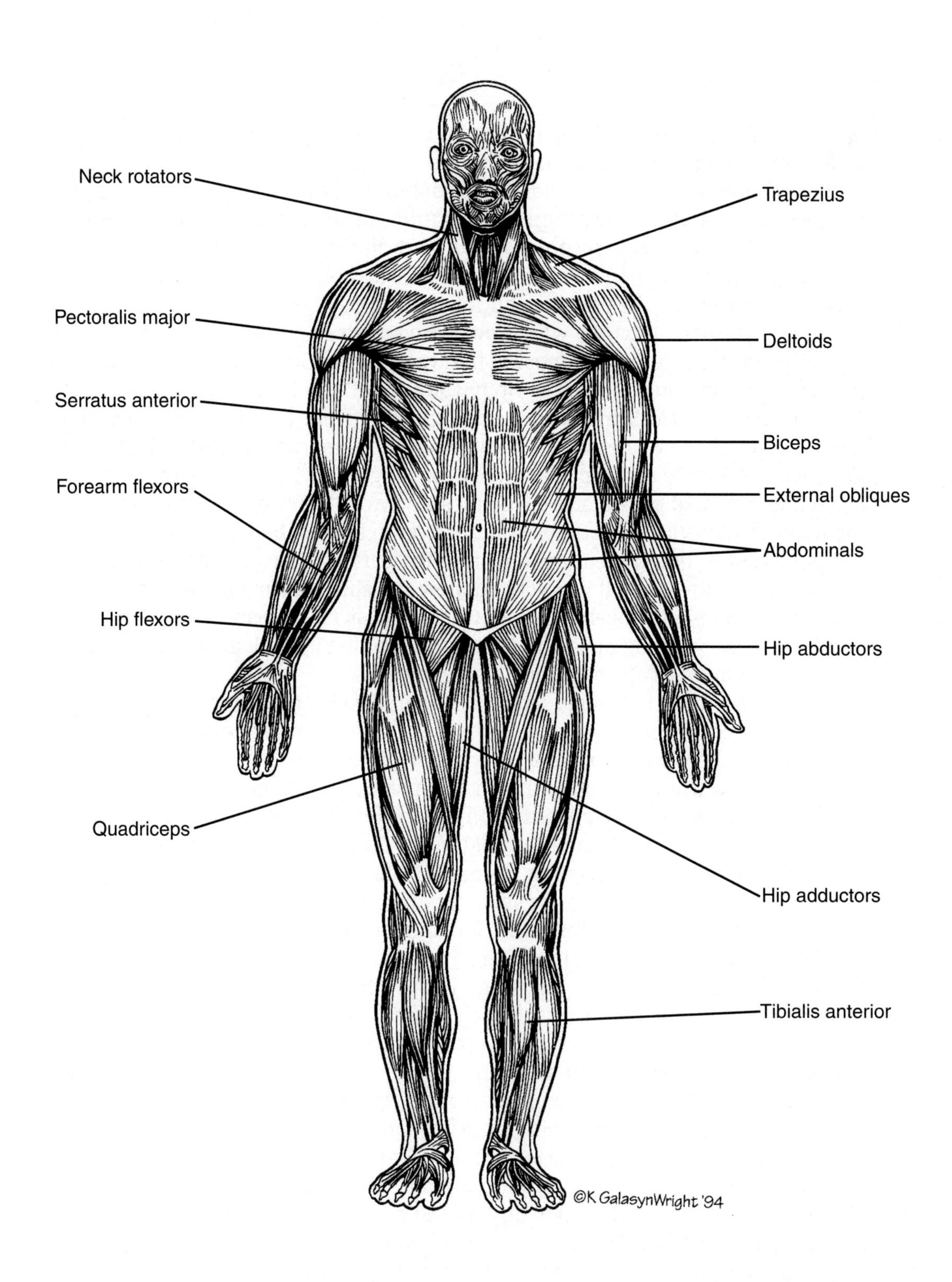

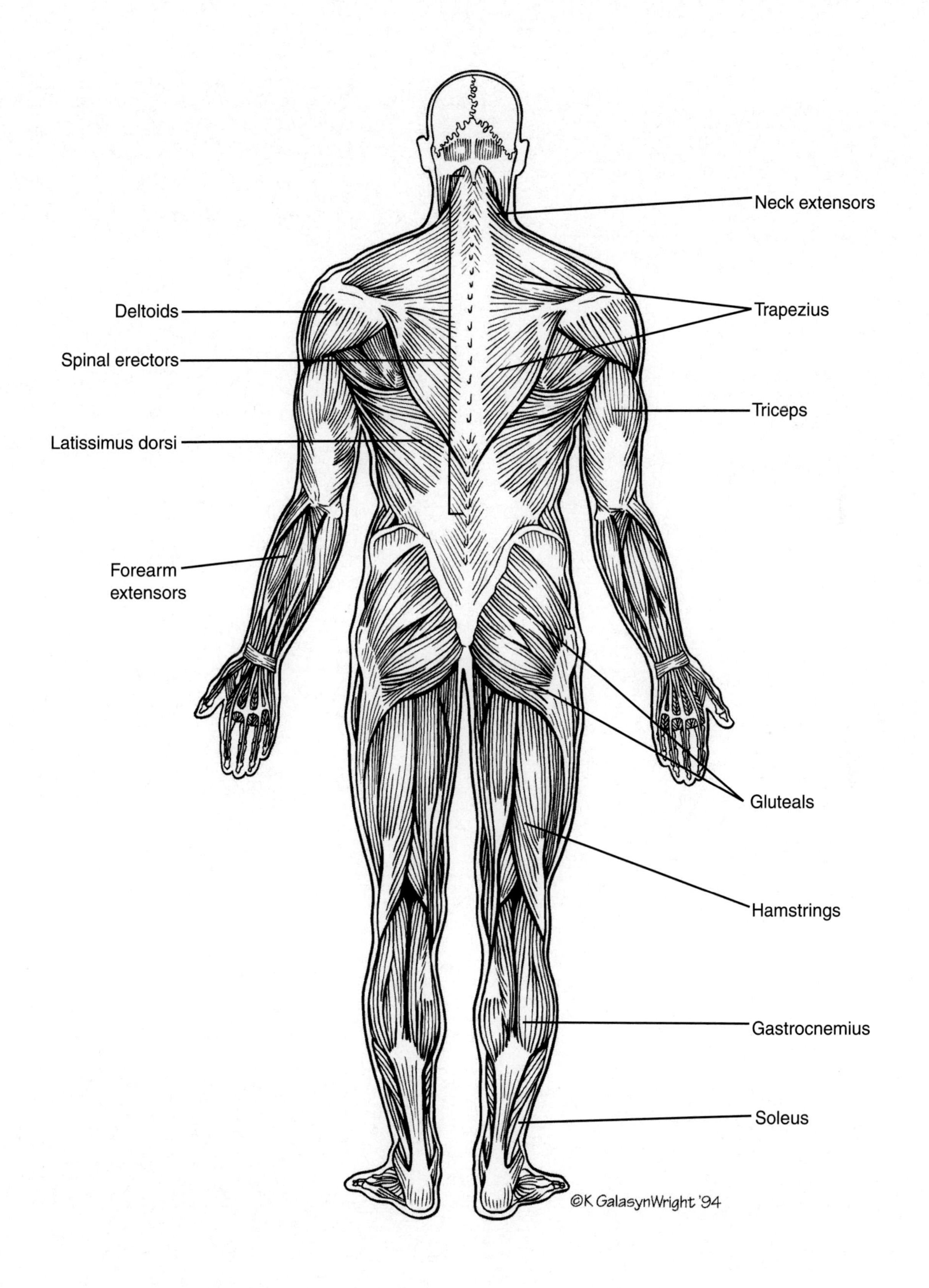
Neck extensors
Deltoids
Trapezius
Spinal erectors
Triceps
Latissimus dorsi
Forearm
extensors
Gluteals
Hamstrings
Gastrocnemius
Soleus
©K GalasynWright '94

PART I

Building Blocks for Massive Muscles

The first part of this book analyzes the subject of genetic potential. You will learn the role of genetics in bodybuilding potential and how to accurately assess your own physique as you begin your quest to develop your body. You will also learn how to train your body correctly from the ground up for the most effective bodybuilding workouts and how to strike the nutritional balance your body needs to become lean and muscular at the same time.

Chapter 1

Sizing Up Your Body's Potential

The first question most people ask themselves when they begin bodybuilding is, "What will my body look like after several years of training?" Many become interested in the sport after looking at photos of bodybuilders in magazines. It is hard to imagine that the human body (especially your own human body) could achieve the incredible muscle development shown in the magazines.

This brings up the question of genetics. Genetic potential is one of those terms that is often brought up by both novices and experts alike, but rarely explained. Many professional bodybuilders are described as "genetic freaks" to explain their incredible muscle development. But what exactly do we mean by genetics, how does it apply to bodybuilding, and how much does it factor into developing the physique you desire?

Your Genetic Potential

Genetic potential for bodybuilding can be divided into several categories. You may be genetically gifted in some areas and lacking in others. Some genetic traits are predetermined and are not subject to change, for example, your height or the color of your eyes. However, overcoming certain genetic traits through exercise and nutrition to build your ideal body is what bodybuilding is all about.

Before you can do that, however, you must recognize what your genetic potential is. This chapter analyzes all the physical factors that determine how far your physique can develop. Be aware that this is just the groundwork, and that potential is just that, potential. How far you develop your physique is up to you. The physiques of many of today's most accomplished bodybuilders showed no signs of their superstar potential. To quote a line from the movie *Terminator 2: Judgment Day,* "The future is not set; there is no future but what we make for ourselves."

Bone Structure: Basic Framework

The first category for determining your genetic potential is your bone structure. Just as all architectural masterpieces are, initially, built upon a great structure a great physique begins with the bones on which it is constructed. Bone structure can either make or break a good physique.

Larry Scott

The ideal structure for bodybuilding is composed of wide shoulders and a narrow waist. This look is exemplified by bodybuilding legend and Mr. Universe Steve Reeves. The wide shoulders combined with a narrow waist give the body the V-taper that is highly regarded among bodybuilders. Other bodybuilding champions who have this look are Sergio Oliva and Lee Haney, both multiple Mr. Olympia winners.

If you were lucky enough to be born with naturally long clavicles and narrow hips, you are already one step ahead of most bodybuilders. Those who were not blessed in these areas can still work hard to create this illusion. Bodybuilders such as Larry Scott and Rich Gaspari are two good examples. Both of these champions were born with narrow shoulders and wide hips. However, by building inches of muscles onto the sides of their deltoids and lats while keeping their waists streamlined, they were able to create the illusion of the V-taper.

A big rib cage is another asset for bodybuilding success. A deep rib cage adds depth to the upper body, which creates potential for greater size. Standard bodybuilding poses such as the front double biceps, the front lat spread, and the side chest pose look much more impressive with a big rib cage. Can you imagine Arnold Schwarzenegger hitting his patented side chest pose without that great rib cage of his?

The size of the bones themselves is also important for bodybuilding success. A heavy, thick bone structure may be a plus in sports such as football, rugby, and powerlifting, but it may impede physical symmetry in bodybuilding. On the other hand, a very slight bone structure may limit the amount of muscle mass you can carry on your frame, and it may limit the amount of weight you can use in your training.

The length of the individual bones determines the look of the physique. Some bodybuilders have a short torso and long legs. Long legs make the bodybuilder look taller on stage. Bodybuilders with short torsos and long legs, such as Samir Bannout, Lee Haney, and Ronnie Coleman, usually possess superior back development, but they have difficulty developing their legs.

Other bodybuilders have long torsos and short legs. These bodybuilders may look shorter onstage than they actually are because of the length of the legs. Bodybuilders with long torsos and short legs, such as Nasser el Sonbaty and Mike Mattarazzo, usually have excellent leg development, but they have difficulty building a good back. Recognizing what type of structure you have allows you to concentrate on certain muscle groups that may lag behind the rest of your body.

Muscle Shape: Beauty Is in the Eye of the Beholder

The shape of the individual muscle is determined by where it is attached. Muscle shape is unique for each person and creates diversity among bodybuilders. Some shapes are more pleasing than others. When a bodybuilding judge refers to a competitor's symmetry, he is talking about to how the muscles flow together to create an overall pleasing appearance. The hope of all bodybuilders is that the shape of their muscles work together to create an attractive physique.

If you examine the bodybuilding champions over the years, you will see a variety of muscle shapes. Steve Reeves sported what were later referred to as "square pecs," because his chest muscles were attached to his sternum in a square shape. Chris Dickerson, on the other hand, had pectoral muscles that were more rounded. Neither of these bodybuilders trained their pecs to achieve this specific look. This is the way the muscles were shaped at birth. No amount of training could have changed the overall shape. The training only allowed the muscles to get bigger.

If a muscle is attached lower on the bone, that muscle will look longer when fully developed and will create a more pleasing appearance. For example, Larry Scott, the first Mr. Olympia, was renowned for his full, thick biceps. Larry trained very hard to develop his arms, but he was also blessed with biceps that were attached extremely low on his humerus bones. Franco Columbu, on the other hand, was not so fortunate when it came to biceps attachments. Franco, who also won the Mr. Olympia title, was born with biceps attached much higher on his arm. However, he did not let that stop him from working hard to develop arms that were good enough to win the top title in bodybuilding.

Sometimes, a muscle is not attached at the ideal position, but this does not mean that outstanding development of that muscle is not possible. Albert Beckles, a Mr. Universe who presented one of the most incredible physiques in the 1980s, has some of the greatest arms in the history of the sport. A closer look at Albert's biceps attachment, however, reveals that the muscle is attached rather high. When he flexes his arm, the biceps juts up at a vertical angle creating one of the most peaked biceps ever seen on a bodybuilding stage.

Although it may be difficult to determine the shape of your individual muscle groups until they begin to get bigger, the following are the ideal muscle attachments and shapes for each muscle group.

Chest When the pectoral muscles are attached long (farther down the sternum) and wide, they have greater potential for growth. Square pectorals look more symmetrical than rounded pecs. However, the square shape tends to look flat unless the pecs are fully developed. Round pecs can appear developed even at the beginning stages because of their shape. On the downside, round pecs can look bottom heavy if the lower portion is too developed.

Arnold Schwarzenegger is a good example of a bodybuilder who inherited the ideal shape for the pectorals. Arnold has a chest that is attached far down his sternum and out wide. After years of training, he was able to develop a pair of pecs that is considered among the best in the history of bodybuilding. However, photos of Arnold when he began training do not indicate their enormous potential. The shape was there, but the development brought out the true potential of his chest.

Back Several large and small muscle groups encompass the back. The biggest muscle in the back is the latissimus dorsi, often referred to as the lats. The lower the lats are attached on the back, the bigger they will appear when fully developed. A condition known as high lats, where the lats are attached higher on the back, is normally looked down upon by bodybuilding judges.

The attachment of the lower lats also determines how much of the low back is visible from the rear. Berry DeMey, one of the best professional bodybuilders during the 1980s, had lower lats that were attached somewhat high on the inside of his low back. This revealed more of his lumbar region. At his peak, DeMey was known for his "Christmas tree" low back because of the extreme definition he displayed in this area.

In contrast, Lee Haney, eight-time Mr. Olympia, had lats that were attached very low on his back, including the inside of his low back. This latissimus attachment allowed Haney to develop extremely impressive lats, but it did not allow room for DeMey's Christmas tree low back.

Arnold Schwarzenegger

The trapezius muscles, located at the top of the back, are triangular and are normally attached in the same areas on all bodybuilders. The lower traps may be attached a little higher or lower, but the disparity is not as great as with the lats.

Lee Haney

Bodybuilders such as Franco Columbu, Lee Haney, and Samir Bannout all have latissimus dorsi muscles that attach low on their backs. Not coincidentally, these champion bodybuilders are all known for outstanding back development. There is no doubt that the muscle attachment of each of these athletes contributed to their ultimate development.

Deltoids The deltoid muscles over the shoulders are composed of the anterior (front) head, the lateral (side) head, and the posterior (rear) head. The muscle attachments for the deltoids are more uniform among bodybuilders and do not show the disparity in length that muscles such as the biceps and the lats may reveal.

If there is variation, however, and the lateral head of the deltoids is attached lower on the arm, it may detract from the overall width of the upper body. This lower attachment creates the illusion of long deltoids, rather than the ideal look of capped-off shoulders.

The anterior and posterior heads of the deltoids can also vary in their attachment. Many bodybuilders who develop great delts have attachments in favorable positions that allow maximum development. Bodybuilders who are well known for their incredible deltoids are Lee Haney, Mike Christian, and Kevin Levrone. The location of their attachments contributed to their outstanding deltoid development.

Biceps The biceps muscle is the showpiece of the body. Whenever someone asks you to flex your muscle, they are asking to see your biceps. The biceps may be attached long or short. It may also have a variety of shapes, most notably long or peaked.

The ideal biceps has a long attachment with a high peak. This look is displayed by many bodybuilders, especially Arnold Schwarzenegger, who had biceps that were both thick and long but also highly peaked. This outstanding development and shape allowed him to display his arms in a variety of poses that helped him to win Mr. Olympia seven times.

You can determine the length of your biceps muscle by holding your arm out straight with your palm up. Pinpoint the spot in which your biceps muscle is attached to the tendon in the crook of your arm.

Boyer Coe

You cannot change the point of attachment; you can only develop the biceps muscle itself. As your biceps begins to develop, you can determine if the muscle has a long or peaked shape. You can slightly alter the natural shape of your biceps through further development and the type of movements you use to train this muscle. Biceps exercises are discussed in Part II.

The biceps muscle consists of two heads. Sometimes, these two heads are exactly the same length. Sometimes, the lengths of the two heads are different. Boyer Coe, multiple Mr. Universe winner, had an inner biceps head that was a little shorter than the outer head. This created a unique shape and allowed him to display a distinct "split" between the two heads. Boyer used this unique genetic trait to his advantage in his posing routines by emphasizing the biceps split in one of his poses. It allowed him to stand out from all the other competitors because no one else could hit that pose the way he did.

Bill Pearl

Triceps The triceps are more diverse in their shape than the biceps. Because there are three heads (inner, middle, and outer), the shape of the triceps muscle varies from bodybuilder to bodybuilder.

A triceps muscle with a middle head attached low on the humerus bone has more growth potential than one with the middle head attached higher. The same concept applies to the inner head. If the inner head is attached near the elbow, the muscle will have greater growth potential than if it is attached higher. The outer head of the triceps can create the illusion of width in the upper arm when standing relaxed and facing the front. A longer outer head also contributes to the growth potential of the triceps.

Bodybuilders Mike Mentzer, Bill Pearl, and Skip LaCour had triceps muscles attached low on the arm, which they developed into outstanding triceps over their careers. Arnold Schwarzenegger's triceps had a very long inner head, although the middle head was not attached quite as low. However, the combination of the long inner head and the shorter middle head created great separation, which he displayed in poses from the rear.

If the triceps muscle is attached higher up on the arm, there is less potential for growth. Sometimes, as in the case of Arnold's triceps, one head is attached farther down than another. It's unusual for all three triceps heads to attach low on the arm. Consider yourself fortunate if you are one of the few with three heads attached low on the arm.

Forearms The muscles of the forearm consist of the extensor muscles (brachioradialis and extensor carpi radialis among others) and the flexor muscles (flexor carpi radialis, flexor carpi ulnaris and the palmaris longus) on the underside of the forearm. As with the other upper-arm muscles, the lower the attachments are on the forearm, the greater the potential for growth.

The forearm muscles, like the calf muscles, are heavily influenced by genetics. Most bodybuilders with outstanding forearms and calves were born with them and didn't have to do much work to develop them.

Sergio Oliva, Bill Pearl, and Lee Priest have great forearm development. All of these champions also have low attachments for the flexor and extensor muscles.

Abdominals The abs have been dubbed "the six-pack" in recent years. However, based on your genetic makeup, you may be stuck with only a two-pack or a four-pack. However, if you are fortunate, you may possess an eight-pack!

Mohammed Makkawy

The shape of your abdominal muscles and how many abdominal muscles you display is determined by genetics. A true six-pack has two upper abdominal muscles, two middle abdominal muscles, and two lower abdominal muscles. In addition to the abs, the external oblique muscles located over the rib cage contribute to the overall abdominal region. Some individuals have abdominal muscles that are set close together while others have a distinct line, called the linea alba, which runs vertically between the abdominal muscles. The linea alba is not noticeable in some, and in others it creates a gap between the abdominals.

The external oblique muscles located on either side of the abdominals are thicker and more pronounced on some bodybuilders than on others. This is not always a function of training, although working the external obliques will create a thicker muscle. The shape and thickness of these muscles is also determined by genetics.

Tom Platz

Champion bodybuilders who have developed outstanding abdominals include Mohammed Makkawy, Thierry Pastel, and Ahmad Haidar. Two bodybuilders who stand out in the area of external oblique development are Robby Robinson and Shawn Ray. Boyer Coe, on the other hand, always struggled with his abdominals because of the genetic make-up of this area.

Quadriceps The quadriceps muscle, located on the front of the thigh, has four distinct heads. These heads are called the rectus femoris, vastus lateralis, vastus medialis, and vastus intermedius. The quadriceps muscle varies in shape and insertion points from bodybuilder to bodybuilder.

The ideal shape of the quadriceps muscle includes a fully developed vastus medialis (nicknamed the "teardrop muscle") and rectus femoris, as well as a rounded vastus lateralis (located on the outer thigh). If the heads of the quadriceps are attached in a short or narrow position, it creates an inferior look. One of the most important aspects of a well-shaped quadriceps muscle is an impressive sweep created by a vastus lateralis muscle attached wide at the side of the thigh. This quadriceps sweep balances the width of the upper body and presents a proportionate physique.

Many champion bodybuilders have displayed outstanding quadriceps development. Tom Platz, Tim Belknap, and Jay Cutler are known for their incredible legs. All of them have fully shaped quadriceps, including a wide vastus lateralis muscle on the outside of the quads, which adds width to the legs.

Calves The muscle attachment and shape of the calf muscles, similar to the biceps, is easy to determine. Just stand on your toes while looking at the back of your lower leg and pinpoint the muscle attachment on the tendon. A low insertion point means the muscle is longer, which translates into more growth potential. A calf with a high insertion point has limited growth potential because the muscle is short.

Two major muscles form the calves. The first is the gastrocnemius, the large, heart-shaped muscle that is prominent on the back of the leg. The other is the soleus, which lies underneath the gastrocnemius and can be seen in the middle of the gastrocnemius from the back. Both muscles are usually the same length.

The ideal calf muscle is attached low on the leg and is shaped like an upside down heart. Calves vary in shape among individuals, but the fuller the muscles of the calves, the more impressive they look when developed. Several top professional bodybuilders have outstanding calf development. Three who immediately come to mind are Chris Dickerson, Mike Mattarazzo, and Dorian Yates.

Chris Dickerson

The muscles on your body overlap and flow into one another to create the symmetry of your physique. As a bodybuilder, it is your job to recognize which areas lack the ideal shape and do your best to correct the imbalance.

Muscle Cells: Quantity Matters

One of the most interesting roles genetics plays in bodybuilding is determining the number of muscle cells found in each muscle group. This inherited number of cells is largely responsible for the amount of mass you can develop.

Take a good look at any bodybuilding champion, and it is relatively easy to determine which muscles have a generous number of muscle cells and which don't. Some muscle groups seem to grow with little or no effort, while others seemingly resist growth no matter what the bodybuilder does.

Mr. Universe Kal Szkalak is a good example. Kal won the 1976 Amateur Athletic Union (AAU) Mr. America and the 1977 International Federation of Bodybuilders (IFBB) Mr. Universe and was touted in the magazines as the next Arnold. He had entered and won five competitions—a perfect record. Kal had an incredible upper body with huge, peaked biceps, a thick, full chest, and a broad and muscular back. However, Kal's leg development was way out of proportion with his upper body development. His calves were small and underdeveloped, and his quadriceps, although possessing some separation, were also too small to match his great upper half.

I remember attending a seminar by Boyer Coe in which he talked about the disparity between Kal's upper- and lower-body development. Boyer said he had witnessed Kal training legs at the World Gym in California and that Kal trained his legs very hard, and they still refused to match his incredible upper body. The reason is the number of muscle cells Kal inherited. He obviously was born with more than his fair share in the upper body, but was shortchanged when it came to the legs.

Sometimes you can predict which areas of the body have been blessed with lots of muscle cells even before you begin training. They are the areas with some degree of development even without training. However, muscles that are initially underdeveloped are not necessarily that way because they have few muscle cells. Some muscle groups respond quickly when trained properly, while others may take more time. It's very difficult to determine until you actually begin training each area.

Another interesting theory of muscle development is hyperplasia. Hyperplasia occurs when the number of muscle cells increase as a response to exercise. It has been believed for years that muscle growth is due to hypertrophy, or the growth of the individual muscle fibers. However, evidence now suggests that muscles may also grow because of the multiplication of muscle fibers, or hyperplasia.

Most of the research on hyperplasia has been performed on animals such as birds, rats, and cats. Jose Antonio, PhD, recently performed a study on a bird in which he used weights to progressively overload one wing and stretch the anterior latissimus dorsi muscle. The overload scheme started with a weight that was 10 percent of the bird's weight and increased by 5 percent up to 35 percent. Two days of rest preceded an increase in weight. After 28 stretch days, this study produced the greatest gains in muscle mass recorded in an animal or human model of tension-induced overload—a 334 percent increase in muscle mass with a 90 percent increase in fiber number!

In addition to the weight-induced stretch in this study, other studies on animals have used regular muscular exercises to study hyperplasia. In one study, cats trained to perform a wrist flexion exercise increased the number of muscle fibers in the forearms from 9 to 20 percent. In another study, rats performed a squat exercise in response to an electrical stimulus and increased the number of muscle fibers in the plantaris muscle (a plantar flexor muscle on the back of the leg) by 14 percent.

Studies on human muscle-cell hyperplasia are difficult to conduct because of the inability to count the muscle fibers in a human. Scientists and researchers have come up with one method for getting around this obstacle; they try to determine muscle hyperplasia by measuring the cross-sectional area of an athlete's muscle fibers and comparing it to those of a sedentary person.

However, the evidence from these cross-sectional measurements has produced inconsistent results. For instance, one study showed that the arm circumferences of elite bodybuilders and powerlifters were 27 percent greater than those of sedentary controls, yet the cross-sectional areas of the athlete's muscle fibers in the triceps brachii muscle were the same as in the control group. Other studies have demonstrated that bodybuilders have larger fibers rather than more fibers when compared to a control population.

These recent studies on muscle-cell hyperplasia indicate that exercise-induced stress (hypertrophy) may cause muscle cells to multiply as well as increase in thickness. This is exciting news if hyperplasia allows a bodybuilder to develop a genetically weak muscle group through extensive resistance training.

Fiber Type: Type Equals Size or Endurance

In addition to the number of muscle cells, genetics also determines the type of muscle fiber that is predominant in the muscle cell: white (fast twitch) or red (slow twitch).

Red muscle fibers are best for endurance activities. They are also called slow-twitch fibers because of their slow contraction time and high resistance to fatigue. Slow-twitch muscle fibers contain a lot of mitochondria (often referred to as the powerhouse of the cell because it is responsible for ATP synthesis, the process by which the body produces energy) and more capillaries that surround each muscle fiber. The capillaries make it possible for the muscle to use oxygen for energy.

White muscle fibers, on the other hand, are well suited to anaerobic activities such as sprinting, throwing the shot put, and weightlifting. They are quick to fatigue because of their fast contraction time and the higher glycogen content of the cells. These fibers contain fewer mitochondria and capillaries than red muscle fibers.

White muscle fibers can be further classified into two separate categories: fast oxidative (type IIa) and fast glycolytic (type IIb). Type IIb fibers contain lots of glycogen and high levels of the enzymes required for producing energy without oxygen. They also contain very few mitochondria and rely on glycolytic enzymes for their energy.

Type IIa fibers are a combination of the slow-twitch muscle fibers and the type IIb fast-twitch fibers because they contain the best of both fiber types. Type IIa fibers are moderately resistant to fatigue and are relatively dense in mitochondria and capillaries. However, they also have high levels of creatine phosphate and glycogen, as well as high glycolytic and oxidative enzyme activity. This makes type IIa fibers well suited for aerobic activities that require a great deal of power such as a 400-meter race.

For bodybuilding you want a greater percentage of type IIb muscle fibers. These fibers, according to Chris Aceto in his book *Understanding Bodybuilding Nutrition and Training,* are capable of growing by 100 percent in size, while the type IIa fibers can grow by only 25 percent. Thus, if you have inherited a greater percentage of type IIb muscle fibers than type IIa, you will be able to build bigger muscles through training.

Most people have an equal percentage of fast-twitch and slow-twitch muscle fibers in each muscle. Some muscles are composed of mostly fast-twitch or mostly slow-twitch fibers. For example, the soleus muscle in the calf is mostly slow-twitch. The hamstrings, on the other hand, are almost all fast-twitch.

To determine your muscles' composition, you must biopsy individual muscles. This painful procedure involves sticking a needle into a muscle and removing several fibers for examination. A less painful method of evaluation allows you to determine your fiber type through training. Perform an exercise with 80 percent of your one-rep maximum (1RM). If you can do fewer than 7 repetitions with that weight, your muscles are composed of more than 50 percent fast-twitch muscle fibers. If you can perform more than 12 repetitions with 80 percent of your 1RM, your muscles are more than 50 percent slow twitch. If you can do between 7 and 12 repetitions, then the muscle group has an equal proportion of fibers.

One problem with this testing method is that it is hard to isolate a specific muscle when performing an exercise. For example, if you use the bench press to determine the muscle composition of the pectoral muscles, you also have to take into account that the anterior deltoids, triceps, and other upper-body muscles are involved in performing the bench press exercise.

You could, however, use an isolation exercise to determine the fiber type of specific muscle groups. For example, you could use the leg extension exercise to test the quadriceps muscle or the dumbbell fly to test the pectoral muscles. The results would not be precise, but close enough to help you determine the growth potential of your muscles based on their fiber type.

Training the muscles with traditional bodybuilding methods (using basic exercises with a weight that allows a maximum of 10 repetitions) targets the type IIb muscle fibers. If you have a majority of slow-twitch muscle fibers in a particular muscle group, it is not possible to convert them over to type IIb fast-twitch fibers. However, it is possible that many of the type IIa intermediate fibers will take on some of the qualities of the type IIb fibers.

Even if a muscle is composed mostly of slow-twitch fibers, heavy training that targets the type IIb fast-twitch fibers will increase the size of the muscle. This is because the fast-twitch fibers have a larger cross-sectional area than slow-twitch fibers. As a result, the fast-twitch fibers take up much more space than the slow-twitch fibers, leading to greater size in that muscle. Of course, if the muscle is mostly type IIb fast-twitch fibers, the growth potential is even greater.

Endurance athletes have a greater percentage of slow-twitch fibers, which allows them to run great distances before becoming fatigued. Similarly, the high percentage of fast-twitch muscle fibers in world-class sprinters gives these athletes a greater advantage in producing muscle force and power. These genetic predispositions come into play in determining a world-champion athlete.

Three Basic Body Types

In the 1940s, Dr. William Sheldon developed the theory for classifying physiques into certain body types. He called this process somatotyping. Sheldon classified all physiques into three broad categories: endomorphs, mesomorphs, and ectomorphs (see figure 1.1).

An endomorph is a naturally heavy or fat person. He or she is characterized by a soft, round body, wide hips, round face, and a heavy, thick bone structure. The endomorph gains fat and body weight very easily and has a hard time maintaining a lean physique.

A mesomorph has the classic athletic or bodybuilder physique. This body type is characterized by wide shoulders and a large chest. A mesomorph is muscular but lean with great natural strength. This is the ideal body type for an aspiring bodybuilder.

The last category is the ectomorph, a naturally skinny person. This physique is characterized by long arms and legs, flat chest, narrow shoulders, a slight bone

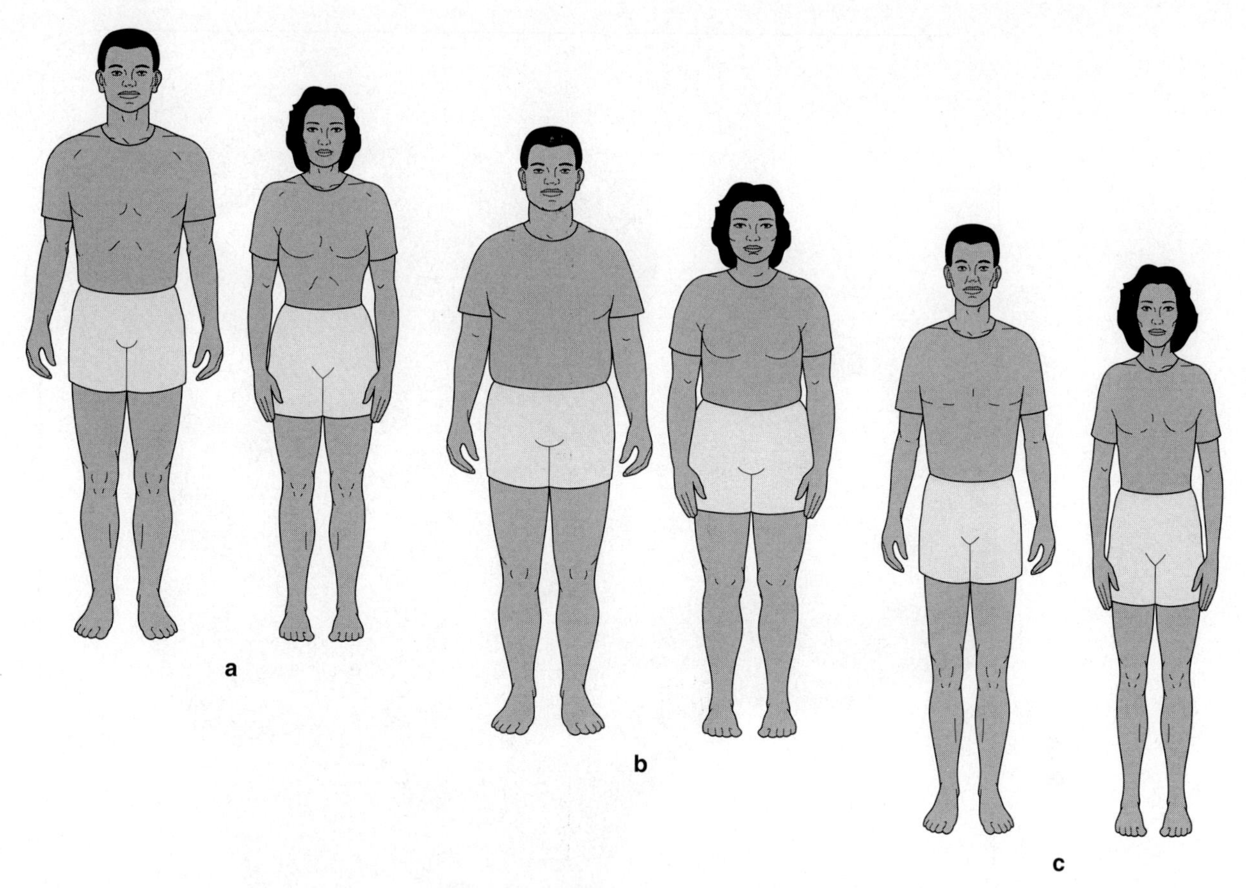

Figure 1.1 Knowing the three categories of body types helps bodybuilders determine their genetic potential: *(a)* Mesomorphs; *(b)* endomorphs; and *(c)* ectomorphs.

Reprinted, by permission, from T.R. Baechle and R.W. Earle, 2000, *Essentials of strength training and conditioning*, 2nd ed. (Champaign, IL: Human Kinetics), 173.

structure, and very little body fat. The ectomorph has great difficulty gaining weight and getting stronger.

If you look at some of the bodybuilding champions from the past, you can see that not all were natural mesomorphs. Many had characteristics of either endomorphs or ectomorphs. The first Mr. Olympia, Larry Scott, was very skinny when he began training; therefore, he could be classified as an ecto-mesomorph. Frank Zane, who developed a very aesthetic physique along the lines of classic Greek sculpture, could also be described as an ecto-mesomorph. Both of these Mr. Olympias had difficulty adding muscle tissue because of their natural ectomorphic tendencies.

Other bodybuilders were naturally heavy when they began training. These bodybuilders found it very easy to add body weight, but had a difficult time getting lean enough to win competitions. Danny Padilla and Dave Draper could be classified as endo-mesomorphs. They both had great size but needed to follow very strict diets to achieve the definition necessary for competition.

Of course, many bodybuilders are ideal mesomorphs. These athletes have little difficulty adding muscle mass to their frames. They seem to grow thick muscles easily and don't face as many challenges as natural ectomorphs or endomorphs do. Casey Viator, Sergio Oliva, and Jay Cutler stand out as natural mesomorphs, individuals who were born to be bodybuilders.

Frank Zane

All champion bodybuilders have mesomorphic characteristics. If they didn't, they could not have made it to the championship level. Someone who is largely ectomorphic or endomorphic does not have the genetic makeup to become a champion bodybuilder. He can certainly improve his physique and, in some cases, dramatically transform his body. But to reach the top of any sport, genetics plays a role to some degree.

Knowing your body type will help you design a training and nutrition program appropriate for your unique physique. This is discussed in greater detail later, but suffice it to say that being aware of your body type will allow you to structure your training and nutrition for optimum results.

Metabolic Rate: Body Type Sets the Pace

Your metabolic rate, or the speed at which your body processes food, is one of the inherited traits that affects your success in bodybuilding. Closely related to the individual body type, metabolism can generally be classified as fast, slow, or medium. Most ectomorphs have fast metabolisms, endomorphs have slow metabolisms, and mesomorphs have medium to medium-fast metabolisms.

Because much of bodybuilding success depends on how lean the body can get, a fast or medium-fast metabolism is an advantage as long as it is not so fast that it becomes nearly impossible to gain muscle tissue. Extreme ectomorphs have difficulty adding any type of body weight because their body processes food so quickly. In addition to being lean, a bodybuilder must also have a substantial amount of muscle tissue. This requires a metabolism slow enough to use the extra calories to process new muscle tissue.

Unlike the bone structure or the attachment of the muscles, the metabolism can change. Generally, your metabolism is much faster when you are young and becomes gradually slower as you age. Even prototypical ectomorphs are able to gain weight after a certain age.

Adding muscle tissue to the body changes metabolism. Muscle tissue, unlike fat, requires calories to sustain its existence. Therefore, the more muscle you have, the more calories you burn at rest. As a result, your metabolism adapts by becoming faster because of the increase in muscle tissue. Some top-level bodybuilders eat a minimum of 4,000 calories a day just to maintain their body weight because of the large amount of muscle tissue they carry.

You can also change your metabolism through your eating habits and training program. Eating several small meals per day increases metabolism by making the body work to digest each meal. In contrast, eating one or two large meals each day slows metabolism because of the increased time between meals. This large gap between meals lowers blood sugar levels, which forces the body to slow during this period of fasting.

Exercise can also increase metabolism. Cardiovascular exercise stimulates metabolism in addition to burning body fat and calories. The more active you are, the more you stimulate your metabolism. Sitting around all day causes your metabolism to become sluggish. Weight training indirectly stimulates metabolism by adding lean tissue (muscle) to the body.

Many mesomorphs have the ideal metabolism: fast enough to prevent excess body fat from accumulating but slow enough to add muscle tissue. Mesomorphs can usually eat more carbohydrates than those with a slower metabolism.

Endomorphs have greater difficulty adding lean muscle tissue without adding fat. Putting on weight is no problem for an endomorph, putting on the right kind of weight is. Many endomorphs eat a diet high in protein and moderate in carbohydrate. Too many carbohydrates add fat more easily on an endomorphic body than on the other body types.

Ectomorphs and those with fast metabolisms also must pay attention to their diets in order to make progress. Each meal is vitally important to making gains. The body must be flooded with calories—carbohydrate, protein, and fat—to have enough nutrients to add muscle tissue.

Analyzing Your Genetics

How can you use this information on genetics to determine your own genetic potential? Some areas of genetics are impossible to determine until you begin training consistently, while others are apparent right from the beginning.

When you first begin training you must determine the following:

1. Body type: Are you primarily ectomorphic, endomorphic, or mesomorphic?
2. Metabolism: Would you judge your metabolism as fast, slow, or medium? Metabolism is closely related to your body type.
3. Bone structure: Look at the width of your shoulders and the depth of your rib cage as well as the width of your hips and waist. Check out the length of your legs and arms. Do you have a long torso and short legs or short torso and long legs? How thick are your joints (wrists, knees, and ankles)?
4. Are any parts of your body naturally muscular? Are any areas underdeveloped?

After six months to a year of training, take photographs of yourself and analyze your physique again, considering the following:

1. Muscle shape: Analyze your muscle groups. Which muscle groups are the ideal shape described earlier in this chapter? Which are poorly shaped? Are any muscle attachments in less than ideal locations (short biceps or triceps, narrow quadriceps, or high lats)?
2. Muscle cells: Do any muscle groups respond quickly to training? Which areas lag behind the others? Are the weak areas a result of poor training or poor genetics?
3. Metabolism: How has your metabolism responded to the bodybuilding program? Is gaining muscle easy or difficult? Is it easy to put on fat, or are you able to stay relatively lean?

Besides this questionnaire, there are several tools at a bodybuilder's disposal to help you objectively analyze your physique. These tools include the mirror, tape measure, scale, photographs and, finally, another person's objective opinion.

Mirror, Mirror on the Wall

Looking at your physique in the mirror allows you to step back and view your body as a whole. If you are thinking of entering a competition, you need to become familiar with looking at yourself in a mirror because this is the same view that the judges will have when analyzing your physique.

It's best to use a full-length mirror or stand back far enough to get a full-length view. One of the biggest mistakes you can make is looking only at your upper body and neglecting to look at your legs. The judges at a bodybuilding competition will look at your physique from head to toe, so you need to analyze yourself in the same manner. Also, check out your body from every angle, not just from the front. Be sure to look at your physique from both sides and from the back.

Let me relate how I analyzed my genetic potential when I was 15 years old. I began training one year earlier, weighing 135 pounds at a height of 5 feet, 8 inches. When I started training, I was thin but slightly muscular. I had been involved in the martial arts for a year or so before I began bodybuilding, so I was not new to exercise. I was performing push-ups and lots of abdominal exercises before I began training with weights.

I would classify myself as an ecto-mesomorph. I was always a skinny kid, but I became slightly muscular when I began regular exercise. I noticed that some areas of my body responded quickly. My biceps had a peak when I was in eighth grade (my classmates used to call me Popeye), and my lats started popping out soon after I began doing chins. These muscles obviously had an ample number of muscle cells.

I took photos of myself after one year of training and analyzed my physique compared to some of the bodybuilders I saw in the magazines. My biceps looked good immediately, but my triceps were not as responsive. My lats were long and wide after one year of training (good muscle attachments), so I knew that was an easy muscle for me. My chest, on the other hand, was pretty flat. However, my pecs were attached wide and long, so I knew the potential was there once I developed more mass. My traps needed a lot more size to balance the width of my clavicles. My deltoids also needed a lot of work. They were very flat with no deltoid cap like the champs I saw in the magazines. My abs had good shape, so I could see that this would be a strong muscle group in the future.

My legs were another matter. I had a severe case of "chicken legs" at 15 years old. My legs were long and thin, and they showed little potential for bodybuilding. However, I was still training at home when I was 15, so my leg training was very limited. Like many bodybuilders, I concentrated on building my upper body at the expense of my legs when I was younger.

My bone structure showed good potential at 15 years old. My clavicles were wide, so I was on my way to displaying the coveted broad-shouldered look of the bodybuilder. My rib cage was also big and full, which I knew would help me in poses such as the front double biceps and side chest. My joints were relatively thin, which would allow my muscles to appear bigger than if I had had thick joints.

Assessing my genetic potential in a front double biceps pose at age 15 after one year of training.

My metabolism was pretty fast at 15, and I don't remember having a weight problem. When I started training, my main concern was gaining body weight and muscle size. As a teenage competitor, I only needed to diet for three to four weeks to be totally ripped.

I never experimented with how many reps I could do at 80 percent of my max to determine what percentage of muscle fiber type I had. My guess is that I am equally distributed with white and red muscle fibers with possibly more white fibers than red. I was always attracted to sports of short duration. I ran some track in the eighth grade, and I competed in the 100- and 220-yard dashes instead of the 440 or the mile. I was also more proficient in the shorter races in swimming than the longer events.

After analyzing my physique, I came to the conclusion that it would be possible for me to be successful as a competitive bodybuilder, but it was going to take time. I had the bone structure to build a good physique, and some muscle groups even responded quickly. However, I was fairly thin and needed to work hard to add muscle mass. I knew it was not going to be easy because I had some ectomorphic characteristics, and I also had a difficult time gaining weight. I was going to have to train heavy and hard to add the muscle size I needed to be a champion. Without this belief in my genetic potential, I might have lost my desire to continue training and building my body.

Also, when using a mirror to analyze your physique, look in the same mirror with the same lighting each time you pose. Different mirrors and different lighting can reflect a totally different look. Of course, you will tend to stick to the mirror that makes you look your best. The key is to be consistent when judging your physique.

Although using the mirror to measure your physique is subjective, there are guidelines for gauging your progress. Look at table 1.1 for the areas of your physique that you should analyze from a relaxed position from the front, sides, and rear.

You can also use the mirror to check your muscularity. Even when you are working on adding size to your physique, the mirror will tell you in no uncertain terms if you are adding too much fat.

When getting ready for a competition, pose in front of a mirror every day. Posing is like anything else—the more you do it, the better you get at it. Presentation is extremely important in bodybuilding competition, and you will learn to present your physique better by practicing daily. Use the mirror to judge if you are getting lean enough for your competition. Chapter 11 explains proper technique for the poses required in a bodybuilding competition.

The Tape Measure Doesn't Lie

In contrast to using the mirror, the tape measure is a more objective method for determining progress in bodybuilding. However, measurements can be misleading. Although the tape measure can be a more honest and objective way of looking at your physique, it is never used to judge a bodybuilding competition. Instead, judges rely purely on how your body looks compared to others. The judges don't care how impressive your measurements are; it's how you look that ultimately matters.

Despite the fact that you are not judged on your measurements during a bodybuilding competition, measuring individual areas is a great way to determine progress. The tape measure is especially useful for gauging progress when you are training to add size or when preparing to enter a competition. You can lie and convince yourself that your physique looks great in a mirror, but you can't cheat the tape measure. If you are losing size in your arms, or your legs are out of proportion to your upper body, the tape measure will tell the story.

When gauging your progress, measure the chest, upper arms, waist, thighs, calves, forearms, and neck. You can also measure the width of the shoulders and the hips, but the seven areas first mentioned are the most important. You can measure these areas yourself, or you can have someone else do it for you. If someone else helps you, make sure the same person measures every time because two different people might measure differently and come up with radically different measurements.

Here is the proper way to measure your physique. The chest measurement determines the size of your pectorals and your lats. Begin with the measuring tape in a straight line around your upper back. Bring the tape under your arms and across your chest. The measuring tape should be centered in the middle of your chest. Do not flex the pecs or the lats, but remain relaxed during this measurement. You are simply trying to determine how big the muscles in your upper torso are.

TABLE 1.1 Reflection Analysis

Mirror view	Target area
Front view	**Shoulders:** Look for a V-taper as the shoulders taper to the waist. **Deltoids:** Check for the cap of the side deltoids. This accentuates the V-taper. **Lats:** The width of the lats should be evident from the front. This will help create the V-taper. **Abdominals:** Developing the abs and oblique muscles will help create the illusion of a small waist in contrast to the delts and lats. **Pectorals:** The outer and lower pecs should be developed, giving a curved appearance to this area. **Biceps:** Take note of how the biceps and forearms appear when standing relaxed to the front. They should be developed enough to appear prominent even when completely relaxed. **Quadriceps:** The quadriceps should be fully developed with a nice sweep to the outer part of the thigh. **Calves:** The calves should be in proportion to the quadriceps. Ideally, the calf muscles are diamond shaped when viewed from the front.
Side view	**Chest and lats:** Make sure that the chest and lats are in proportion. The thickness of the torso muscles is more apparent from the side than it is from the front. **Pectorals:** Look for an imbalance between the upper- and lower-pec development. **Deltoids:** Look for balanced development between the front, side, and rear heads of the deltoid. Many bodybuilders overdevelop the anterior head while neglecting the rear head of the muscle. Also look for the sweep of the trapezius muscle from the side. **Biceps and triceps:** Look for a balance between the biceps and triceps muscles. Both body parts should be fully developed from the top to the bottom. Does the development of the forearm muscles match the arms? **Thighs:** Look at general thickness. The quadriceps should create a curve away from the thigh, and the hamstrings should do the same thing on the rear of the leg. Legs that are underdeveloped and out of proportion will appear straight up and down. **Calves:** The calf muscles should create a curve away from the lower leg. If the legs lack in development, this will be obvious from any view.
Rear view	**Lats:** These expressive muscles should create a sweep to the back from the armpits to the waist. **Traps:** Look for the thickness of the trapezius muscles from the back of the neck tapering down to the shoulders. **Low back:** When in top condition, these muscles should stand out, creating the "Christmas tree" look to the low back. **Shoulders and arms:** The rear deltoids and the triceps will be apparent from the rear. If these muscle groups lack development, they will appear shallow. The forearm muscles will also be visible from the rear, so check their thickness and development from this angle. **Thighs and calves:** You will be able to see the full development of the hamstrings from the rear view. The outer head of the quadriceps will also be visible from the rear if they are well developed. The calves will be in full view from the rear. The diamond is the ideal shape for this muscle group.

Although everyone is different, there are guidelines for determining how you measure up in the world of chest and back development. Arnold Schwarzenegger and Sergio Oliva were rumored to have chest measurements of close to 60 inches. Arnold has claimed a 57-inch chest in his book *Education of a Bodybuilder.* Using this statistic as a measuring stick, any measurement over 50 inches is a pretty big

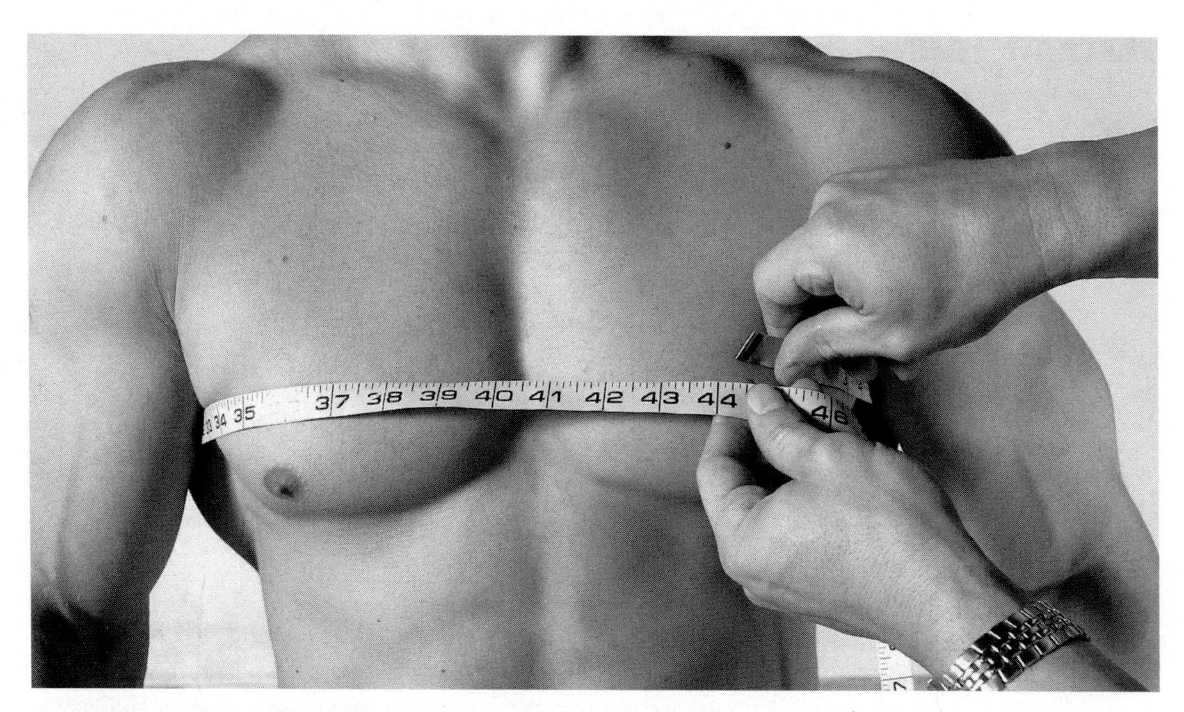

Chest measurement position.

chest. Many bodybuilders begin training with a chest measurement in the 35- to 40-inch range. Of course, this measurement is affected not only by the size and thickness of the pectorals but also the width and thickness of the latissimus dorsi muscles and the depth of the rib cage.

Everyone's favorite area to measure is the upper arm. One of the questions bodybuilders are asked most often is, "How big are your arms?" To properly measure your arms, flex your biceps muscle as hard as you can. Carefully wrap the measuring tape around the highest point of your biceps and the thickest part of your triceps, trying to keep the tape as straight as possible.

The measurement that all arms are judged by is the coveted 20-inch mark. A 20-inch arm is very big, and that is the measurement that most bodybuilders strive to achieve. However, the shape and definition of an arm can make it appear much larger than it really is. A 17-inch arm with an outstanding peak and extreme definition can look like it is three inches larger than it really is.

Measuring the waist is very important. If the waist dramatically increases in size as all the other areas get bigger, chances are that some of the increase is fat and not muscle. However, if the arms, chest, and thighs all increase in size while the waist measurement stays the same or only increases slightly, you can assume that most of the gains are muscle and not fat.

To accurately measure the waist, hold the tape across the back of the waist and bring it around to the front keeping it in a straight line. Measure about one inch below the navel. This area seems to be the spot where the greatest amount of fat accumulates.

Although the accumulation of fat is equally distributed across the body, the waistline is usually the first place to gain fat and the last place to lose it. For this reason, your waist measurement is an excellent way to gauge your body fat. The size of your waist is determined not only by the amount of fat on your body but also by the size of the obliques and abdominal muscles and the width of your hips.

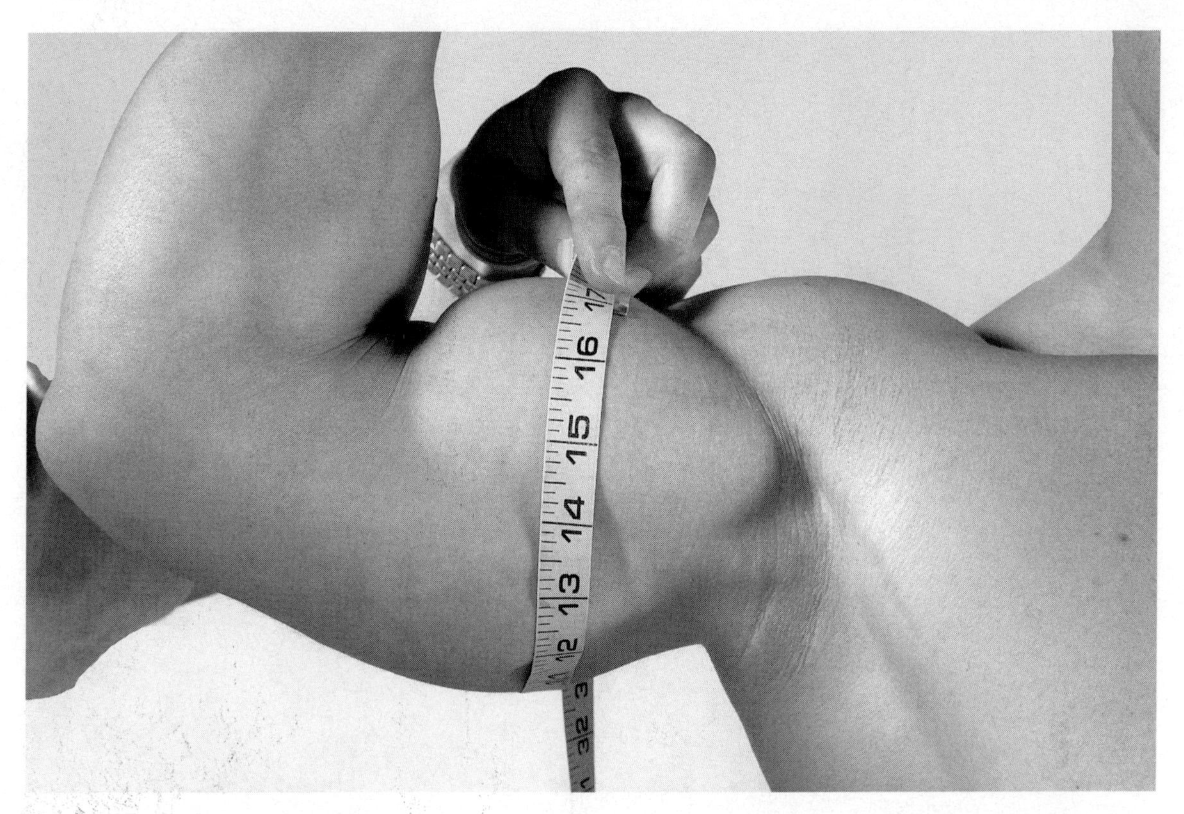

Arm measurement position.

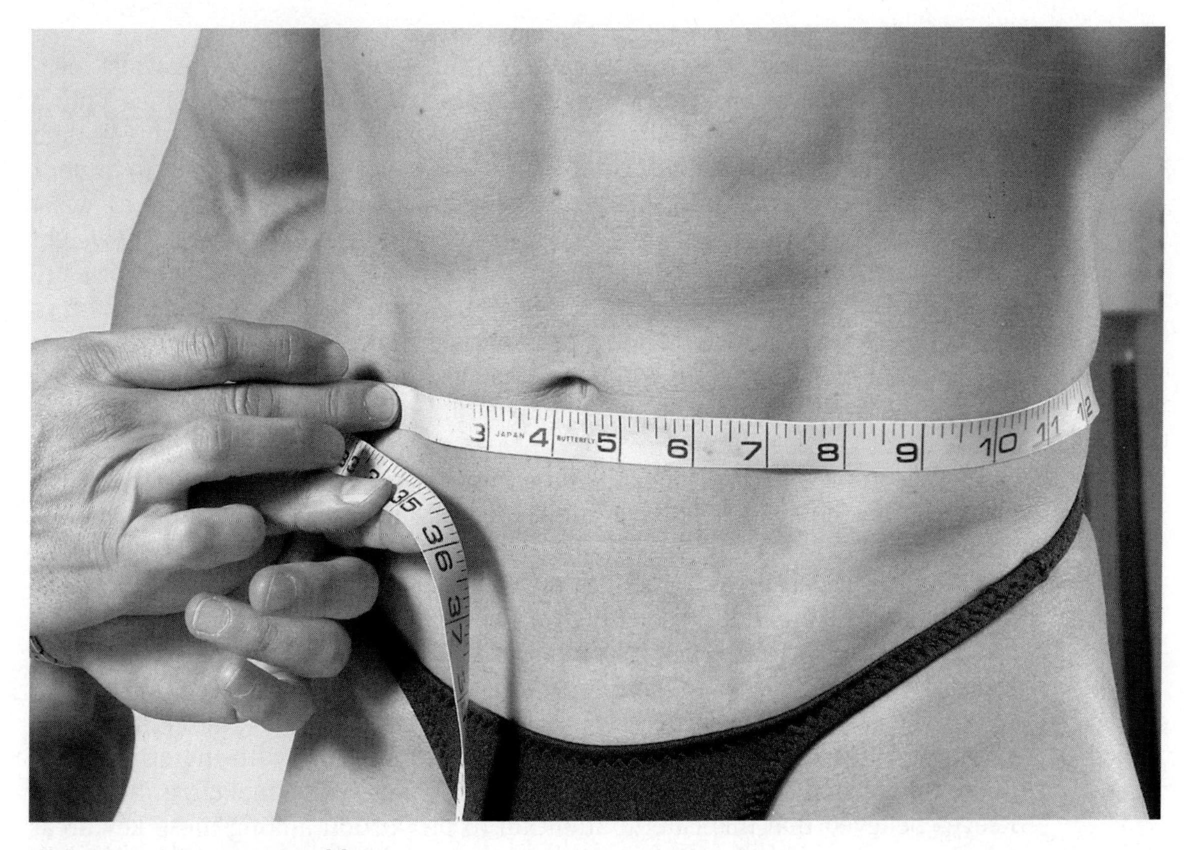

Waist measurement position.

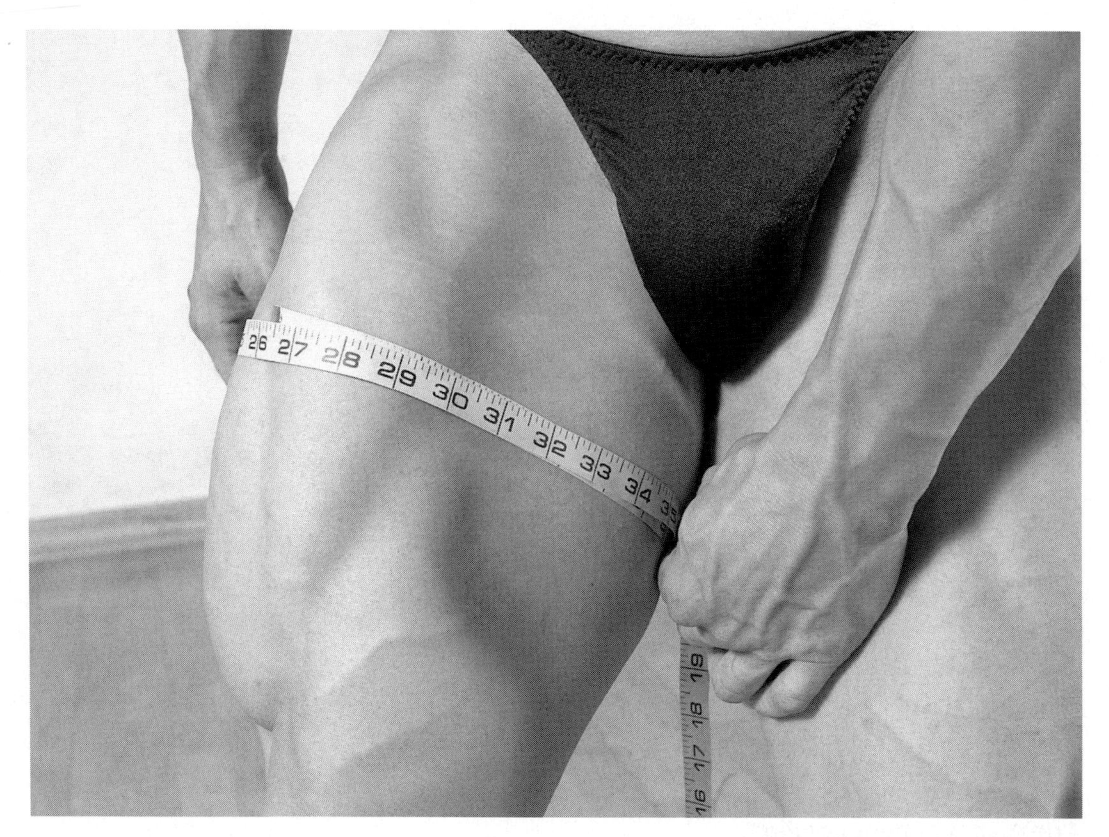

Thigh measurement position.

Some bodybuilders blessed with naturally small hips can achieve a waist measurement as small as 27 inches. This is extremely small when combined with a 50-inch chest. Other bodybuilders shoot for a waist measurement in the 30-inch range. One thing to remember is that your waist measurement will go up as your body weight rises. Even if you achieve a very low body-fat percentage, the waist measurement will go up if you are carrying more muscle and a higher body weight than previously.

It's also important to measure the legs to be sure that the lower body is in proportion to the upper body. It is a beginner's mistake to measure only the arms or chest and ignore the legs. You would never think of training only your upper body at the expense of your legs. So you should track the lower body's progress as you chart your development.

To measure the thighs, wrap the tape around the leg about two-thirds of the way up from the knee. This area is the biggest and provides the most accurate measure.

A very big thigh measurement is anything close to or more than 30 inches. Most natural bodybuilders have thigh measurements between 25 and 29 inches in contest condition. Any measurement over 27 inches is considered a big leg, especially onstage.

When measuring calves, flex the muscles and wrap the tape around the middle of the calf area. The ideal measurement should be in line with the arms. Steve Reeves was noted for having arms, calves, and a neck with equal circumferences. Reeves believed that this careful attention to proportion among these key areas was part of the secret for his beautiful shape and symmetry.

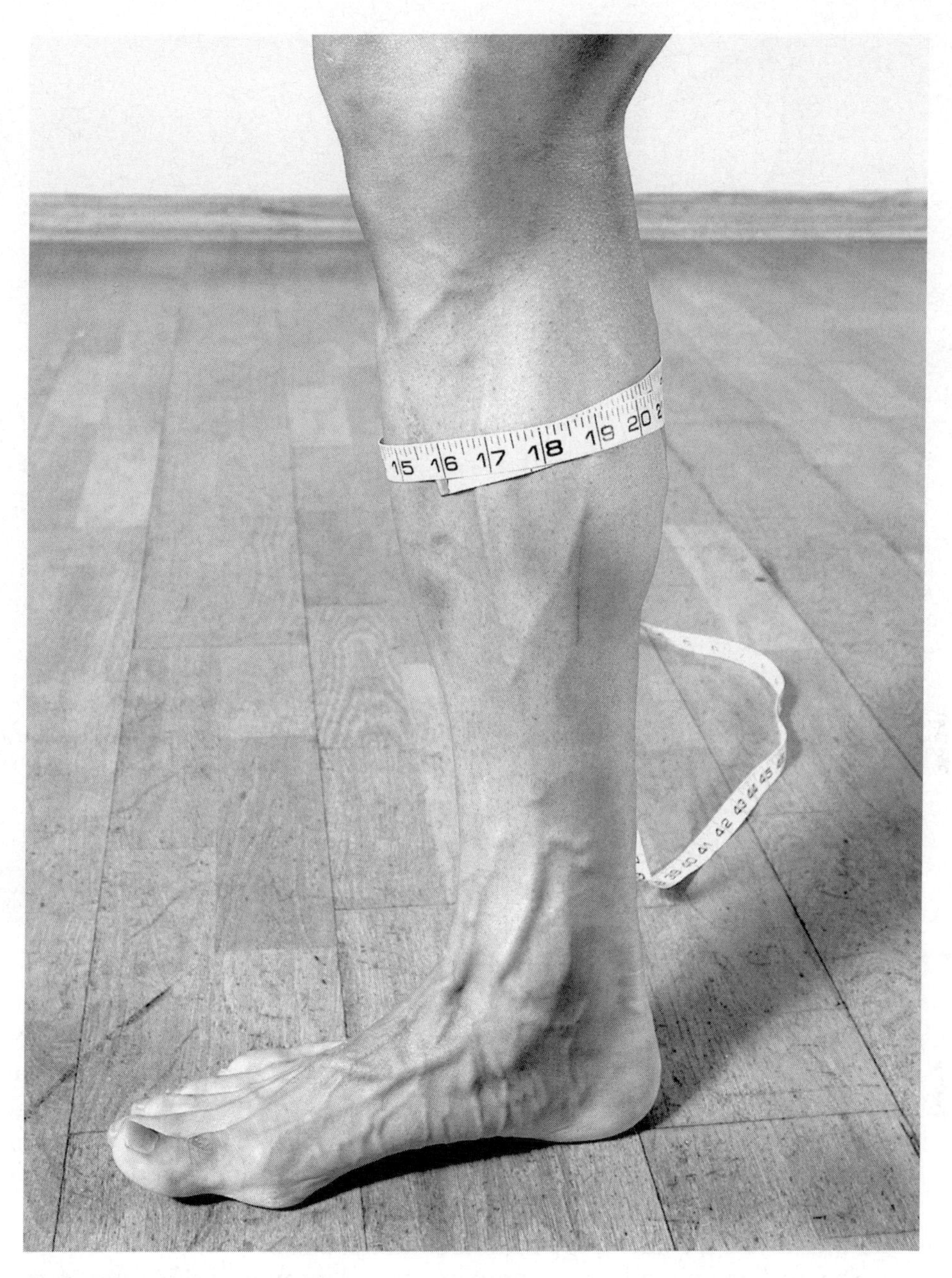

Calf measurement position.

Because the calves should be in proportion to the arms, any calf measurement close to 20 inches is considered extremely well developed. Most bodybuilders with good calf development probably have calves that measure from 16 to 18 inches.

Measure the forearms to determine the proportion of the upper arms to the lower arms. You can measure the forearms while they are relaxed or flexed. I prefer the flexed position. Bend your elbow to a 90-degree angle and flex the forearm muscles by cocking the wrist up.

The forearms usually measure several inches smaller than the upper arm. Lou Ferrigno had forearms that measured 18 inches when he was in his prime. This is very large and should not be considered the norm. A forearm between 13 and 15 inches is a decent measurement for a natural bodybuilder with 17- to 19-inch upper arms.

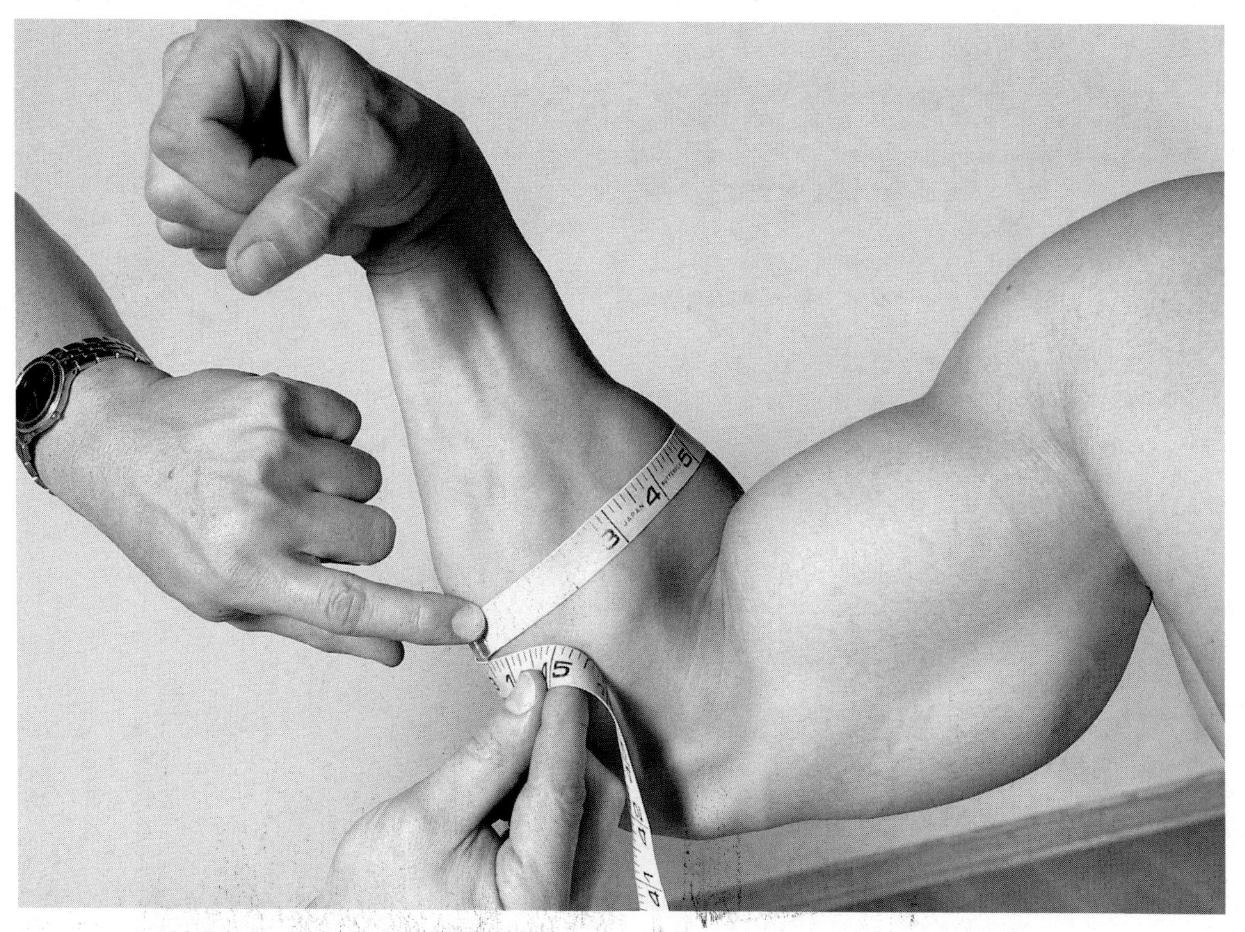

Forearm measurement position.

The last measurement to record is the neck. Most bodybuilders do not train the neck because it grows as a result of exercises for the deltoids and traps. Nevertheless, measure the neck regularly to make sure that it is proportional to the arms and calves. The neck is very easy to measure. Just wrap the tape around the middle of the neck. You may have to look in a mirror to record the correct number if you are taking the measurement yourself.

The neck should measure approximately the same as the arms. A small neck makes the physique appear frail, even if the rest of the body looks massive. A big, thick neck, however, bestows a look of power to the physique. A large neck makes the whole body appear rugged and strong.

Apply the following guidelines to your seven measurements to determine if your physique is in proportion.

1. The neck, calves, and arms should measure within an inch or two of each other. It's not uncommon for the arms to be slightly larger than the calves or neck. However, calves that are more than two inches smaller than the arms are out of proportion.

2. The chest measurement should be 95 percent of both thigh measurements. A bodybuilder with 25-inch thighs should have a chest measurement of 47.5 inches ($25 \times 2 = 50 \times 0.95 = 47.5$).

3. The forearm measurement should be approximately 80 percent of the upper arm measurement. A bodybuilder with 18-inch arms should have forearms that measure at least 14.5 inches.

4. The waist measurement will differ depending on if the bodybuilder is trying to gain weight and add muscle, or if he is losing body fat to prepare for competition. A method for keeping on track during the off-season and for setting a goal during contest preparation is to shoot for a waist measurement that is 70 to 72 percent of your chest measurement during the off-season and only 65 percent of your chest measurement when you are onstage. For example, if your chest measurement is 50 inches in the off-season when you're trying to add muscle, your waist measurement should not exceed 36 inches. For a competition, the ideal measurement for your waist would be 32.5 inches.

These approximations are ideal for my physique, but you can use the same percentages for your body. However, you must be open to making adjustments based on your unique physique. For example, if you were born with a smaller hip structure than I was, you may be able to set a goal for a waist measurement of only 60 percent of your chest measurement.

As you analyze your measurements, keep in mind the ideal proportions of a winning bodybuilder. You want the greatest chest-to-waist differential possible within the limits of your bone structure. You also want your legs to appear in proportion to your upper body when you stand relaxed to the front. It's important that the arms, calves, and neck all appear to be the same size. And don't neglect parts of the body like the forearms. If they are out of proportion to the upper arms, you must train them harder to keep them in balance.

One rule to remember when measuring to mark progress is not to measure yourself too often. Adding muscle takes time. You may get discouraged if you measure too often and see no progress. A good rule of thumb is to measure once every three to four weeks. This is long enough to show progress but not frequent enough to cause discouragement.

Scale and Body-Fat Percentages

Most people use the bathroom scale to gauge how fat they are. However, as all bodybuilders know, muscle weighs more than fat, so the scale may not accurately reflect how much muscle or fat is on your body. But when you use a scale in conjunction with body-fat calipers, you get a much better idea of how much fat and muscle you're carrying.

Calipers measure skinfold thickness, which lets you estimate how much body fat you have. The calipers measure the subcutaneous fat, which is located between the skin and the muscle. This subcutaneous fat makes up your body-fat percentage. The lower your body fat, the more defined your physique appears.

Skinfold thickness measurements are taken at various sites on the body (see figure 1.2). Some of the sites, such as the legs and arms, tend to stay lean even in the off-season. Others, like the abdominals, tend to accumulate fat quickly and are usually the last areas to lose body fat. For this reason, the combination of the skinfold measurements determines body-fat percentage.

If you weigh yourself at the same time that you take the skinfold measurements, you can get a better understanding how much fat compared to muscle mass you have. Trying to determine if you are making progress and gaining muscle simply

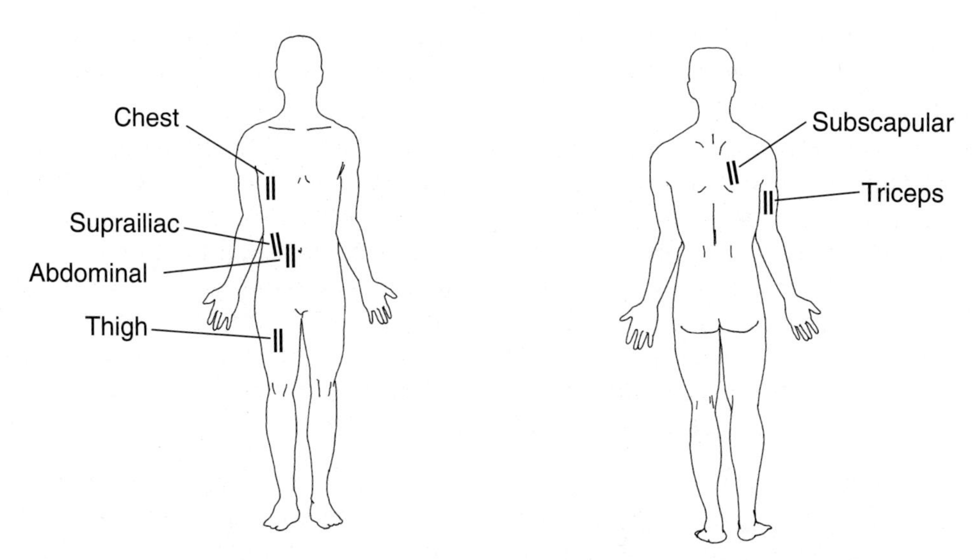

Figure 1.2 Skinfold sites.

Adapted, by permission, from L.T. Mackinnon, C.B. Ritchie, S.L. Hooper, and P.J. Abernethy, 2003, Exercise Management: Concepts and Professional Practice (Champaign, IL), 111.

by weighing yourself is often misleading. Taking skinfold measurements along with weighing yourself is a better option for accurately assessing your progress when gaining muscle and losing fat.

At each measurement site illustrated in the figure above, pinch the skin and measure the thickness using skinfold calipers. The measurements should be recorded and measured in millimeters. The measurement sites and the proper way to take the measurements are as follows.

Chest: Locate the area halfway between the nipple and the shoulder on the outside of the chest. This area is approximately one and a half inches away from the nipple. Pinch the skin with one hand and measure the thickness of the skinfold with the caliper.

Abdominal: Pinch the skin one inch to the side of the navel and measure the skinfold vertically. The abdomen is the area that accumulates fat the quickest, and this measurement will show the greatest change when dieting.

Thigh: The proper site for this measurement is halfway between the top of the thigh and the knee. Pinch the skin and measure the fold vertically. If you tend to hold water or skin thickness in the thighs, this site will show dramatic changes between the off-season and precontest.

Suprailiac: This site is one and a half inches above the pelvic bone. Pinch the skin and measure the skinfold diagonally.

Triceps: The site is located on the back of the arm at the midpoint of the triceps. Pinch the skin and measure the thickness vertically.

Men use the sum of the chest, abdominal, and thigh measurements to estimate their body-fat percentage. Women use the sum of the triceps, suprailiac, and thigh measurements to estimate their body-fat percentage. Use the measurements and your age to figure your body fat. The following formulas will help you determine your own body-fat percentage. These formulas give a measure of body density (D). To convert body density to body fat, use the following equation:

$$\% \text{ Body Fat} = (495/D) - 450$$

Males

$$\text{Density} = 1.10938 - (0.0008267 \times \text{sum of chest, abdominal, thigh}) + (0.0000016 \times \text{square of the sum of chest, abdominal, thigh}) - (0.0002574 \times \text{age}).$$

Females

$$\text{Density} = 1.0994921 - (0.0009929 \times \text{sum of triceps, suprailiac, thigh}) + (0.0000023 \times \text{square of the sum of triceps, suprailiac, thigh}) - (0.0001392 \times \text{age}).$$

For men, a body-fat percentage between 10 and 25 percent is appropriate for optimum health, and 5 to 10 percent is ideal for a competitive bodybuilder. Women should shoot for 18 to 33 percent for top health and 12 to 22 percent for competition. Women naturally carry a higher body-fat percentage than men, so their ideal percentages are slightly higher.

For a competitive bodybuilder, the percentages are much lower than for an average person just trying to stay in shape. Even in the off-season, a body-fat percentage of 25 percent is too high. However, 10 to 12 percent body fat is lean enough to be an asset when it is time to diet down for a competition. Likewise, a female bodybuilder should strive to keep her body-fat percentage close to 18 percent during the off-season if she wants to get down to 10 to 12 percent for a competition.

Body-fat percentages and body weight are two more objective methods for gauging your progress. Although measuring your body fat through skinfold measurements is not the most accurate way to determine your body composition (underwater immersion is the most accurate method), you will be able to assess your progress or lack of it with regular measurements. Just be sure that the same person takes your measurements each time (unless you are doing them yourself) so that the measuring technique is consistent.

When dieting for a competition, measure your body-fat percentage and measure yourself with the tape every three to four weeks. In the off-season, bring out the calipers every four to six weeks. Instead of body-fat percentages, use the size of your waist as a barometer of fat levels.

Body-fat percentage is another objective measurement that, in the end, doesn't mean anything when it comes to bodybuilding competition. Just because a person has 5 percent body fat doesn't automatically mean that he will beat someone with 7 percent body fat. Other factors determine who wins a bodybuilding competition. Often a person with a low body-fat percentage doesn't look as lean as the number suggests. Remember, the bottom line is how you look. Body-fat percentages may help you to stay motivated and assess your progress, but the judges don't care what your body-fat percentage is, and you shouldn't make it a big deal either.

Photos Tell the Story

Next to the mirror, photos are probably the best way to analyze your physique. They allow you to study your body in the same way that the judges at a bodybuilding competition do. Although photos lack the three-dimensional aspect, they provide an excellent tool for examining and analyzing your physique that may be missed when looking in a mirror.

When taking photographs of your physique, follow the same guidelines you use to look in the mirror. Take the photos in the same place and at the same time to provide an accurate comparison. This is particularly important when taking photos outside.

Be sure to wear clothing that reveals your physique. Posing trunks are good in the final few weeks before a competition. Training shorts are fine if you are merely attempting to analyze areas that need work. Don't wear sweat pants or a tank top as they will cover your body and hide areas that may need improvement.

If weather conditions and the time of the year are right, take your photos outside. The sun brings out more detail than indoor lighting. As any professional photographer will tell you, if you don't take the photos at the right time of the day, the sun will cast harsh shadows that cover most of your body. These photos will provide little feedback. I've been told that the best time for taking photos of your physique is either two hours after sunrise or two hours before sunset. The sun is low enough at these two times of the day to avoid harsh shadows. However, standing outside in posing trunks in January doesn't work in most places, so you may need to stay inside.

No matter where you take the photos, remember that different backgrounds produce different effects. A black background makes you appear more defined, and a white backdrop makes you look bigger but with less definition. Avoid taking photos in front of a distracting background such as a brick wall or a waterfall. Your physique should be the dominant subject in the photo so that you can properly analyze each picture. If at all possible, take the photos in the same place each time.

Instruct your photographer to include your whole body in each picture. Don't cut off the legs or the calves. Digital cameras allow you to see the images immediately after snapping the shutter. This instant feedback lets you make sure you've gotten your whole body in the photo, and if not, gives you a second chance.

If you don't want to rely on finding someone to take the photos, use the timer on your camera or purchase a timer for your camera that snaps the shutter after a certain amount of time. If you plan to take photos regularly, this may be a good investment. The automatic timer allows you to take photos whenever and wherever you please.

Just like when you are in front of the mirror, take photos in a variety of poses to determine your strengths and weaknesses. At a minimum, you should have photographs of yourself standing relaxed from the front, both sides, and the rear plus the seven mandatory poses. You can also include some of your favorite poses.

When analyzing your photos, look for the same things you would look for in the mirror: development, proportion, symmetry, and condition. Because bodybuilding is about developing your muscles, development should be your first goal. Analyze each photo and note which muscle groups seem to be growing and which are lagging behind.

Physique photographs can be taken as often as every week (if you are in the final stages before a competition) or as infrequently as once a year. For example, when I am dieting for a contest, I take photos weekly during the final 12 weeks of preparation. When the level of body fat is reduced to the single digits, you can see changes every week.

An Objective Eye

A final method of analyzing your physique is to have someone look at your condition. This person needs to be someone you can trust to give you an honest assessment of your physique. They also need to be educated about the sport of bodybuilding so they know what they are looking at. Finding a person who is both informed and objective can be harder than you think. Most people will not tell you the brutal truth for fear of hurting your feelings. Although they are trying to make you feel better, it will do you no good to have someone "lie" to you and tell you look good when you really don't. It's better to hear the truth about your physique, even if it hurts, so you can make the changes necessary to improve your physique. I was lucky to have the advice of my brother, Don, when I was competing. I could rely on Don to be honest with me when I was getting ready for a competition, because I knew he would tell me the truth and he was very intelligent when it came to analyzing a bodybuilding physique. This advice was invaluable to me for my contest preparation because I was able to gauge my progress based on his objective opinion.

Power of the Mind

One thing to keep in mind about genetics and bodybuilding is the power and influence of the mind. Believing that your genetics are bad for building your body will influence your determination and desire to develop your physique. Many of the bodybuilding champions who have been role models for generations started off with less than stellar physiques, and yet they went on to create championship bodies.

Early pictures of Mr. Olympia Franco Columbu reveals a physique that did not look like a future bodybuilding champion. Franco was short with narrow shoulders and bowed legs and was downright skinny. Frank Zane was also very thin when he began bodybuilding. The symmetry and shape were there, but it was up to Frank to develop his physique into the work of art that it later became. Even the Incredible Hulk himself, Lou Ferrigno, was painfully skinny as a teenager. Lou obviously had great potential for bodybuilding, but he wasn't aware of it until he began lifting. He soon developed one of the most massive physiques the sport has ever seen. Many times it is impossible to determine how good you can eventually become until you try.

Now that you've decided to see how far you can go in the sport of bodybuilding, chapter 2 describes training methods to build massive muscles.

Chapter 2

Training Methods for Adding Mass

Three factors contribute to gains in muscle size. These are resistance training, nutrition, and recuperation. The first step in this process is training. Bodybuilding training tears down muscle tissue through weight training. The muscle fibers themselves are damaged during intense weight training involving the right amounts of resistance and repetitions. The fibers then grow bigger and stronger through the process of adaptation. This adaptation period occurs in the days following a workout and the process is accelerated through proper rest and nutrition. However, because muscles adapt to the stress you impose on them through training, you must progressively increase the intensity. If you always use the same resistance and intensity, the muscles have no incentive to respond, and they stop growing. We start this chapter with the initial techniques for mass building then move into four traditional methods for increasing intensity.

Building Mass Through Repetitions

Let's begin with repetitions. The optimal number of reps is debatable. Some bodybuilders believe that only low reps make the muscle grow, while others point to bodybuilding legends such as Serge Nubret who developed incredible muscle size using relatively light weights and high repetitions.

The number of reps you perform in any given set depends on your goals. If your goal is to get stronger, you use a different repetition scheme than someone who wants to develop maximum muscle size. See table 2.1 for the correct repetition patterns.

TABLE 2.1 Correct Repetition Patterns

Type of reps	Range of reps	Uses	Exercises	Tips
Low	1-5	Developing strength and power	Bench press Squat Deadlift	Schedule sets of triples (3 reps) and doubles (2 reps) into your training routines. Low reps build strength first and muscle mass second. To gain both size and strength, perform a few sets of 6-12 reps, then include heavy sets that allow only 3-5 reps at the end to build strength. Basic exercises such as the bench press, squat, and deadlift are perfect for low reps. If you have a high proportion of fast-twitch (white) muscle fibers, you will respond better to low reps than someone with equal proportions of fast- and slow-twitch fibers or more slow. If you suspect you have a greater proportion of fast-twitch in a certain muscle group, train that area with heavy resistance and 4-6 reps.
Moderate	6-10	Developing muscle size and strength	All of the basic exercises	Resistance that keeps the number of reps in the 6-10 range is best for muscle growth because it thickens the muscle fibers, pumps the area surrounding the muscle cells (the sarcoplasm) with blood and other nutrients, and puts the muscle fibers under tension long enough for growth to occur. Sets of 6-10 reps make the muscles bigger first and stronger second. The amount of time a muscle is under tension is critical to growth. Very low reps do not keep the muscle fibers under tension long enough to promote growth. Athletes who primarily use low reps may be very strong, but they aren't as big as those who use high reps.
High	12-20	Muscle growth due primarily to the increase in capillary size in the muscle cell instead of the increased thickness of the muscle fibers themselves.	Basic or isolation exercises	Higher reps require less resistance during the set. The decreased resistance results in less muscle strength and more endurance. Higher reps also pump more growth-producing blood into a muscle.

(continued)

Type of reps	Range of reps	Uses	Exercises	Tips
High *(continued)*				The pump-type of workout (12-20 reps) does not affect the growth of the muscle fibers as much as heavy training with 6-10 reps per set. High reps are valuable for muscle groups that do not readily respond to low or moderate reps. Quite often, a stubborn muscle group does not share the same nerve-to-muscle connection as other muscle groups. In other words, the stubborn muscle groups do not pump up as easily as the faster growing muscles. For less-responsive muscle groups, use high reps to pump more blood into the area. Do more reps with less resistance or superset two exercises to force more blood into the muscle group. This additional "pump" at the end of a workout helps stubborn muscle groups respond when 6-10 reps with heavy resistance does not work.
Extremely high	50-100	Shocking the muscle to promote growth	Machine or dumbbell isolation exercises	Extremely high reps can shock the muscle to promote growth. This training method may provide benefit because it is different from conventional training methods. More than 15 reps do not usually increase muscle size. However, those with a greater proportion of red (slow-twitch) muscle fibers may find high reps better for making progress because of the greater tension time. Low reps may provide slow progress to those with predominantly slow-twitch fibers. However, because most of the growth of muscle fibers occurs in the fast-twitch type IIb muscle fibers, even those with slow-twitch fibers will benefit from heavy resistance and moderate reps. To increase tension time for slow-twitch fibers, use supersets or drop sets. These methods allow heavy resistance but increase the tension time necessary for growth.

Incorporating Reps Into a Workout

The most effective way to incorporate repetitions into a workout and obtain benefits from a combination of a high, moderate, and low number of reps in one workout is the pyramid system of training. In the pyramid system you use a light weight for the first set and perform 12 to 15 repetitions, and then add weight in each succeeding set while decreasing the repetitions.

This training method safely warms up the muscles by beginning with light resistance and slowly adding more as the workout continues. Beginning a workout with heavy weights is almost guaranteed to cause injury. The muscles, as well as the joints, tendons, and ligaments, need time to warm up. By starting with a weight that is 50 percent of your heavy working set (a set at a weight that allows a maximum of six reps) and doing 12 to 15 repetitions, you force blood into the muscles, warming up the area before your heavy sets.

Table 2.2 provides an example of a pyramid system using the bench press exercise. Pyramid training allows you to use a variety of resistances through a range of 6 to 12 repetitions. Each succeeding set is heavier than the previous one, which prepares the body for the maximum set while continuing to pump growth-producing blood into the muscles.

Another variation on the pyramid system is to warm up with gradually increasing weight but to limit the number of repetitions (table 2.3). This method eliminates the possibility of "burning out" or fatiguing the muscles being trained by doing too many repetitions in the warm-up sets.

TABLE 2.2 Pyramid Option 1: Maximum Working Weight 315 Pounds

Set	Weight in pounds	Number of reps
1	135	12
2	225	10
3	275	8
4	315	6

TABLE 2.3 Pyramid Option 2: Maximum Working Weight 315 Pounds

Set	Weight in pounds	Number of reps
1	135	10
2	225	3
3	275	1
4-6	315	6

Which method of pyramid training is better? Both have benefits. However, the first method allows you to train the muscles through a variety of repetitions even though the early sets are considered warm-ups because you do not work to failure. In pyramid option 1, the pectoral muscles are working and definitely benefiting from sets of 225 pounds for 10 reps and 275 pounds for 8 reps.

Most advanced bodybuilders who use this method of pyramiding keep the resistance for the warm-up sets the same after they reach a certain level of strength and development. However, they still strive to increase the resistance used in the final set or sets. They do this because the final heavy sets are the ones they take to failure. The sets before this serve as a warm-up for the muscles, tendons, and ligaments. Remember, it is the final, gut-wrenching reps that are responsible for the growth of type IIb muscle fibers, the fibers that can double in size.

On the other hand, if you are not as advanced, you will have to increase the resistance on all sets, including the warm-ups. If a bodybuilder with one year of experience uses the following routine on the bench press: Set 1 – 135 pounds for 12 reps, set 2 – 155 pounds for 10 reps, set 3 – 175 pounds for 8 reps, and set 4 – 205 pounds for 6 reps, the weight for all of the sets, even the warm-ups, will increase as he or she gets bigger and stronger. Remember that the muscles benefit from every set, not just the last few heavy ones.

The second method of pyramid training is effective for bodybuilders who are very advanced or are getting ready for a competition. Advanced bodybuilders are more likely to reach a sticking point or a plateau in their strength levels. If these bodybuilders hold off on the warm-up sets, they will be stronger on the working sets and should be able to increase their strength over time. Competitive bodybuilders limit their strength when they cut back their caloric intake to prepare for competition. But they can more effectively use the strength they have by limiting the number of reps during the warm-up sets and going all out on the final working sets.

The drawback to pyramid option 2 is that although three warm-up sets are performed before the working sets, this may not be enough to warm up the muscles and tendons. Of course, one solution is to add more warm-up sets before the working sets.

Pyramid training outlined in option 2 seems to work best for bodybuilders who respond well to low repetitions. Because they limit the number of reps in the warm-up sets, these bodybuilders work in the one- to six-rep range predominantly. For bodybuilders with a disproportionate number of white muscle fibers, limited reps in the warm-up sets probably works best. For those with an equal number of red and white muscle fibers, the first method of pyramid training is a better option.

Note that the pyramid system is not necessary for every exercise. You should, however, use it for the first exercise for a particular muscle group to warm it up fully.

Volume vs. Intensity

Arnold Schwarzenegger was the king of bodybuilding in the 1970s. He performed approximately five sets each of four to six exercises for each target area for an average of 20 to 30 sets per area while training six days a week. Every magazine article of this era recommended and outlined similar programs. Because Arnold was the best, the vast majority of the other bodybuilders followed his lead. This included every bodybuilder from the Mr. Olympia level to the rank novice training in the basement.

The reasoning behind the high number of sets was that every target area is composed of different muscles, and each must be trained for full development. The back, for example, includes the upper lats, the middle back, the lower lats, and the low back. Therefore, the back needs a minimum of four exercises to attain full development. Five sets of each of these four exercises require a minimum of 20 sets to train the area completely. If you add in another movement for lat thickness and maybe one more to work the smaller muscles of the upper back, your back routine now consists of 30 sets. Using this theory, even a single muscle like the biceps requires at least 20 sets. These include an exercise each for the upper and lower areas of the biceps, plus another exercise each for the outer and inner heads.

On paper, it makes sense to include an adequate number of exercises to fully train each muscle. The problem is that the body is not a machine and cannot perform set after set without creating an energy deficit. Because a limited amount of energy is available for each training session, it does not take long to overtrain individual muscles and the overall body as well.

Despite the obvious shortcomings of high-volume training for each muscle group, most of the world's bodybuilders trained this way because that was the conventional wisdom. Nearly every bodybuilding magazine at the time recommended 20 to 30 sets for each target area if you wanted to get big.

Then, a young bodybuilder by the name of Mike Mentzer came along. Mike placed second in the 1975 International Federation of Bodybuilders (IFBB) Mr. America contest and appeared to have potential and a reasonable future. However, one year later, Mike surprised everyone by showing up much bigger and dramatically improved to destroy the competition at the 1976 IFBB Mr. America. Suddenly, he had a shot at winning the Mr. Universe contest. Mike Mentzer became bodybuilding's rising star.

When Mike gave interviews for the magazines after his Mr. America win, he surprised everyone by revealing the radical training routine that had been responsible for his incredible improvement in the last year. Mentzer admitted that he had trained just three days per week for his Mr. America victory. What was even more shocking was that he did a maximum of five sets per target area—five sets total, not five sets per exercise!

Mentzer explained that he used to train like every other bodybuilder: 25 to 30 sets per target area and working out six days per week. This regimen had produced an impressive physique, one that was good enough to place high in national events, but he felt he had reached a plateau. His body was not growing as fast as he felt it should considering the amount of time he was spending in the gym each week. It was only after completely changing his training routine that he was able to make the improvements he needed to win the Mr. America title.

Mentzer theorized that training intensity and not training volume accounted for the growth of muscle tissue. He also explained that a bodybuilder could train hard or he could train long, but he could not do both. In other words, every bodybuilder using 20 to 30 sets per target area was not training as hard as he could. Instead, he was pacing himself to complete the large number of sets. Mentzer explained that trying to perform high volume at maximum intensity was similar to trying to sprint a marathon. It is physically impossible.

Mike Mentzer's radical theories on training and intensity revolutionized the sport of bodybuilding. Previously accepted ideas on the number of sets required to develop muscle were now looked at suspiciously. Mentzer's philosophy on training hard and not long made sense. It wasn't long before bodybuilders all over the world began to change their training programs.

You can determine how many sets to use for each target area by figuring out how many exercises it will take to train the muscles to the maximum. The basic exercises, which use several muscle groups to produce the movement, are the most effective; however, the involvement of multiple muscle groups also makes them more difficult to perform. For example, the squat is a much more demanding exercise than the leg extension because with the squat, you are using the muscles of the thighs, lower back, glutes, and hips. With the leg extension exercise, you are only using the quadriceps muscles to perform the movement and the exercise becomes much less demanding than a basic exercise such as the squat. These exercises require a lot more energy, and they stress the body as a whole much more so than isolation exercises. Isolation exercises or exercises that concentrate on only a specific area of a muscle are not as taxing to the system, and they do not promote maximum muscle development like the basic exercises do.

This is not to say that isolation-type movements should be avoided. They have their place in a bodybuilding program, particularly when preparing for a competition. However, when it comes to developing the muscles to their potential, the basic exercises are the only way to go.

Although exercise routines for each target area are explained in detail in part II of this book, table 2.4 provides a general overview on how many sets each muscle group requires.

TABLE 2.4 Overview of Sets

Target area	Type of exercise	Number of sets	Tips
Chest	2 basic exercises and 1 or 2 isolation exercises	10-12	Use 3 or 4 sets for each basic exercise (not including warm-ups) and 2 or 3 sets for the other exercises.
Back	1 exercise for the upper lats, 1 or 2 exercises for the thickness of the middle lats, 1 exercise for the lower lats, and l exercise for the low back	12-15	Use 3 or 4 sets for the first 3 exercises (focusing on the width and thickness of the lats), 2 or 3 sets for the lower lats, and 3 sets for the low back.
Deltoids	1 pressing exercise for the front delts, 1 exercise for the side delts, and 1 exercise for the rear delts	9-12	Any type of pressing movement as the basic exercise for the delts and as the primary movement for the front deltoids. If another exercise is included for the side delts and the rear delts, you will have to use at least 3 exercises to train the delts.
Traps	Shrug movements with barbells or dumbbells	4-6	The trapezius muscle is often trained with the delts because both are involved in many of the same movements. The traps are trained with a limited range of motion and do not need a lot of exercises for full development. A good trap workout can be achieved with only 1 or 2 exercises for 2-4 sets for each movement.

(continued)

TABLE 2.4 ***(continued)***

Target area	Type of exercise	Number of sets	Tips
Triceps	Extension movements and pressing exercises	9-12	The triceps is composed of three different heads: the outer head, the inner head, and the middle head. 3 or 4 sets of 3 different exercises will fully train all three heads.
Biceps	2-3 exercises of 2-3 sets each Curling movements with both barbells and dumbbells.	6-9	Because the biceps is small, it does not require a lot of sets to fully work it.
Quadriceps	2 basic exercises such as squats and leg presses for an average of 4 sets each plus an additional shaping exercise	11 or 12	Although the quadriceps muscle is large and is capable of a tremendous amount of work, the basic exercises for the quads are demanding. Numbers of sets are unrealistic and could result in overtraining.
Hamstrings	2 exercises for 3 or 4 sets each	6-8	Leg curls are the primary movement for the hamstrings and should be performed from a variety of angles: lying, seated, and standing. Stiff-leg deadlifts also build the hamstrings.
Calves	2 exercises of 3 or 4 sets each	6-8	The calves are a relatively small muscle group and typically slow to respond. They must be trained intensely; however, this doesn't necessarily mean lots of sets.
Forearms	1 exercise for the upper forearms and 1 exercise for lower forearms for 3 sets each	6	The forearm muscles can be stubborn. Train this group consistently with relatively high reps.
Abdominals	Off-season, 1 exercise for the upper abs and 1 exercise for the lower abs for 3 sets each; precontest training, 2 exercises for the upper abs and 2 exercises for the lower abs for 3 or 4 sets each.	6 in the off-season and 12-14 for precontest training	Superset the upper- and lower-ab exercises during the workout. It's possible to perform 3 or 4 ab exercises in a row with no rest between movements.

Total Sets for Mass Building

When deciding on the number of sets for each area of the body, you must consider the total number of sets for the workout. The body has a finite amount of energy for each workout. Too many sets in a training session negatively affects not only the workout but also future progress.

When the goal for each training session is to get bigger, you must follow three rules. The first is to use the basic exercises. The second is to perform these exercises with enough intensity to produce growth. The third is to complete enough sets to produce growth, but limit the volume to avoid overtraining. Too many sets hamper your ability to recuperate from workouts, which interferes with your progress in the long run.

If you perform the basic exercises with heavy weights and at a high intensity, you must reduce the number of sets per workout, otherwise your progress will come to a standstill. High volume combined with high training intensity leads to overtraining.

Many bodybuilders are overtraining in their workout regimens and are not even aware of it. They become used to doing a large number of sets for each body part and never really train the muscles as hard as they could. If they are truly training hard using the heaviest weights possible for the right number of reps and combining this high intensity with a high number of sets to train each muscle group, it will not take very long before they become overtrained.

The symptoms of overtraining include a general feeling of fatigue, not looking forward to the next training session, decreased strength during the workout, loss of muscle mass and an increased resting heart rate. If you listen to your body, you will be able to determine if you are overtraining just by the way you are feeling.

Many bodybuilders used to high-volume training (an average of 20 sets or more per target area) are shocked at how much stronger they become when they reduce the number of sets. Your body recuperates more easily when you use fewer sets, but push each one to the limit.

A good rule of thumb is to limit the number of sets per workout to 25 or fewer when training to gain size. To keep the sets moderate, you must decide before beginning the workout how many sets and exercises you will do. A plan for the workout will keep you on track and prevent you from adding sets or exercises during the workout.

For example, if you are scheduled to train chest and arms during an off-season workout, you could break down your workout as follows: 10 sets for the chest, 8 for the triceps, and 6 for the biceps, for a total of 24 sets in the workout.

This limited number of sets lets you work out at 100 percent intensity. Without this number in mind, you might be tempted to add sets for each muscle group and end up with too many sets overall.

Increasing Intensity

Bodybuilders use four methods to increase intensity. These involve manipulating the training session in the following ways:

- Adding resistance
- Adding volume
- Using the same resistance and volume in less time
- Extending the set past the point of failure

Some methods are better than others when it comes to building muscle mass. The traditional belief is that heavy resistance and low reps are superior for building size. Training with heavy weights is one of the best methods for getting big. However, other training concepts are also excellent for building massive muscles.

Training Method 1: More Resistance

An old saying among bodybuilders advises, "Go heavy or go home." This statement reflects the training philosophy of lifting heavy resistance to build size. The more resistance used, the bigger the muscles will become.

However, for heavy training to be effective, you must follow several guidelines. First, use appropriate weight and proper form. Lifters trying to move weights that are too heavy tend to sacrifice form in an effort to push the weight up. Resistance so heavy that you can't control it keeps you from working your muscles properly, which can lead to serious injury. Lifting maximum weight correctly requires intense concentration.

When training with heavy weight, you must use the proper number of reps. As discussed in chapter 1, a very limited number of repetitions builds strength rather than muscle size. Therefore, to build muscle size with heavy resistance, you must perform at least six repetitions.

Training the muscles with heavy weights is the first step toward developing massive size. All of the biggest bodybuilders in the sport initially developed their physiques by training with increasingly heavier weights. This process of forcing the muscles to adapt to a greater resistance results in bigger and stronger muscles. These results are not possible using lighter weights.

Forcing the muscles to adapt to a heavier training load is called the principle of progressive overload. It's a very simple process. If you have been using 150 pounds on squats for three sets of 10 reps, increasing the weight to 160 pounds for three sets of 10 reps places an overload on the muscles, an overload it is unaccustomed to. The muscles have no choice but to grow bigger and stronger in order to adapt to the new resistance.

Anyone hoping to increase muscle size and strength must train according to this overload principle. The bigger you want your muscles to become, the heavier you must train them. The 150-pound squats from the earlier example need to progress to 200 pounds, then to 250 pounds, and eventually to 300 pounds. This constant increase in resistance is the "secret" to developing massive muscle size. If you don't continue increasing the weight, your muscles will quickly adapt to the current workload and resist further growth.

Cycling Your Weight

Although the progressive overload principle is the foundation for training to gain size, used by itself it eventually presents a problem: at some point the body reaches a sticking point, and further strength increases become nearly impossible as the body nears its physical potential. The more developed your strength and muscle mass, the more difficult it becomes to make progress.

One solution is to use the same technique that powerlifters and weightlifters use. Their primary goal, after all, is to lift heavier weights. That's how their competitions are judged.

Powerlifters know that lifting heavier and heavier weights eventually leads to a plateau, and that the body will not get stronger just by increasing the weight. If this were true, there would be no limit to the amount of weight a person who trained consistently could lift.

To get stronger, powerlifters and other strength athletes divide their training programs into cycles of 6 to 12 weeks. A strength cycle uses the same exercise each week, but varies the number of reps and the weight from week to week to give the muscles time to recover between workouts. If all goes well and the correct weights were utilized during the cycle, the bodybuilder should have greater strength when the cycle is finished.

For example, table 2.5 outlines a nine-week strength cycle for the bench press exercise. A nine-week cycle allows you to increase the weight gradually so that you finish the cycle able to lift more weight than when you started. Although not listed in the table, the workout starts with a few warm-up sets. When choosing the weight for the cycle, be sure to select a weight that you can lift by yourself. Don't use a weight that requires help from a spotter. This will not build your strength, only that of your spotter. It's crucial to leave your ego at home and work with weights that are right for you.

I used the cycle in this illustration to overcome a sticking point on the bench press. At that point in my career, I could bench press 300 pounds for five repetitions. However, I had been stuck at that weight for weeks and could not do more reps with that weight. I didn't think going heavier was the answer because 300 pounds was already too heavy. For this cycle, I chose a beginning weight that I knew I could handle for the required number of reps. If I had miscalculated and

TABLE 2.5 Cycle and Weight Selection

Week	Weight in pounds	Reps	Sets
1	290	5	3
2	295	4	3
3	300	3	3
4	295	5	3
5	300	4	3
6	305	3	3
7	300	5	3
8	305	4	3
9	310	3	3

picked a weight that was too heavy or too light, I either would not have been able to complete the cycle, or I would not have challenged myself enough to gain strength.

Three to five reps is the best range for building strength and power. However, each workout in table 2.5 uses three sets so that the muscles can gradually adapt to the new weight. Being able to complete the required repetitions in all three sets on your own and in control, rather than struggling with the last heavy set, helps you feel like you can master the increasingly heavier weights.

Choose a weight for week one that is lighter than what you are capable of. After the first week, the resistance will increase throughout the rest of the cycle. If you begin the cycle with a weight that is too heavy, you will most likely reach a sticking point before the end of the nine weeks. Also remember that you want to have a little bit left over when you finish each workout. The goal is to gradually increase your strength by slowly overloading the muscles with a greater resistance each workout. Working yourself to failure will most likely shortchange your strength before the cycle is complete.

When you go back to your standard way of training after using a power cycle, you should notice an increase in strength. By gradually working with heavier weights each week, your strength will increase and you will overcome any sticking points you may have encountered during your training.

If you use cycles in your training, choose a basic exercise. This is important because basic exercises involve multiple muscle groups and are better suited to developing strength and power than isolation exercises are. And as an added bonus, all the muscle groups involved in the exercise will be stronger after completing a power cycle. The strength gained through an isolation exercise would be limited to a single muscle group; therefore, the gains in strength would be minimal.

Forced Reps

Forced reps are an advanced training method that extends a set past the point of failure. A training partner or your own free hand helps finish the repetition after your muscles fail. You can apply as many as three forced reps to an exercise if you use them correctly.

When I was 20 years old I trained very heavy to get bigger. I used weights that allowed me to do only six to eight reps because this is the best repetition range for building size and strength. However, I reached frequent sticking points, so I often used forced reps to get past them and advance to heavier weights.

As a means of getting stronger, I used a very heavy weight for my last set and attempted to eke out at least three reps on my own before reaching failure. Because this low number of reps is not enough to build muscle mass, my training partner stood by during my final set to give me a little assistance for two more reps.

Forced reps with heavier-than-normal weights let me work with weights I never would have been able to reach if I had stuck with the six- to eight-rep guidelines. This push for greater strength is the opposite of cycling weights to increase strength. However, it seemed to work for me. I increased my strength during this growing period of my bodybuilding career. For example, my maximum on the incline dumbbell press was the 110-pound dumbbells. I could do five or six reps with this weight, but they were difficult. Attempting to use the 120-pound dumbbells would have been too much to handle.

By using the forced reps method, I had my training partner stand by as I grabbed the 120 pound dumbbells for my final set. I was able to eke out 3 good reps on my own before reaching failure. At this point, my partner gave me a little assistance by pushing my elbows so I was able to complete another 2 reps on my own.

I don't recommend forced reps for every workout. Pushing to a point of failure and beyond overly stresses the nervous system. However, forced reps are effective if they are used occasionally to make the workout more intense or, as in this example, to accustom the muscles to heavier weights. Bill Pearl recommends that you leave the gym with something left over to contribute to the next workout instead of pushing to the point that you have nothing left. I think this is excellent advice.

The forced reps principle, shown here during seated dumbbell presses, is key to adding mass and advancing to heavier weights.

The problem with forced reps is that your training partner may apply too much help and end up doing most of the work. It's important that you and your partner understand that only minimal help will be given during forced reps and only when the muscle cannot lift the weight on its own.

Controlling the Negative

The eccentric portion of a repetition is when the weight returns to its starting point. This is also referred to as the negative part of a repetition. Many exercise physiologists have theorized that the negative portion of each rep causes the most damage to the muscle fibers, which later contributes to their growth. It is also agreed that the negative part of the repetition builds strength and power more than the concentric part of a repetition. The descent, or the eccentric part, of a rep is very important in getting stronger.

Mr. Olympia Dorian Yates explained that he was able to build his incredible strength by controlling the eccentric part of each repetition during his workouts. Dorian executed perfect form with every exercise. He had complete control over the negative portion of each rep, lowering the weight very slowly to the starting point before using an explosive contraction to complete the repetition.

Mike Mentzer occasionally used purely negative repetitions during his professional career. Two training partners lifted an extremely heavy weight into position. From there, Mike lowered the weight very slowly, emphasizing the eccentric portion of the repetition. After the training partners returned the weight to the starting position, Mike did another repetition, again emphasizing the negative.

Because the eccentric muscle contraction during the negative portion of a repetition is stronger than the concentric contraction during the positive part, you can use much greater resistance for negatives. This increased resistance and emphasis on the eccentric portion of each rep builds great strength.

Negative reps seem to work best with (surprise!) the basic power movements. Because you will use heavy weights, it is much safer to perform exercises that call upon several muscle groups rather than singling out one particular muscle group in an isolation exercise. Because negative reps impose intense stress on the body, the chance of injury increases. Therefore, it is important to warm up properly.

Use negative reps with basic upper-body exercises such as the bench press, incline press, military press, chin-ups, deadlifts, and close-grip bench press. You can also use them on lower-body movements such as squats, leg presses, hack squats, leg extensions, and leg curls. Pushing movements such as the bench press, incline press, military press, and close-grip bench press are especially well suited to negative reps. The concentric movements in squats or deadlifts can be very intense without the emphasis on the negative, and therefore, are not the best choice.

One drawback to negative reps is finding two partners to lift a very heavy weight just so you can lower it slowly. However, if you can find the help necessary, negative reps can be very effective for increasing strength and power.

Because of the intense stress on the muscles and tendons when using extremely heavy weights for eccentric training, use this training method for a maximum of six weeks at a time and no more than two or three times a year. Too much emphasis on negative repetitions overstresses the tendons and causes more harm than good. Also, schedule your training so that you do not use the eccentric training principle on too many movements during the week. Limit yourself to one or two movements per cycle to avoid excessive stress on the muscles, joints, and tendons. Too much of a good thing is not appropriate when it comes to intense training.

Power Rack Partials

Another technique for improving strength on the basic exercises is partial repetitions in a power rack. Placing pins at specific locations in a power rack limits the range of motion for an exercise, allowing partial reps. For example, if you want to build more strength for the lockout position in the seated military press exercise, set the pins so that at the lowest point of the movement the bar is even with your forehead. By performing only the last quarter of the exercise, you focus on the lockout portion. This limited range of motion allows you to use heavier weights, which eventually develops more strength in this portion of the exercise.

Partial reps in the power rack can help you overcome a sticking point in an exercise. For example, if you seem to get stuck on the bench press exercise in the middle range of the movement, you could work on this particular portion of the movement by using a power rack. By setting the pins so that the bar rests several inches above the chest (right where the bar seems to get stuck when doing bench presses), you could do multiple sets of bench presses focusing on this particular sticking point. By working the area in which you are weak, you will eventually develop strength to overcome the sticking point.

Power movements such as the bench press, deadlifts, squats, military press, and the close-grip bench press are perfect for partial reps in the power rack. If you decide to use this training method, concentrate on exercises that are difficult to perform. Use the specific area of the movement that you have identified as your sticking point. Spend four to six weeks doing three to five sets of five to six reps in this specific area of the movement.

If you spend six weeks working on a certain area of an exercise with the prescribed number of sets and reps, you will build strength in that movement. Partial reps in the power rack follows the rule of specificity, which states that if you want to improve a skill, you must practice it.

The exercises on the following pages are the recommendations for using the power rack to develop strength in a specific area of an exercise.

Bench press (lockout): Set the pins several inches below the point where your arms would be completely straight. Begin the exercise with the bar resting on the pins and forcefully push the bar to the lockout position *(a)*. Hold the lockout for several seconds before slowly lowering the bar to the resting position on the pins *(b)*. Wait for a couple of seconds before pushing the bar back to lockout. Because this exercise uses a very limited range of motion, you should be able to use more weight than in a full bench press exercise.

a

b

Bench press (midpoint): Set the pins approximately 10 inches from the lockout position in the power rack *(a)*. Push the bar from a resting position on the pins, the midpoint, to lockout and hold for two seconds before lowering the weight to the pins *(b)*. Avoid bouncing the bar off the pins; this will not develop strength in the sticking point.

a

b

Bench press (starting point): Set the pins so the bar rests directly above the chest, making the upper arms parallel with the bench *(a)*. Begin each rep from this point, pushing the bar straight up to lockout *(b)*. Lower the bar slowly to the pins and wait one second before pushing the bar back up. This develops explosive power from the bottom position of the bench press.

a

b

Deadlifts (half reps): Set the pins in the power rack so that the bar rests just below the knees *(a)*. Beginning the exercise here diminishes the contribution of the legs, hips, and low back, focusing instead on the upper back and traps. Slowly rise to an upright position *(b)*. You can use more weight in this half rep than in a full deadlift.

a

b

Squats (lockout): Although it is rare to reach a sticking point at the top of the squat position, partial reps from this position can build power and size in the upper thighs. Set the pins in the power rack at the same level as the upper rib cage *(a)*. This position produces a quarter-rep squat. Just as you can with the half deadlift, you can use more weight in a partial rep squat exercise. Begin with the bar resting on the pins and push the bar up to the standing position *(b)*. Lower the bar slowly to the resting position. Pause for a second, then push the weight back up to the standing position. This exercise was a favorite of Mike Mentzer, who used an enormous amount of weight for this movement as a means of building bigger legs.

a

b

Squats (midpoint): If squats are tough for you, and it's difficult getting past the midpoint, use the power rack to work that weakness. Set the pins at waist level and squat until the bar approaches the pins *(a)*. Push the weight up before the bar rests on the pins *(b)*. Starting the exercise from the bottom position where the pins are set would work the low back more than the thighs. By doing repetitions in this range of motion, you increase the power in the midpoint of the squat.

a

b

Squats (bottom position): If you like doing full squats, but are weak coming out of the hole, this exercise is perfect for adding strength in the bottom position. Set the pins at the same spot as for a full squat position *(a)*. Begin the exercise from the bottom and concentrate on coming out of the hole explosively *(b)*. You can do the repetitions continuously at this point or start each rep from a dead stop to build more power. Keep your upper body very tight and concentrate on using the legs when coming out of this precarious position. You will probably have to use less weight than you use with standard squats because of the awkward starting point.

a

b

Military press (midpoint): The sticking point on the military press exercise usually occurs at the midpoint. This is where the triceps help push the weight to the lockout position. Set the pins on the power rack so that the bar is at eye level and push the bar overhead *(a)*. Beginning at this position will overcome the sticking point. Lower the bar slowly to the pins and rest one second before pushing it overhead *(b)*. Three sets of five or six reps is ideal for building strength at the midpoint.

a

b

Close-grip bench press (midpoint): Similar to the military press, the sticking point on the close-grip bench press occurs at the midpoint of the exercise. Setting the pins in the power rack approximately five inches above the chest will help build strength at the lockout position *(a)*. You will be able to lift more weight to the lockout position by starting the exercise at the midpoint *(b)*. Rest the bar on the pins for one second before doing another repetition.

a

b

Training Method 2: More Volume

As you move past the beginning stages as a bodybuilder, one way to make your workouts more intense is to add exercises and, consequently, more sets. If you had been training your chest with three sets of bench presses and three sets of incline presses, then add three sets of flys to your chest routine, you have increased the workload for your chest. Your chest muscles will adapt to this advanced workload by getting bigger.

Of course, how much workload, or volume, a muscle can take is limited. To attempt to get bigger by adding more and more sets is foolish. After the intermediate stage, you are better served by increasing the intensity of a workout rather than adding more sets. "Harder, not longer," is the mantra espoused by advanced bodybuilders everywhere.

However, increased volume can place more stress on a muscle to make it grow. Advanced bodybuilders whose muscles have become accustomed to performing a particular number of sets need to change something to get their muscles growing again. They can train heavier and possibly cut back on the number of sets. They can also keep the weight the same but add more volume, thus increasing the total workload. Although high-intensity advocates warn that overtraining is sure to result whenever volume increases, history and experience show that there is more than one way to skin a cat or to make a muscle grow.

10 Sets of 10

Training intensity and volume are inversely related. If the intensity of a workout goes up, the volume must fall. As Mike Mentzer has repeatedly preached in his sermons on training intensity, "You can train hard or you can train long, but you can't do both."

However, despite the prevailing attitude about intensity and duration, it is possible to make a workout more intense by adding volume. More sets can equate to more work for a muscle. More work can be interpreted as greater intensity even if each set is not being taken to failure.

One popular training method that increases intensity by adding volume is called 10 sets of 10. The athlete uses this technique with one exercise (preferably a basic exercise such as squats or bench presses) and performs 10 sets of 10 repetitions.

Of course, you must lower the volume of the rest of the workout for this part of the body, or overtraining will result. If you normally do four or five sets of squats and decide to double that number, you must reduce or eliminate the number of sets for the rest of your leg workout to accommodate the extra workload.

The intensity for the workout will come from the total workload imposed on the muscles and not from the intensity of each set. If each set were taken to failure, it would be impossible to perform all 10 sets without first reducing the resistance or the number of reps. Each set must be worked hard but within limits. Total failure is not necessary and will, in fact, prevent you from finishing the workout.

If you were going to use the 10 sets of 10 training method, follow these guidelines. First, choose the right weight. It should be moderately heavy but not so heavy that you will reach failure before doing all 10 sets. Because you will perform 10 sets of 10 repetitions with this weight, a weight that barely allows you to do 10 reps is obviously too heavy. You would not be able to complete more than two or three full sets.

I used a program similar to the 10 sets of 10 for my leg routine. In 1996, I was squatting heavy in an attempt to build up my thighs. Beginning in January, I pushed myself every workout to use heavier weights on leg presses and squats. By April, my knees started to rebel from the abuse.

Then my quadriceps tendon on both legs became inflamed. At first, my knees ached for two or three days. After another month or two of heavy training, my quadriceps tendon stayed inflamed for five days after an intense workout. It got to the point where my knees would just start to feel good when it was time to work them again. My knees were getting worse each week, and I knew I needed to cut back on the intensity. However, I didn't want to stop training my legs heavy because I wanted to build more size.

I read an article in a bodybuilding magazine that explained the 10 sets routine. In that routine, you did 10 sets of only one exercise per target area. However, instead of doing 10 reps for each set, the article then outlined a progressive program where the resistance increased each week.

My training partner and I decided to give this routine a try. My knees couldn't stand going heavier anyway, so I was game for increasing the total workload instead by adding volume instead of weight. We decided to use squats for our 10 sets routine.

We warmed up by riding a stationary bike for six minutes. Afterward we did two sets of 12 to 15 reps of the leg press exercise. Because the leg press uses many of the same muscle groups as the squat, it's a perfect exercise before moving on to the target exercise.

When we finally began squatting, we did a few warm-up sets to get our bodies accustomed to the movement. We used 135 pounds for 12 reps for our first set. On our second set, we squatted with 225 pounds for 10 reps. For our final warm-up set, we used 315 pounds for 8 reps. Then we were ready to begin the real workout.

We used 365 pounds on our first week of the program. Because we were required to do 10 sets of five repetitions in our first workout, we picked a weight that we could do 10 reps with and used that for 10 sets of five reps.

Table 2.6 outlines the plan we put together for our cycle of 10 sets of squats.

The routine was deceptively brutal. When we attempted 365 pounds for 10 sets of five reps on

Squats are a great exercise to use with high-volume training.

our first week, it seemed too easy. After all, we were accustomed to using well over 400 pounds during our standard workouts; 365 pounds was a warm-up weight for us. After several sets of squats, I began to think I had made a mistake estimating how much weight to use . . . until we got to the sixth set. The last four or five sets became tough as the total workload started to take its toll.

We soon discovered that 10 sets of squats with a heavy weight (even with limited reps) was extremely difficult. It became as much a mental workout as a physical one. After all, the prospect of getting under a heavy barbell 10 consecutive times would break the will of any normal person!

It helped to have a training partner who was going through the same torture I was. A mental technique that made the workout easier to overcome was drawing a hash mark on a piece of paper every time my partner and I completed a set. This helped me keep track of how many sets I had left, but it also helped me to take each set one at a time. Thinking about how tough set number eight was going to be when I was only on the third would not help me through this self-imposed torture.

Thankfully, the results were well worth the hard work. I measured my legs before and after the seven-week, 10-sets program and was overjoyed to find that my legs had grown almost two inches. That's an amazing gain, especially in less than two months. So much for the argument that the only way to grow is through more intensity with less volume.

TABLE 2.6 Sample Cycle of 10 Sets for Squats

Week	Weight in pounds	Reps	Sets
1	365	5	10
2	385	4	10
3	405	3	10
4	385	5	10
5	405	4	10
6	425	3	10
7	405	6	10

Because there is no formula for determining the correct weight on a particular exercise for 10 sets of 10 reps, use your best judgment. Choose a weight where 10 repetitions are relatively easy. You should be able to easily handle the weight, yet still feel the muscles working. If, for example, you normally use 315 pounds for 10 reps of squats, you may want to use 275 pounds for 10 sets of 10 reps. Even this weight may be too heavy. You won't know until you try.

When using this training technique, 10 sets should be difficult to complete. If performed correctly, it should become progressively more difficult to complete all 10 repetitions in the last five sets. If you can do all 10 without struggling on the last few sets, the weight is too light.

Use a spotter for all 10 sets. Your goal is to completely exhaust a muscle group by bombing it with high sets and high reps. This high-volume training program shocks the muscles into responding and is a great technique for a stubborn muscle group that doesn't respond to your current routine.

This routine works because the intensity gradually increases through a progressive workload. You can determine the total workload by multiplying the resistance used by the sets performed by the number of reps.

$$\text{Resistance} \times \text{sets} \times \text{reps} = \text{total workload}$$

Using this formula for the 10 sets program I used for my legs, you can see that the workload gradually increased over the seven-week program (table 2.7). Similar to the cycling principle, the workload increased overall but not every week. Instead, it cycled to allow recuperation and, therefore, greater gains at the end of the cycle.

A high-volume approach like this is great for shocking stubborn muscles that don't respond to traditional means of training. The 10-sets leg routine was extremely intense and could not be followed continuously without risking injury or burnout. Use this type of high-volume shock program only two or three times a year, taking several months before using it again.

TABLE 2.7 Sample Seven-Week, Ten-Sets Program for Legs

Week	Weight in pounds	Reps	Sets	Total pounds
1	365	5	10	18,250
2	385	4	10	15,400
3	405	3	10	12,150
4	385	5	10	19,250
5	405	4	10	16,200
6	425	3	10	12,750
7	405	6	10	24,300

Training Method 3: Same Resistance and Volume in Less Time

Another method for increasing training intensity is to speed up the workout. By maintaining the same resistance and the same volume, but taking less rest between sets, you increase the intensity of the training session. The decreased rest periods put more stress on the muscles.

Many bodybuilders choose this method for increasing intensity when preparing for a competition. The goal of competitive bodybuilders is to decrease their body fat and develop a hard, refined look while maintaining the size and fullness of the muscles. By decreasing their rest periods, they hope to harden up by adding an aerobic component to the workout.

Another reason to train faster when preparing for a competition is the drop in strength many bodybuilders experience because of the reduced caloric intake. By training with less rest instead of more weight, you maintain the intensity of the workout and don't have to try to train heavy when your strength is diminished. However, in order to make the workout more intense, you must lift the same weight while decreasing the rest periods. Training lighter and faster does not necessarily make the workout more intense.

Lee Labrada, a top professional, used to train much more quickly when he was preparing for a competition. The increased pace helped create the hard and finished look he was renowned for. Natural bodybuilder Ronald Coleman also trained quickly during his contest preparation. Ronald timed himself during his workouts to ensure that his rest periods between sets were only 60 seconds. After his time was up, he picked up the weights for another set.

Although training intensity goes up when the speed of the workout increases, the amount of weight you can lift at this fast pace most likely goes down. If you want to lift heavy weights, you must take a considerable amount of rest between sets to allow the muscles to fully recuperate. Powerlifters and bodybuilders who lift heavy weights sometimes take up to five minutes between sets of basic, mass-building exercises such as deadlifts and squats. These longer rest periods allow your muscles to restore the creatine phosphate and adenosine triphosphate (ATP), which fuel your muscles, to their optimum levels so that the muscles can continue working and gaining strength.

If your goal is to get bigger and stronger, this training method may not be for you. It is difficult to increase strength when taking short rest periods.

Supersets

Another method for completing a workout at a faster pace is to use supersets. A superset consists of two exercises with no rest between the two movements. Supersets can involve exercises for opposing muscle groups (like the chest and back or the biceps and triceps) or two exercises for the same muscle group.

The most common method of supersetting is to combine exercises for opposing muscle groups. Because opposing muscle groups do not use the same muscles to produce movement, you do not run the risk of being too fatigued to perform the second exercise.

Many bodybuilders have used supersets to increase muscle mass. Although it is most common to use heavy weights with extended rest periods between sets to gain size, supersets can shock a muscle into responding and growing larger. It is even possible to use maximum weights when supersetting two exercises for opposing muscle groups.

This increase in strength is due to the pump that takes place in the opposing muscle groups. For example, if you are supersetting a chest exercise with a back exercise, the pecs, front delts, and triceps that are pumped from the chest exercise help to make you stronger when you perform the exercise for your back. When you go back to the chest exercise, the pump your lats, biceps, and rear delts received will help make the chest movement easier to perform.

Strength coaches often recommend pumping up an opposing muscle group with a light weight before attempting a heavy set for your target muscle group. If you are bench pressing a heavy weight, for example, you can make the movement easier by pumping up the lats with a light set of lat pull-downs. The pump in your lats and biceps will make those muscle groups feel more buoyant and the opposing muscles, the pecs and triceps, will feel stronger when performing the bench press. It's a strange phenomenon, but it works.

Any muscle groups that are opposite from each other are ideal for supersetting. The following are examples of how you could combine muscle groups into a workout using supersets:

Chest and back superset

- Bench press and wide-grip chins
- Incline press and barbell rows
- Flys and seated cable rows

Biceps and triceps superset

- Barbell curls and close-grip bench press
- Incline curls and lying triceps extensions
- Preacher curls and triceps push-downs

Quadriceps and hamstrings superset

- Squats and leg curls
- Leg press and stiff-leg deadlifts
- Leg extensions and lunges

Front- and rear-deltoid superset

- Military press and bent-over lateral raises
- Seated dumbbell press and barbell rows to the chest

Preexhaustion Another method of supersetting is to combine two exercises for the same muscle group. This is called preexhaustion and uses an isolation exercise supersetted with a basic exercise to exhaust a muscle to failure. Perform an isolation exercise first to target the working muscle. After the muscle is exhausted, immediately perform a basic exercise that uses several muscle groups to bring the muscle to total failure.

If using the preexhaustion training technique for your legs, combine an isolation movement like leg extensions with a basic movement like squats. After several warm-up sets, use a weight on the leg extensions that allows a maximum of 12 repetitions. Perform this set to failure.

After completing the set of leg extensions, jump off the machine and head to the squat rack. The bar should already be loaded with the weight you intend to use. Get under the bar as quickly as possible and begin squatting. Your quadriceps should already be exhausted. However, the other muscle groups involved in the squat—glutes, low back, and hips—allow you to continue to work the quads. This exercise combination lets you work a muscle to complete exhaustion.

The preexhaustion method works so well because when using a heavy, basic exercise that involves several muscle groups, you can't isolate and work a specific muscle. On squats, for example, in addition to working the quads, you also work the glutes, hips, and low back. In fact, many bodybuilders complain that their low back becomes exhausted before the quads are worked thoroughly. In the bench press, the front deltoids and triceps are involved and could give out before the pecs are fully worked. The isolation exercise preexhausts the target muscle.

The following exercise combinations put the preexhaustion principle into effect:

Chest	Dumbbell flys followed by bench press
Back	Dumbbell pullovers followed by barbell rows or chins
Deltoids	Side lateral raises followed by military press or dumbbell press
Triceps	Triceps push-downs followed by dips or close-grip bench press
Biceps	Concentration curls followed by close-grip underhand chins
Quadriceps	Leg extensions followed by leg press or squats
Hamstrings	Leg curls followed by stiff-leg deadlifts
Upper abs	Crunches followed by incline sit-ups or cable crunches
Lower abs	Reverse crunches followed by hanging knee raises

A modified preexhaustion method includes an isolation exercise for a targeted muscle and a basic exercise that includes that muscle, but doesn't superset the exercises. Instead, simply rearrange your exercise sequence so that the isolation movement comes before the basic exercises. This also allows you to feel the muscle you are trying to work by first isolating it.

For example, perform leg extensions first in your leg routine. Do the full number of sets you normally would do, then move on to a basic exercise like squats or leg press. The quadriceps should be somewhat fatigued by the time you get to the second exercise. Follow this training method for any part of your body.

Supersets for the same area Another way to use supersets is to perform two exercises back to back for the same part of the body. These are usually two isolation exercises, especially if you're doing them at the end of your workout. Because this training technique increases the working time, or tension time, for a particular muscle group, you can use it to bring up an area that is lagging.

If a certain muscle group has a greater percentage of red muscle fibers, or if it does not seem to respond because of inefficient muscle–nerve connections, combining two exercises for the same muscle group could help to overcome these limitations. Training a muscle to failure using one exercise then immediately following with another exercise for the same muscle, increases the working time and brings more blood to the working muscle. The greater the pump, the better you will be able to feel the muscle working and the faster it will respond.

Superset two exercises for the same area at the end of a heavy workout. Choose two isolation exercises. Combining two basic exercises or even a basic exercise with an isolation exercise may be too difficult at the end of the workout. After completing the meat-and-potatoes portion of the workout (the basic exercises performed with heavy weights for 6 to 10 repetitions), superset two exercises to finish the muscle group and force as much growth-promoting blood into the area to get it to respond. There is no better feeling than a muscle pumped to the maximum after training all the white muscle fibers with the basic movements.

This superset method can be used for any area of the body, and at any point in the workout. If you have a muscle that resists growth, supersetting two exercises for the same muscle could make a difference.

Training Method 4: Extending a Set Past Failure

As mentioned earlier, Mike Mentzer believed in very few sets, taking each to failure. In fact, he used several training methods to push his muscles past the point of failure. In addition to training very heavy on the basic exercises, Mentzer used forced reps, drop sets, and the rest pause method to force his muscles to grow.

These training techniques are very stressful, but Mentzer was able to get away with an extremely low number of sets, sometimes as few as five sets per body-part, by training his muscles to total failure with each set. However, these training methods stress the nervous system; therefore, you must use them cautiously. Some bodybuilders reduce the potential for excessive stress by using steroids and other performance-enhancing drugs that help to lower cortisol levels. Cortisol is a hormone that the body produces when it is under great stress—a catabolic hormone that tears muscle tissue down. A natural bodybuilder, on the other hand, must be very careful when using intense training techniques such as these. Too much stress on the nervous system can cause overtraining, which prevents muscle growth.

If you do add one of these intense training techniques to your workouts, incorporate them gradually and monitor the results. If you feel overtrained or sore all the time, or if you feel that your strength or muscle mass is declining, cut back or eliminate these training methods for a while. The feedback techniques for analyzing your progress discussed in chapter 1 will help you determine if these techniques are working for you or against you.

Another thing to keep in mind is to add these advanced training methods one at a time. Instead of using forced reps, negatives, and the rest pause method all in one week or in one workout, use only one and note the results. This allows you to rate the effectiveness of each training method on its own.

Forced Reps

We've already discussed forced reps as a way to build strength. But forced repetitions can also take a muscle past the point of failure. When a muscle cannot contract anymore during a heavy resistance workout, a training partner provides just the right amount of assistance to help lift the weight. This allows you to complete several more repetitions beyond the point of failure.

Forced repetitions should allow you to perform a maximum of three additional reps. Any more than that means your partner is doing the majority of the work, and you are just along for the ride. When applied properly, each additional rep beyond the point of failure should be exceedingly difficult. If your partner gives you too much or not enough help, the set will not be as effective as it could have been. A partner accustomed to training with you and able to sense how much help you need and when you need it is extremely valuable.

Forced reps are a way to increase training intensity. But use them sparingly; you don't want to have to rely on a partner to complete a workout. You also don't want to over stress your nervous system by pushing too many sets past the point of failure.

Limit forced repetitions to two or three sets per target area. For example, if you are training chest and using the bench press, incline press, and flat bench flys for a workout, use a set of forced reps on the last heavy set of bench presses and incline presses. During the rest of the workout, perform the work sets only to positive failure.

Forced repetitions are more effective with exercises for smaller muscles than for bigger ones. This is most likely due to the extreme stress of training a large muscle group with heavy weights. Performing squats and deadlifts with maximum weight is tough enough without extending the set past failure. In contrast, an extra rep or two on barbell curls or triceps push-downs causes less overall stress on the body because the affected muscle is small.

Drop Sets

Drop sets are an excellent way to increase intensity. After reaching failure in a set, the lifter uses a lighter weight for the next set. A drop set can be used several times during a set, dropping a lighter weight to keep the set going two to four times. Continuing the set beyond that would most likely compromise the form and quality of the set.

This training technique is excellent for a muscle that is stubborn and doesn't respond to traditional training methods. The reductions in weight allow the muscle to continue working after it has reached failure with a heavy weight. The combination of heavy weight and high repetitions is ideal for reaching hard-to-hit muscle fibers and forcing them to grow.

Although drop sets can be applied to any muscle group, they are more effective with smaller groups, such as the deltoids and calves. Drop sets with a muscle group as big as the thighs or back would be exhausting because of the weights you would be able to use.

To perform a drop set on a set of side lateral raises for the deltoids, begin by doing as many repetitions as you can with your heaviest weight. Immediately after finishing the last rep, put down the dumbbells and begin another set with dumbbells that are 10 pounds lighter. Perform reps with this weight until you reach failure. Then grab another set of dumbbells that is 10 pounds lighter and do a final set of as many repetitions as possible. This drop set consists of three sets within a set. At this point, your deltoids are worked to exhaustion.

Incorporate drop sets on the final set or two of an exercise to thoroughly work the muscle. See table 2.8 for an example of a typical workout for side lateral raises with the addition of drop sets.

Another muscle group that responds well to drop sets is the calves. The calves are typically stubborn and often resist growth. Because the muscle fibers of the calves are accustomed to being used all day when we walk or stand, training must be intense before they will respond.

TABLE 2.8 Typical Side Lateral Sets and Reps

Sets	Dumbbell weight in pounds	Reps
1	40	12
2	45	10
3	50	8
4	55	8
	45	8
	35	6-8
5	Same as set 4	Same as set 4

In addition, the calves are the farthest major muscle group from the heart. This makes it difficult to pump up these muscles with the traditional 6- to 10-rep method of training. Many bodybuilders who train their calves like any other muscle group come away disappointed with their results. To get the calves to grow, they must be trained with both high repetitions and heavy weights. How can you possibly do high reps when using a heavy resistance? Drop sets, of course!

Use drop sets with donkey calf raises. Support one, or even two, guys on your back in addition to a weight belt strapped around your waist. With this resistance on your back, do 15 repetitions. At this point, one of the partners jumps off your back. Continue to pump out the reps, trying for 10 to 15. After you can do no more reps, the other partner jumps off your back. Then do as many reps as possible with just the weight belt.

This drop set totals 35 to 40 reps. This high number of repetitions allows you to train all the muscle fibers in the calves including the difficult slow-twitch fibers. However, the heavy resistance used at the beginning of the set activates the fast-twitch fibers that contribute to the size of a muscle group. Also, getting a pump is definitely not a problem with the extremely high number of repetitions performed in the set.

Drop sets can be used for any exercise and for any muscle group. They are particularly effective with exercises using a machine or dumbbells because it is easier to drop the weights quickly. Barbell exercises are difficult with drop sets because of the difficulty in removing the weights. One or two training partners makes the process much easier.

Rest Pause

Mike Mentzer made the rest pause training technique popular in the late 1970s. It involves very heavy resistance lifted one repetition at a time. After each rep is a 10-second pause before attempting another rep. This method allows the use of near maximum weights because of the pause between reps. These longer rest periods allow your muscles to restore the creatine phosphate and adenosine triphosphate (ATP), which fuel your muscles, to their optimum levels so that the muscles can continue working and gaining strength.

To illustrate how this training method works, let's use the incline bench press as an example. If you could perform incline bench presses with 275 pounds for six reps, you could conceivably use 295 pounds for incline presses using the rest pause technique. To begin, take the loaded bar off the rack and perform one full repetition before returning the bar back to the rack. Wait for 10 seconds and take the bar off the rack for another repetition. Continue in this manner for at least five reps.

This technique is very intense because of the near maximum weights used for every repetition. It's like doing a series of one-rep maximum lifts all in one set. Most strength training experts recommend performing one-rep maximum lifts infrequently to avoid injury and overtraining. For this reason, you should limit rest pause training to one set per workout and no more than once per week.

Basic exercises using weights that can be set down between repetitions are most effective with this training method. Pressing movements such as the bench press, incline press, and military press are ideal. Arm exercises such as barbell curls and close-grip bench presses also work well with this method, as do leg movements such as the squat and leg press. Back exercises such as barbell rows, T-bar rows, and deadlifts are not suited for this training technique. Putting the weight down and picking it up again causes too much strain on the low back.

The rest pause technique has not gained much popularity over the years. This could be due to its inconvenience. Most bodybuilders prefer to do continuous repetitions to achieve a pump in the muscles. Performing rest pause reps stresses the muscles, but the pump isn't prevalent because of the stop-and-go technique. Another reason this technique isn't popular is the sheer effort involved. Performing a near maximum repetition over and over requires as much mental effort as physical exertion. Perhaps it is too tough for most bodybuilders to perform consistently.

Because rest pause training allows you to train a muscle group with heavier weight than you are accustomed to, use this technique to gain size when you are already using heavy weight. Although you must be cautious with this intense training method, go ahead and give it a try.

Determining the proper number of sets and repetitions is the key to planning an effective workout for each target area. And progressively increasing your intensity ensures that the muscles continue to grow. Now it's time to learn how to split up these workouts and spread them throughout the week to create a training routine.

Performing Split Routines for Fast Progress

When bodybuilders begin a training program, they train the total body in one training session by performing a basic movement for each muscle group. This method of training works well for the beginning bodybuilder whose muscles are unaccustomed to weight resistance training. After six to twelve months of training the total body two to three times a week consistently, the strength and development of the muscles will have improved considerably and the muscles will need more work (volume and resistance) in order to progress further. This progress can be accomplished through a split routine in which the muscle groups are split up and trained on different days instead of the whole body being trained in one workout. This split routine is necessary when additional exercises and sets are added to the workout in order to make the training more demanding for the individual muscle groups.

The optimal training split is essential for progress in bodybuilding. To see gains, you must balance your workload and intensity with sufficient rest. If you tip the scale too much in one direction, you won't see progress. Most bodybuilders try to do too much and err on the side of overtraining

When using a split routine for building muscle mass, the most effective exercises must be combined with enough rest and recuperation to allow size and strength gains. Do not try to follow a pro bodybuilder's routine in the hope that you will be able to equal his development. Most professionals use performance-enhancing drugs, which greatly enhance their ability to recuperate and grow from high-volume training. Following the same program without the help of those drugs is certain to lead to overtraining and lack of progress.

Rules for Designing a Training Routine

Because there are so many factors to consider when designing a training program, it can be a confusing process. You must decide what exercises to include and how many sets for each movement. How intense should a set be? How many total sets will you do in the workout? And finally, how many days per week should you train? Is it beneficial to train six days a week, or should a drug-free bodybuilder train just three or four days?

Rule 1: Balance intensity and recuperation When designing a training routine, intensity will determine how much recuperation you need.

An advanced bodybuilder can generate much more intensity than a beginner for several reasons. One is that his muscles are more neurologically efficient, which translates into more muscle fiber activation when using heavier weights. Because he uses more of his muscle fibers, he requires more recuperation than a beginner or intermediate trainer.

A beginning bodybuilder can train each muscle group as many as three times per week, but limit himself to one exercise for each muscle group while he begins to develop muscular coordination and strength. During this initial stage his muscles are also becoming more neurologically efficient when contracting under heavier loads. These changes must happen before training can cause the muscles to grow. As the beginner becomes more advanced, he adds exercises to develop each area of the body. He also begins to use more resistance as he becomes stronger. This increased volume and resistance necessitate more recuperation between workouts. Training a muscle before it has fully recuperated compromises its development and strength and can lead to overtraining and injury.

Rule 2: Consider exercise type when planning recuperation The type of exercises you perform in a training session greatly affects the amount of recuperation you need. Multijoint exercises such as squats, deadlifts, power cleans, bench presses, barbell rows, and military presses are more stressful on the nervous system and demand a much greater energy output than isolation exercises such as flys, lateral raises, and concentration curls. Therefore they require more recuperation.

Rule 3: Schedule only as many sets as you need It is important to perform the right number of sets. Too many can lead to not only overtraining an individual muscle group but also depleting the central nervous system, especially if you are doing too many intense basic exercises.

As a general rule, limit the number of sets per session to 25 when training two target areas or 35 sets per session when training three or more. This eliminates the tendency to add less effective exercises or throw in superfluous sets and ensures that you use only the most effective movements for the optimal number of sets.

Rule 4: Schedule rest days No training takes place on rest days. On these days, the entire body rests, which allows recuperation.

Some bodybuilders split up their training by area of the body and train five or six days in a row. They believe that because they train a different muscle group each day, it doesn't matter how many days a week they train, as long as they are not overtraining a particular muscle group. What they are forgetting is that every time they work out, they work not only a certain muscle group, but also the entire body. The central nervous system is particularly affected by high-intensity weight training with near maximal weight.

If you have performed a brutal workout with heavy squats or deadlifts, you can relate to how wiped out these make you feel the next day. Don't underestimate the stress that certain exercises place on the system as a whole. If you train hard day in and day out with no regard for overall recuperation, your progress is sure to hit a brick wall.

Bodybuilders who are accustomed to training every day are amazed at how much progress they make when they schedule rest days after intense weight training sessions. A full day of rest is essential after pushing the body to the limit.

In bodybuilding circles some believe there is no such thing as overtraining, only undereating and undersleeping. In other words, you can train as hard and as often as you like as long as you supplement it with enough nutritious food and sleep. This philosophy was most likely started by a bodybuilder who also supplemented his training with performance-enhancing drugs. Extremely intense training tears down the body and demands adequate recuperation to rebuild it. Eating and sleeping more is not enough for a drug-free bodybuilder.

Mass-Building Routines

An intermediate and advanced bodybuilder can use many different types of split routines. Typically, you split up your training by target area so that you train the entire body in two to four days. You have many options for grouping areas of the body.

Routine 1: Two-Day Push-and-Pull Split

This routine is great for intermediate bodybuilders who want to build size and strength. It uses basic exercises and heavy weights in a limited number of sets (see tables 3.1-3.4, pages 74 and 75).

The push-and-pull split divides the body into pushing muscles (chest, delts, and triceps) and pulling muscles (back and biceps). Because the emphasis is on heavy training and plenty of rest, train the thighs with the back and biceps to decrease your time in the gym.

Because this routine works a large number of muscle groups in one training session, the sets per workout are limited, and each exercise emphasizes several muscle groups per movement. This is an intense routine that trains each muscle group twice per week. Advanced bodybuilders will probably require more rest for each target area because they use heavier weights, and they have greater muscle activation. This is also a great routine for intermediate bodybuilders attempting to gain size and strength. In fact, I increased my body weight from 205 pounds to 230 in eight months with this routine.

The goal for each week should be to increase the amount of resistance for each exercise. Strive to perform one more rep or use five more pounds during each workout. Muscles will grow bigger and stronger only through the use of heavier weights and more intensity.

TABLE 3.1 Monday Workout: Chest, Deltoids, Triceps, and Calves

Target area	Exercise	Sets	Reps set 1	Reps set 2	Reps set 3	Reps set 4
Chest	Bench press	4	10	8	6	6
	Incline press	3	8	6	6	
	Flys	3	10	8	6	
Deltoids	Standing military press	4	10	8	6	6
	Upright rows	3	10	8	6	
	Barbell shrugs	4	12	10	8	6
Triceps	Push-downs	3	10	8	6	
	Weighted dips	3	10	8	6	
Calves	Standing calf raises	4	12	10	8	8

TABLE 3.2 Tuesday Workout: Thighs, Back, Biceps, and Abs

Target area	Exercise	Sets	Reps set 1	Reps set 2	Reps set 3	Reps set 4	Reps set 5
Thighs	Squats	5	12	10	8	6	6
	Hack squats	3	10	8	8		
	Leg curls	3	10	8	6		
	Stiff-leg deadlifts	3	8	6	6		
Back	Wide-grip chins	3	12	10	8		
	Barbell rows	4	10	8	6	6	
	Seated cable rows	3	10	8	6		
Biceps	Barbell curls	3	10	8	6		
	Incline curls	2	8	6			
Forearms	Wrist curls	3	12	10	10		
Abs	Incline sit-ups	3	20-30	20-30	20-30		

Rather than using the same exercises for a muscle group both times you work it during the week, you use different exercises. This prevents muscle staleness. For example, the chest workout uses barbell exercises on Monday and dumbbell exercises on Thursday. Squats are performed during both thigh workouts, but with a different number of repetitions. The Tuesday thigh workout is the heavy leg day while the Friday leg workout uses moderate weight and higher repetitions. The heavy squat workout on Tuesday is followed by hack squats, while the moderate squat workout on Friday precedes heavy leg presses. All of the exercises are basic movements that build the greatest amount of muscle mass.

TABLE 3.3 Thursday Workout: Chest, Deltoids, Triceps, and Calves

Target area	Exercise	Sets	Reps set 1	Reps set 2	Reps set 3	Reps set 4
Chest	Dumbbell bench press	4	10	8	6	6
	Incline dumbbell press	3	8	6	6	
	Dumbbell pullovers	3	12	10	10	
Deltoids	Seated military press	4	10	8	6	6
	Side lateral raises	3	10	8	6	
	Power cleans	3	8	6	5	
Triceps	Close-grip bench press	3	10	8	6	
	Lying triceps extensions	3	8	6	6	
Calves	Donkey calf raises	3	15-20	15-20	15-20	

TABLE 3.4 Friday Workout: Thighs, Back, Biceps, and Calves

Target area	Exercise	Sets	Reps set 1	Reps set 2	Reps set 3	Reps set 4
Thighs	Squats	4	12	10	10	8
	Leg press	4	12	10	8	8
	Dumbbell leg curls	4	10	8	6	6
Back	T-bar rows	4	10	8	6	6
	One-arm dumbbell rows	3	8	6	6	
	Deadlifts	3	10	8	6	
Biceps	Seated dumbbell curls	3	10	8	6	
	Preacher barbell curls	2	8	6		
Forearms	Wrist curls	3	12	10	10	
Abs	Hanging knee raises	2	20-30	20-30		

Also, note that heavy deadlifts are reserved for Friday, the same day as the squats with moderate weight. Because heavy deadlifts and heavy squats stress the low back muscles, they should not be scheduled for the same day. Because stiff-leg deadlifts emphasize the hamstrings rather than the low back, and they generally are performed with lighter weights, they can be done on the same day as heavy squats.

Routine 2: Two-Day Alternate Split

This routine is similar to the first: each target area is trained twice per week with an emphasis on basic exercises (see tables 3.5-3.8, pages 76-77). However, it does not train the thighs and back in the same workout. Because these are the two largest muscle groups in the body, many bodybuilders find it too difficult to train them in the same workout. Another reason to train them on separate days is that both of these target areas can tolerate heavy weights and require a tremendous amount of energy to train correctly.

The alternative to the push-and-pull routine combines the chest, back, and deltoids in one workout and the thighs and arms in the other. The chest and back are opposing muscle groups; one uses the pushing muscles and the other uses pulling muscles. The deltoids are involved in both target areas. The front delts are indirectly affected during chest training, and the rear delts are involved in back training.

Because the thighs are a big muscle group and are demanding, they are combined with the relatively small muscle groups of the arms. The biceps and triceps, similar to the chest and back, are opposing muscle groups so you train the pushing and pulling muscles of the arms in the same workout.

Many bodybuilders love the feeling of working opposing muscle groups. It magnifies the pump, and this superior blood flow encourages muscle growth.

For this workout program, use dumbbells for the chest workout on Monday and barbells for the chest workout on Thursday. The workout on Thursday also features a superset routine between the chest and back. Supersetting these two muscle groups provides a significant pump and can increase the size of the upper body. When you are finished with this workout, your whole upper body (chest, back, shoulders, and arms) should be pumped to the max.

As with the first training routine, heavy squats are performed on Tuesday and moderate squats on Friday. Stiff-leg deadlifts are trained on the same day as heavy squats, and regular deadlifts are performed on the same day as moderate squats.

TABLE 3.5 Monday Workout: Chest, Back, Deltoids, and Calves

Target area	Exercise	Sets	Reps set 1	Reps set 2	Reps set 3	Reps set 4
Chest	Dumbbell bench press	4	12	10	8	6
	Incline dumbbell press	3	8	6	6	
	Dumbbell pullovers	3	12	10	10	
Back	Wide-grip chins	3	12	10	8	
	T-bar rows	3	10	8	6	
	Hyperextensions	3	20	15	15	
Deltoids	Standing military press	4	10	8	6	6
	Upright rows	3	10	8	6	
	Bent-over lateral raises	3	10	8	6	
Calves	Seated calf raises	3	20	15	15	

TABLE 3.6 Tuesday Workout: Thighs, Arms, and Abs

Target area	Exercise	Sets	Reps set 1	Reps set 2	Reps set 3	Reps set 4	Reps set 5
Thighs	Squats	5	12	10	8	6	6
	Hack squats	3	10	8	6		
	Dumbbell leg curls	4	10	8	6	6	
	Stiff-leg deadlifts	3	10	8	6		
Triceps	Close-grip bench press	3	10	8	6		
	Lying triceps extensions	3	10	8	6		
Biceps	Barbell curls	3	10	8	6		
	Incline curls	2	8	6			
Forearms	Wrist curls	3	12	10	10		
Abs	Incline sit-ups	2	20-30	20-30			

TABLE 3.7 Thursday Workout: Chest, Back, Deltoids, and Calves

Target area	Exercise	Sets	Reps set 1	Reps set 2	Reps set 3	Reps set 4
Chest and back superset	Bench press supersetted with wide-grip chins	4	10	8	6	6
	Incline press supersetted with barbell rows	3	8	6	6	
	Dumbbell flys supersetted with seated cable rows	3	10	8	6	
Deltoids	Seated military press	4	10	8	6	6
	Side lateral raises	3	10	8	6	
	Barbell shrugs	3	10	8	6	
Calves	Donkey calf raises	3	20	15	15	

TABLE 3.8 Friday Workout: Thighs, Arms, and Abs

Target area	Exercise	Sets	Reps set 1	Reps set 2	Reps set 3	Reps set 4
Thighs	Squats	4	12	10	10	8
	Leg press	4	12	10	8	8
	Dumbbell leg curls	4	10	8	6	6
	Deadlifts	3	10	8	6	
Triceps	Push-downs	3	10	8	6	
	Dips	3	10	6-8	6-8	
Biceps	Seated dumbbell curls	3	10	8	6	
	Preacher curls	2	8	6		
Forearms	Wrist curls	3	12	10	8	
Abs	Hanging knee raises	2-3	15-25	15-25	15-25	

Routine 3: Three-Day Push-and-Pull Split—3 on, 1 off

Bodybuilders who progress beyond the intermediate level often spread their training over three days so they can train fewer muscle groups in one session (see tables 3.9-3.11, pages 78-79). This reduces the number of sets performed in one workout. It also allows a bodybuilder the luxury of training only two major muscle groups with as much intensity as possible before ending the workout rather than training three or four muscle groups in one workout.

In the three-days-on, one-day-off routine you train the whole body over three days before taking a rest day. This allows four days of rest between workouts for a particular muscle group compared to the three days of rest in the two-day split. The three-days-on, one-day-off routine trains each muscle group twice in an eight-day period. The two-day split trains each muscle group twice per week.

A push-and-pull routine eliminates the possibility of overtraining because all the pushing muscles are trained together, and all the pulling muscles are trained together, leaving no chance of overlapping the smaller muscle groups and overworking them or training them too often.

The three-day split is easier to follow because it alleviates the need to train the legs on the same day as the back and biceps. Because training the legs is physically demanding, especially when using substantial weight, they are trained with the abs only. Although some people like to work the calves with the thighs, they often cannot be worked maximally after a taxing thigh workout. Also, the calves can be worked more often than most muscle groups and respond well to two workouts during the three-day split.

Because the leg exercises make up the majority of the work on its training day, it is best to place the leg workout between the two upper-body workouts. This division allows the upper-body muscles a day of rest while the thighs are worked. This schedule provides proper recuperation for each muscle group, which is critical as the resistance and intensity of the workouts increases.

The total number of sets in each workout is slightly lower than in the two-day split. Where the two-day split averages 32 sets per workout, the three-day split averages 27 sets per workout. However, three workouts are performed consecutively to train the whole body instead of two workouts. The additional volume and exercises in a three-day split more fully develops the muscles and further increases the size and strength gained from the two-day split.

TABLE 3.9 Day One: Chest, Deltoids, Triceps, and Calves

Target area	Exercise	Sets	Reps set 1	Reps set 2	Reps set 3	Reps set 4
Chest	Bench press	4	10	8	6	6
	Incline press	3	8	6	6	
	Flys	3	10	8	6	
Deltoids	Military press	4	10	8	6	6
	Side lateral raises	3	10	8	6	
	Barbell shrugs	4	10	8	6	6
Triceps	Lying triceps ext	3	10	8	6	
	Weighted dips	3	6-10	6-10	6-10	
Calves	Standing calf raises	4	12	10	8	6

TABLE 3.10 Day Two: Abs and Thighs

Target area	Exercise	Sets	Reps set 1	Reps set 2	Reps set 3	Reps set 4	Reps set 5
Abs	Incline sit-ups	3	20-30	20-30	20-30		
	Incline knee raises	3	20-30	20-30	20-30		
Thighs	Squats	5	12	10	8	6	6
	Leg press	4	12	10	8	6	
	Leg curls	4	10	8	6	6	
	Stiff-leg deadlifts	3	10	8	6		

Table 3.11 Day Three: Back, Biceps, and Calves

Target area	Exercise	Sets	Reps set 1	Reps set 2	Reps set 3	Reps set 4
Back	Wide-grip chins	3	12	10	8	
	Barbell rows	4	10	8	6	6
	Seated cable rows	3	10	8	6	
	Deadlifts	3	10	8	6	
Biceps	Barbell curls	3	10	8	6	
	Incline curls	2	8	6		
Forearms	Reverse curls	2	10	8		
	Wrist curls	2	10-12	10-12		
Calves	Donkey calf raises	4	15-20	15-20	15-20	15-20

Routine 4: Three-Day Alternate Split—3 on, 1 off

Exercises in a three-days-on, one-day-off routine don't have to be divided into pushing and pulling motions. A popular three-day split works the chest and arms together on the first day, followed by thighs on the second, and finishes off with the shoulders and back on the third (see tables 3.12-3.14, page 80).

Because the arm muscles are small, it is easy to train them in the same workout as the chest. Many bodybuilders prefer training the biceps and triceps in the same workout. The shoulders, traps, and back are involved in many of the same exercises so it makes sense to work these areas together. Another advantage to this routine is that you train the back the day after thighs. Because the low back muscles are used indirectly in heavy squats, it is difficult to train the back with exercises like deadlifts and barbell rows before training thighs. By working the back the day after the thigh workout, you don't have to eliminate from the back workout exercises that also work the low back.

TABLE 3.12 Day One: Chest, Deltoids, Triceps, and Calves

Target area	Exercise	Sets	Reps set 1	Reps set 2	Reps set 3	Reps set 4
Chest	Bench press	4	10	8	6	6
	Incline press	3	8	6	6	
	Flys	3	10	8	6	
Triceps	Close-grip bench press	4	10	8	6	6
	Lying triceps extensions	3	8	6	6	
Biceps	Barbell curls	3	10	8	6	
	Incline curls	2	8	6		
Forearms	Reverse curls	2	8-10	8-10		
Calves	Standing calf raises	4	12	10	8	6

TABLE 3.13 Day Two: Abs and Thighs

Target area	Exercise	Sets	Reps set 1	Reps set 2	Reps set 3	Reps set 4	Reps set 5
Abs	Hanging knee raises	3	20-30	20-30	20-30		
	Crunches	3	20-30	20-30	20-30		
Thighs	Squats	5	12	10	8	6	6
	Leg press	4	12	10	8	6	
	Leg curls	4	10	8	6	6	
	Stiff-leg deadlifts	3	10	8	6		

TABLE 3.14 Day Three: Deltoids, Traps, Back, and Calves

Target area	Exercise	Sets	Reps set 1	Reps set 2	Reps set 3	Reps set 4
Deltoids	Military press	4	10	8	6	6
	Side lateral raises	3	10	8	6	
	Barbell shrugs	4	10	8	6	6
Back	Wide-grip chins	3	12	10	8	
	Barbell rows	4	10	8	6	6
	Seated cable rows	3	10	8	6	
	Deadlifts	3	10	8	6	
Forearms	Wrist curls	2	10-12	10-12		
Calves	Donkey calf raises	4	15-20	15-20	15-20	15-20

Routine 5: Three-Day Alternate Split—1 on, 1 off, 2 on, 1 off

Another alternative to the three-day split is adding another rest day to the split (see tables 3.15 and 3.16, pages 81 and 82). Instead of training three days in a row, you train one day, take the next off, then train the rest of the body over the next two days before taking a second day off.

TABLE 3.15 Routine A: Three-Day Split

Target area	Exercise	Sets	Reps set 1	Reps set 2	Reps set 3	Reps set 4	Reps set 5
Day one: chest, back, and calves							
Chest	Bench press	4	10	8	6	6	
	Incline dumbbell press	3	8	6	6		
	Flys	3	8	6	6		
	Dumbbell pullovers	2	10	8			
Back	Wide-grip chins	3	12	10	8		
	Barbell rows	4	10	8	6	6	
	Seated cable rows	3	10	8	6		
	Deadlifts	3	8	6	6		
Calves	Standing calf raises	3	12	10	8		
	Seated calf raises	3	12-15	12-15	12-15		
Day two: rest day							
Day three: legs and abs							
Abs	Hanging knee raises	2	20-30	20-30			
	Crunches	2	20-30	20-30			
Legs	Squats	5	12	10	8	6	6
	Leg press	4	10	8	6	6	
	Leg curls	4	10	8	6	6	
	Stiff-leg deadlifts	3	10	8	6		
Day four: deltoids, arms and calves							
Deltoids	Military press	4	10	8	6	6	
	Side lateral raises	3	10	8	6		
	Bent-over lateral raises	3	10	8	6		
	Barbell shrugs	4	10	8	6	6	
Triceps	Close-grip bench press	3	10	8	6		
	Lying triceps extensions	3	8	6	6		
Biceps	Barbell curls	3	10	8	6		
	Incline curls	2	8	6			
Forearms	Wrist curls	3	12	10	8		
Calves	Donkey calf raises	3	15-30	15-30	15-30		

Of course, you could also train two days in a row, take a day off, train the remaining muscle groups and then take a second day off. See the following list for two examples of how a training routine can be constructed using these guidelines.

Routine A	**Routine B**
Day 1: Chest, Back	Day 1: Chest, Arms
Day 2: Rest Day	Day 2: Legs
Day 3: Legs	Day 3: Rest Day
Day 4: Shoulders, Arms	Day 4: Shoulders, Back
Day 5: Rest Day	Day 5: Rest Day

TABLE 3.16 Routine B: Three-Day Split

Target area	Exercise	Sets	Reps set 1	Reps set 2	Reps set 3	Reps set 4	Reps set 5
Day one: chest, arms, calves							
Chest	Bench press	4	10	8	6	6	
	Incline dumbbell press	3	8	6	6		
	Flys	3	8	6	6		
	Dumbbell pullovers	2	10	8			
Triceps	Close-grip bench press	3	10	8	6		
	Lying triceps extensions	3	8	6	6		
Biceps	Barbell curls	3	10	8	6		
	Incline curls	2	8	6			
Calves	Standing calf raises	3	12	10	8		
	Seated calf raises	3	12-15	12-15	12-15		
Day two: abs, legs							
Abs	Hanging knee raises	2	20-30	20-30			
	Crunches	2	20-30	20-30			
Legs	Squats	5	12	10	8	6	6
	Leg press	4	10	8	6	6	
	Leg curls	4	10	8	6	6	
	Stiff-leg deadlifts	3	10	8	6		
Day three: rest day							
Day four: deltoids, traps, back, calves							
Deltoids	Military press	4	10	8	6	6	
	Side lateral raises	3	10	8	6		
	Bent-over lateral raises	3	10	8	6		
	Barbell shrugs	4	10	8	6	6	
Back	Wide-grip chins	3	12	10	8		
	Barbell rows	4	10	8	6	6	
	Seated cable rows	3	10	8	6		
	Deadlifts	3	8	6	6		
Calves	Donkey calf raises	3	15-30	15-30	15-30		

This three-day split still spreads the training over three days, but the additional rest day (usually between the thigh and back workouts) allows additional recuperation between workouts for each muscle group. Instead of training each target area once every four days, this routine trains each area once every five.

Routine 6: Four-Day Split—Advanced Program

Because larger and stronger muscles generate stronger contractions, move greater resistance, and damage more muscle tissue, an advanced bodybuilder must focus his training and limit each workout to only two major muscle groups per session. The effects of high-intensity training require more days off between workouts so that muscles can fully heal. Therefore, the workouts should be split and spread over four days, which provides five days of rest between each muscle group.

A four-day split should separate workouts for thighs and back with a day between them because the exercises for both of these target areas work the low back muscles. Squats and stiff-leg deadlifts performed on the thigh training days stress the low back muscles. And exercises such as barbell rows and deadlifts also stress the same muscles. Anyone who has strained his or her low back will tell you it is an injury you do not want to risk. These muscles provide stability to the upper body. They are so important during power movements that if they become impaired, effective workouts are all but impossible.

Similarly, the muscles of the shoulders are stressed during chest and deltoid workouts. Therefore, you should separate workouts for these two muscle groups by at least 48 hours. Training deltoids the day after training chest or vice versa could eventually strain the shoulders to the point of injury.

Here is an effective way to divide the target areas into a four-day split:

Day 1: Chest, triceps, and calves

Day 2: Abs and thighs

Day 3: Deltoids, traps, and calves

Day 4: Back, biceps, forearms, and abs

You could also divide target areas in a four-way split like this:

Day 1: Chest, biceps, and forearms

Day 2: Thighs and calves

Day 3: Deltoids, traps, and triceps

Day 4: Back, traps, and calves

The first routine is for bodybuilders who prefer training the chest with the triceps and the biceps with the back. These muscle groups are indirectly involved with one another; therefore, the smaller muscles of the arms have the advantage of increased blood supply and warmed-up joints and tendons before they are trained, which reduces the chance of injury.

Another advantage to training these areas together is that it minimizes the chance of overtraining the smaller muscles of the arms. The heavy workouts for the chest, shoulders, and back stress the arm muscles. If you train the arms by themselves or in separate workouts later in the week, they could become overworked. You eliminate this problem by training the triceps with the chest and the biceps with the back.

The first routine separates the deltoids and traps and works them on their own day; therefore, it is effective for bodybuilders who want to concentrate on these areas. The deltoids are a complex muscle group that often requires several exercises to train completely. Combining deltoid training with another area can limit the amount of work you can devote to this muscle group. Training them by themselves eliminates this problem. Of course, this four-day split follows the rules stated earlier for separating the thigh and back workouts along with the chest and shoulder workouts by one day.

The second routine is similar to the first, except it does not train the triceps and chest together or the biceps and back together. This training split combines biceps with chest and triceps with the deltoids.

The advantage of this split is that the arm muscles will grow stronger by training them on different days than the chest and back. This allows you to use greater weight on the arm exercises, which leads to increased size. This routine also separates the biceps and back and the triceps and chest by at least 48 hours to avoid any overlapping muscle groups.

If your back doesn't respond well to training, this routine is ideal because it trains the back by itself. The back can handle very heavy weight and intense workouts, and its demands from each training session are great; therefore, it's difficult to combine the back with other target areas.

A training program composed of the right exercises plugged into an optimal training routine is the first step in developing muscles and a winning physique. However, after you have completed your work in the gym, you must continue to build your body through proper nutrition. The food and supplements you consume are crucial to physique development. Now let's move on to the very important area of nutrition.

Eating for Maximum Results

Bodybuilding is one of the few sports in which nutrition is as important as training. Although a good nutrition program can make a big difference for any athlete, it is absolutely critical for a bodybuilder. Without the proper nutrients, bodybuilders are not able to build the muscle mass and strength needed for success in their sport. The proper nutrition program is also vital for competition. A low percentage of body fat (being ripped) is essential to winning a contest. All things being equal, the most ripped competitor will take home the winner's trophy.

Developing the right nutrition program can be difficult because, as Charles Gaines noted in his classic book, *Pumping Iron,* "it allows the most room for mistakes." To be a successful bodybuilder, you must understand the role that the three macronutrients—protein, carbohydrate, and fat—play in developing muscle mass. You also must know how to organize these nutrients into a daily eating plan that allows maximum absorption and assimilation.

Building muscle size and reducing body fat are the keys to success in bodybuilding, and neither can be attained without a superior nutrition program. The training, no matter how intense and concentrated, is only the beginning of developing your physique. It's what you do away from the gym that determines how far you will go in bodybuilding.

Creating an Anabolic Environment

Of the three macronutrients, protein is the most important because of its ability to rebuild tissue. Often termed the building block of muscle, protein is the only macronutrient that repairs and rebuilds damaged muscle tissue after intense exercise. For this reason, protein is critically important for all athletes engaged in strenuous activity, particularly bodybuilding.

Protein: Food for Muscles

Protein is made of various combinations of molecular units called amino acids. Of the 22 amino acids, eight are essential because the body cannot make them on its own. They must be obtained from food. Foods that contain these eight essential amino acids are known as complete protein foods.

Food that can be grouped in the meat or dairy category is a complete protein source. A bodybuilder who wants to add muscle to his frame should focus on complete protein food sources such as milk, cheese, eggs, beef, chicken, turkey, and fish. Complete protein foods, even though they contain the eight essential amino acids, vary in their amino acid makeup, which is why it is wise to include a wide variety of protein foods. For example, if you eat only chicken for your protein needs, you will limit yourself to the amino acid makeup of chicken. Arnold Schwarzenegger stressed eating a wide variety of foods to meet protein requirements. See table 4.1 for some high-protein foods.

Many carbohydrate foods also contain an ample amount of protein. Whole-grain foods such as oatmeal, beans, and wheat bread contain a moderately high amount of protein as well as lots of carbohydrate. However, any protein that comes from a plant or grain source lacks some of the eight essential amino acids and cannot be considered a complete protein food. These foods are a welcome addition to a healthy bodybuilding diet, but they should not be the main source of protein for building muscle.

Many bodybuilders advocate eating an extremely high amount of protein to build more muscle mass. The standard recommendation for protein consumption can vary from 1 to 2.5 grams per pound of bodyweight. Using these guidelines, a 200-pound bodybuilder would eat anywhere from 200 to 500 grams of protein per day. This is a very wide range. What exactly is the right amount?

Consuming prodigious amounts of protein does not guarantee greater muscle mass. The rule for nutrition is this: It's not what you eat that counts, but what you eat, digest, and assimilate. What good is it to take in a huge amount of protein that your body cannot possibly digest and use?

Some of the confusion over protein consumption comes from articles written by professional bodybuilders in the bodybuilding magazines. As we've already discussed, most, if not all, professional bodybuilders use steroids in their training. One of the biggest benefits of steroids is that they force the body to use more protein by preventing the liver from eliminating it. A natural bodybuilder will not be able to assimilate the huge amount of protein that a bodybuilder using steroids can. He will use what is needed, and then his body will eliminate the rest as waste or will store the extra calories as fat. A good guideline for a natural bodybuilder is to consume 1.25 to 1.5 grams of protein for each pound of bodyweight. Using the example above, a 200-pound bodybuilder would eat between

200 and 250 grams of protein per day to provide his muscles enough protein to build additional muscle tissue.

Some nutritionists recommend protein consumption based only on lean body weight (muscle tissue) and not total body weight. This makes sense because the plan is to feed the lean muscle tissue, not the excess body fat. A bodybuilder carrying a lot of adipose tissue would consume too many calories of protein if he used the earlier guideline for protein consumption based solely on body weight. For example, if a bodybuilder weighed 250 pounds with 17 percent body fat, his lean body weight would be 207.5 pounds. If this bodybuilder consumed 1.25 grams of protein per pound of lean bodyweight, his protein consumption would be approximately 260 grams of protein per day. If this same bodybuilder used the formula for each pound of total body weight, he would consume 312.5 grams of protein per day, which is probably too much when you add in the protein from the carbohydrate foods he will eat during the day.

It is easier to digest large amounts of protein if you eat several small meals per day, rather than two or three big meals. If you need to eat 300 grams of protein a day, you must shove in 100 grams per meal if you only eat three meals a day. On the other hand, if you consume that same 300 grams of protein spread over six meals, you only need to consume 50 grams at each meal.

Another benefit to several small meals a day is that you will be able to properly assimilate more of the protein. What good is it to eat 300 grams of protein a day if you won't use it efficiently? Eating smaller meals with sufficient protein every two and a half to three hours is the best method for making sure that the muscles can use the tissue-building protein.

TABLE 4.1 Amounts of Protein in Protein-Based Foods

Serving Size	Calories	Protein
10 egg whites	170	35 grams
4 eggs	300	25 grams
4 oz low-fat cottage cheese	100	16 grams
2 oz cheddar cheese	220	14 grams
2 oz low-fat Swiss cheese	180	16 grams
8 oz skim milk	90	9 grams
6 oz turkey breast	180	40 grams
6 oz ground turkey	220	48 grams
6 oz chicken breast	180	36 grams
4 oz sirloin steak	230	34 grams
4 oz lean ground beef	290	30 grams
4 oz salmon	200	28 grams
4 oz flounder	110	22 grams

Carbohydrate: The Energy Source

The next crucial macronutrient a bodybuilder needs is carbohydrate. Carbohydrate is important not only because it is the number one source of fuel for the body, but also because it plays a very important role in building muscle.

The intense weight training required to build muscle is an anaerobic form of exercise because it uses sugar (carbohydrate), not oxygen, for energy. Anaerobic training is intense, and its duration is short. In contrast, aerobic exercise uses oxygen to fuel the training session. It is much less intense and can be performed much longer. Aerobic exercise develops cardiovascular capacity. Anaerobic exercise works the muscular system more than it works the cardiovascular system.

Carbohydrate is the preferred source of energy for the body. Protein and fat can be utilized for energy if there are no carbs available. However, it is much easier and more efficient for the body to break down sugars (carbohydrates) for energy. Anaerobic exercise, such as high intensity weight training, requires adequate amounts of carbs to fuel the workout. If you are low on carbs, you will not have the energy to sustain your muscles through heavy, intense training.

Carbohydrate is also crucial if you are trying to get bigger. Many young bodybuilders concentrate on eating protein, which is important for building muscle tissue, but they forget that carbohydrate also plays a critical role in increasing muscle size. It helps in the recovery and recuperation that takes place after a workout when the muscles repair themselves and grow.

Complex Carbohydrate vs. Simple Carbohydrate

Not all forms of carbohydrate are created equal. Some are complex, while others are simple. It is important to understand the difference between the two because your body absorbs and uses them very differently.

Simple carbohydrate sources are often referred to as simple sugars, and the body breaks them down very quickly. Simple carbohydrate sources include fructose (fruit sugar), sucrose (table sugar), and lactose (milk sugar), as well as most refined foods sold in grocery stores for easy consumption. Almost any packaged food you find in the grocery store contains some type of refined sugar.

Bodybuilders must avoid simple carbohydrate foods because they cause the pancreas to secrete high levels of insulin to handle the sudden rise of sugar in the bloodstream. As a result, simple sugar is often shuttled directly into the fat cells for storage. This is especially important when you are preparing for a competition and need to lose as much subcutaneous fat as possible.

Complex carbohydrate foods are also made up of sugar, but the sugar molecules are strung together to form longer, more complex chains. Complex carbohydrate sources also include fiber, which makes them more difficult for the body to break down and digest. As a result, the insulin response is not as dramatic, and the food is broken down more slowly.

The slower digestion rate of the complex carbohydrate translates into less fat deposition. Complex carbohydrate is more likely to be stored as glycogen (stored sugar) within the muscle cells rather than in the fat cells. For this reason, most of your carbohydrate calories should come from complex sources.

Carbohydrate and Fiber

Fiber is found only in plant foods, not in meat or dairy products. The fiber content of the food you eat greatly reduces its absorption rate in the stomach. This reduces the amount of insulin released, which provides a steady blood sugar level. Bodybuilders should know how much fiber is contained in the foods they eat (see table 4.2 for some fiber-rich foods), and try to eat 40 to 50 grams of fiber per day for maximum benefits.

Fiber can be categorized into two groups, soluble and insoluble. Soluble fiber, which dissolves in water, slows the rate that the stomach empties, which delays the absorption of glucose from the bloodstream. It can also lower cholesterol levels. This type of fiber is found in fruit, oats, barley, psyllium, and some beans.

Insoluble fiber doesn't dissolve in water and passes through your digestive system largely unchanged. Insoluble fiber is commonly found in cereals, wheat bran, and in the stalks and peels of fruits and vegetables. Insoluble fiber accelerates intestinal transit and delays glucose absorption.

It is essential to eat plenty of complex carbohydrate that is as close to its original form as possible. Refining foods generally strips away fiber, leaving you with a food that is quickly absorbed by the body. For example, brown rice contains lots of complex carbohydrate and enough fiber to ensure slow absorption into the muscle cells, which makes it ideal for bodybuilders. However, rice cakes are a poor food choice for bodybuilders. Although they are made exclusively from rice (at least the sugar-free kind are), processing and refining the rice strips it of much of the fiber found in the original food source. In the end, rice cakes become a simple carbohydrate that is quickly absorbed by the body. And as already discussed, this rapid absorption rate leads to storing simple carbohydrate as fat.

TABLE 4.2 Fiber Content in Foods

Food	Grams of fiber
Apple (medium)	4.0
Asparagus (1/2 cup)	1.7
Banana (medium)	3.0
Beans (black, 1 cup)	19.4
Beans (kidney, 1 cup)	19.4
Bread (whole wheat, 2 slices)	6.0
Broccoli (raw, ½ cup)	4.0
Cereal (Wheaties, 1 cup)	2.0
Cereal (Raisin Bran, 1 cup)	5.0
Oatmeal (1 cup)	8.0
Noodles (whole wheat egg, 1 cup)	5.7
Green peas (1/2 cup)	9.1
Baked potato (7 oz)	5.0
Yams (6 oz)	6.8
Brown rice (1/2 cup)	5.5
Whole wheat Spaghetti (1 cup)	5.6
Spinach (1/2 cup, cooked)	7.0

Source: www.wehealnewyork.org/healthinfo.

Carbohydrate Impact on the Glycemic Index

A method for evaluating the absorption rate of carbohydrate is the glycemic index: a system of ranking foods based on their immediate effect on blood glucose (sugar) levels. Foods that quickly break down in the bloodstream have high glycemic-index ratings, while those that are slowly absorbed into the bloodstream are classified as low-glycemic foods. This ranking system is based on the glycemic measurement of glucose, which has a rating of 100 on the glycemic index. Foods with a glycemic-index rating of 50 or less are low glycemic. High-glycemic foods have a rating of more than 50.

Many nutritionists do not put much stock in the glycemic index because these measurements are taken when consuming foods on an empty stomach. Because foods are most often eaten in combination, the glycemic index is often dramatically skewed. A food's fiber and fat content affect how the body digests it. If you consume a simple carbohydrate that has a high glycemic-index rating along with a food that is high in fat or fiber, the absorption of that high-glycemic food will be slowed because of the other foods in the meal.

For example, a banana has a glycemic-index rating of 62, but if you eat it with a high-fiber, low-glycemic food such as oatmeal, the glycemic-index rating of the banana drops. This is because the higher fiber content of oatmeal delays the absorption of glucose from the bloodstream, despite the higher glycemic rating of the banana.

Despite the effect of combining foods, it is still wise to know which foods are highly glycemic and which are low. Because the glycemic index is based on how quickly foods are broken down in the bloodstream, it is best to stick with foods that are high in fiber and close to their original source and skip the refined foods. For example, brown rice has a glycemic-index rating of 59, the more refined white rice has a glycemic-index rating of 88, and even further refined instant rice has a sky-high glycemic-index rating of 91.

The glycemic index of some foods may surprise you. Ice cream, despite its high sugar content, has a glycemic-index rating of 50 compared to waffles, which have a rating of 76. This is because the higher fat content of the ice cream slows its absorption rate, while the lower-fat waffles are more quickly absorbed. But just because a food has a low glycemic index doesn't mean you won't store it as fat. Ice cream, in addition to its high sugar content, also has a higher fat content, which translates into more calories.

Another good example is a Snickers bar, which has a glycemic-index rating of 41 compared to high-sugar, low-fat jelly beans with a glycemic rating of 80. The lower fat content of the jelly beans makes them nearly pure sugar, which raises the blood sugar level immediately. The Snickers bar has a higher fat content, which slows its absorption.

Simply changing the structure of a food can drastically change the way the body absorbs it. A potato, for example, is a complex carbohydrate that contains plenty of fiber in its original form. The body slowly digests a potato baked in its skin. But if you remove its skin and mash it, it becomes easier to absorb and produces a higher insulin response.

Role of Insulin in Building Muscle

Insulin is a hormone released by the pancreas in response to high levels of sugar in the bloodstream. When you eat a carbohydrate food, the bloodstream absorbs the sugar from the carbohydrate from the intestines. The pancreas then secretes insulin as a response to this rise in the blood sugar level. The cells of the body that have insulin receptors bind to the insulin in the blood.

What does any of this have to do with bodybuilding? Understanding the function of insulin and how it helps transport nutrients to the cells explains how important carbohydrates are to building muscle. Since it is the sugar in carbohydrate that is responsible for raising the blood sugar level and causing an insulin response, it is easy to see that carbs are an essential nutrient for bodybuilders.

Whenever carbohydrate is consumed, the blood sugar level is increased, which causes insulin to be released. The insulin acts as a transport mechanism in shuttling the sugar from the carbs to be stored as glycogen in the muscle cells. It also transports the amino acids (from any protein foods that are consumed) into the muscle cells. Both of these nutrients (sugar and amino acids) are extremely important for muscle repair and growth.

What is interesting about athletes, particularly bodybuilders, is that the muscle cells of their bodies become "trained" to become more insulin sensitive while their fat cells become more insulin resistant. This is due to the muscle cells of an athlete's body becoming accustomed to storing glycogen and then using that glycogen for intense exercise. Bodybuilders also eat in a way in which the muscle cells are fed carbohydrate in the correct manner to encourage glycogen storage while simultaneously discouraging fat deposition.

This adaptation of the muscle cells to become more insulin sensitive is a process that occurs over time. A sedentary person who does not normally deplete all the glycogen in his or her muscle cells through intense exercise would not have muscle cells that were insulin sensitive. However, an obese person would most likely have fat cells that are very insulin sensitive because this person's lifestyle has encouraged these cells to adapt in this manner.

Window of Opportunity

Transporting glycogen and amino acids into the muscle cells is particularly important immediately after a workout. Anaerobic training uses carbohydrate for energy. An intense training session should totally deplete glycogen stores, leaving the muscle cells starving for sugar. The 30 to 45 minutes following a workout have become known among bodybuilders as the window of opportunity. By consuming the right nutrients at this critical time, you can optimize recuperation and make significantly greater progress.

In general, bodybuilders should eat complex carbohydrate that contains lots of fiber and is low glycemic. However, you can break this rule immediately following a workout. Because the muscles are depleted, eating slowly digested complex carbohydrate is not the answer. Instead, you want simple sugars that will feed your depleted muscle cells as quickly as possible. Normally, the increased insulin level that follows consumption of simple sugars causes your body to store carbohydrate as fat, but after a strenuous workout, the muscles cells demand sugar; therefore, the simple carbohydrate is transported to the muscle cells instead of the fat cells.

Along with simple carbohydrates, the postworkout meal should also include an easy-to-digest form of protein. Because the simple sugars raises the insulin level, consuming a fast acting form of protein along with the simple carbohydrate transports the amino acids from the protein into the muscle cells along with the carbohydrate. This postworkout meal provides your muscle cells the two nutrients they crave and the two nutrients required to build muscle mass.

Shakes or drinks provide a postworkout meal that is easy to digest and gets into your system quickly. You can make your own by mixing 40 grams of whey protein, which is absorbed quickly, and 60 grams of simple carbohydrate in powder form. Some bodybuilders choose to eat food instead of drinking a shake for their post-workout meal. This is okay as long as the food contains some easy-to-digest protein along with some high-glycemic carbs. A good choice would be a whey protein drink or ground turkey for the protein source combined with mashed potatoes or rice cakes with jelly on them for the quick carb choice. I personally think a shake is both easier and quicker to digest to feed those starving muscle cells but some bodybuilders would rather eat food to save money or because they prefer eating food as opposed to drinking a shake.

Fat: An Alternative Energy Source

The third macronutrient is fat. Fat, like carbohydrate, is a potential source of energy. Excessive fat is easily stored as adipose tissue, or body fat. In fact, of the three macronutrients, fat is the easiest to convert to stored body fat. Simple carbohydrate is the second easiest because of the high insulin levels it induces. Complex carbohydrate is next because of its more complex makeup and its fiber content. Protein is the most difficult to store as body fat. That's not to say that an excessive amount of protein cannot be stored as body fat, just that it isn't stored as easily as the other macronutrients.

When designing a nutrition program, remember that one gram of fat contains nine calories, more than twice the number of calories in one gram of protein or carbohydrate. They each have four. Because of the higher calorie content of fat, many bodybuilders eat a diet very low in fat. If protein builds muscle, and carbohydrate supplies energy in the form of muscle glycogen, why intentionally eat foods high in fat if they don't serve a purpose, they argue.

The truth is that fat is an essential part of any diet and should not be eliminated. In fact, strictly limiting fat interferes with normal bodily processes. Even worse for a bodybuilder, an extremely low-fat diet over time could prevent the body from burning subcutaneous fat. The body has developed several mechanisms to help it survive, and if it interprets a low-fat diet (less than 20 grams a day) as a form of starvation, it may stubbornly hold on to its body fat until it senses it will again be fed adequately.

Good Fat

Just as your body requires complete protein foods to obtain the essential amino acids, it also demands certain types of fat. These essential fatty acids are linoleic acid and alpha-linolenic acid, which the body can transform into any kind of fat it needs.

Linoleic acid (omega-6 fatty acids) and alpha-linolenic acid (omega-3 fatty acids) are referred to as good fat and are required for optimal health. These polyunsaturated fats can be found in canola oil and in oils made from pumpkin seeds, soybeans, and walnuts. Vegetable oils are good sources of the omega-6 fatty acids. Flaxseed oil and fatty fish such as salmon, mackerel, and sardines are an excellent source of omega-3 fatty acids. Omega-3 fatty acids, in particular, are responsible for developing brain tissue. Foods high in omega-3 fatty acids are quickly converted in the body to food for the brain. A bodybuilder should eat oily fish at least three times a week and add one or two tablespoons of flaxseed oil to his or her diet daily to consume a sufficient amount of omega-3 fatty acids. The omega-3 fatty acids, in addition to their health benefits to the brain, help in making the muscle cells more insulin sensitive, which helps to absorb greater amounts of glycogen and amino acids into the muscle cells.

Bad Fat

Saturated fat can be classified as bad because it only serves as an energy source or is stored as excess body fat.

Saturated fat is found in many animal protein foods such as meat, cheese, eggs, and milk. However, these are not the only foods high in saturated fat. Vegetable oils such as palm, palm kernel, and coconut are dangerously high in saturated fat. In addition to making you fatter, saturated fat can also raise cholesterol levels and low-density lipoproteins (LDL). Higher cholesterol levels as well as a higher LDL count can cause plaque buildup, which increases the chance for atherosclerosis.

One method for cutting back or avoiding saturated fat while still eating a diet high in protein is to modify the animal protein food so that it is lower in fat. For example, prime rib and porterhouse steak are higher in fat than other cuts such as flank steak and round steak. Also, egg whites contain virtually no fat, but the yolk contains 8 grams of it. If you consume milk and cheese, select 1 percent or skim milk and low-fat cheese instead of whole milk and regular cheese.

Ugly Fat

In addition to saturated fat, you should also avoid trans fatty acids. Modern food processing methods including heating, hydrogenating, bleaching, and deodorizing alter a fat's natural structure to produce trans fatty acids. These procedures are common to almost all mass-produced fat and oils. Processing changes the natural configuration of fat so that it can't link with your body's cells the way nature intended. These ill-fitting links disrupt cellular metabolism and permit toxic substances to enter the cell. This abnormal cell function has been implicated in both cardiovascular diseases and cancer.

To avoid trans fat, read the labels on your food. Stay away from words such as hydrogenated or partially hydrogenated. Trans fat does not occur in unprocessed foods. It is a direct result of manmade tampering.

Eating Like a Bodybuilder

When most of us were growing up, we were taught to eat three square meals a day. Eating breakfast, lunch, and dinner, we were told, would provide the nutrients essential for good health. However, this traditional plan does not fit into the bodybuilding lifestyle. Simply eating enough nutrients for good health will not build muscle mass. In order to build muscles beyond "normal" boundaries, a bodybuilder must eat far more calories than the average person. And a bodybuilder must eat foods containing the essential nutrients that promote growth. Otherwise, he will continue to look average and not like a bodybuilder.

A bodybuilder needs sufficient calories, protein, carbohydrate, and fat every day to regenerate muscle tissue after tearing it down through intense training sessions. But the way the body digests and absorbs food makes it impossible to consume, digest, and use enough nutrients in just three meals a day. A better plan is to spread your caloric and nutritional intake throughout the day. Many bodybuilders eat six meals a day.

The body can digest and absorb only so much protein at one time. Limiting yourself to 30 to 50 grams of protein at one meal is much more efficient than trying to cram in 80 to 100 grams in one sitting. If your nutrition plan requires you to eat 250 grams of protein a day, you need to consume approximately 42 grams of protein in each of six meals. Spacing meals two and a half to three hours apart should allow you to digest and assimilate this amount of protein.

Multiple small meals also benefit your carbohydrate absorption rate. If you eat too much carbohydrate at one time, the insulin level in the bloodstream rises too high, causing your body to store the calories from the carbohydrate as fat. In addition, eating multiple small portions of complex carbohydrate containing fiber gradually replaces glycogen stores in the muscle cells, giving you plenty of energy for your next training session. However, once you have replenished muscle glycogen, additional carbohydrate is stored as body fat.

Multiple small meals also make it easier to consume the number of calories required to sustain and build muscle tissue. Not only can you absorb the nutrients more efficiently, but you can also eat more in six small meals than trying to stuff yourself with three big meals.

Feed the Muscles: Creating a Diet for Lean Mass

Many bodybuilders new to the sport resist eating several small meals a day, especially if they were brought up to believe that they should eat only three times a day. They cannot understand the concept of eating more to become lean and to lose body fat. A good rule to remember is: Feed the muscles and starve the fat.

Eating at least six small meals a day ensures that the nutrients are transported to the muscle cells, and not to the fat cells. Eating sufficient amounts of complete protein foods and complex carbohydrate feeds the muscles with the amino acids and glycogen they crave after a heavy, intense training session. At the same time, avoiding foods high in sugar, saturated fat, and empty calories starves the fat cells. Eating six meals a day keeps your blood sugar level in check and prevents your insulin levels from going too high, which limits fat deposition.

In addition to more efficient absorption, eating several small meals also stimulates metabolism. Every time you eat a meal, your body must work to digest the food. Your body burns more calories to digest foods containing complete protein and complex carbohydrate. Foods containing refined sugar are quickly digested and do not require the body to work as hard to assimilate them. This process of converting food into energy is called thermogenesis. The energy produced by the body to digest food requires heat. The more heat that is produced, the more calories will be utilized in order to process these foods. Foods containing high amounts of fiber along with complete animal protein have a high thermogenic rate.

Food Preparation: Planning Ahead

As you can imagine, eating six times a day requires planning and preparation. If you don't prepare the meals ahead of time, they may not be ready when it is time to eat. Eating each meal and eating it on time is an essential requirement of bodybuilding. Skipping a meal or not eating at the scheduled time can slow metabolism, decrease blood sugar levels, and possibly cause muscle catabolism (muscle tissue breakdown from lack of amino acids). If you are serious about building muscle, you also must be serious about preparing your food.

Because it is important that the food be available when you need it, the first rule is to buy your food ahead of time. Buying in bulk and storing it in the refrigerator or the freezer ensures that food will be on hand when it's time to eat.

Animal protein foods such as turkey, chicken, steak, and fish are easy to store in the freezer. Cut or separate the meat into 4- to 6-ounce servings and store them individually in small plastic bags. I recommend buying a small scale so you can weigh all of your food so you know exactly how much you are eating. Other protein foods such as eggs are convenient to buy in bulk. If you eat 10 eggs a day, you will go through them pretty quickly. Buying six to eight of the 18-egg cartons will save you trips to the store. And they won't go bad at the rate you use them.

Vegetables, however, are another matter. Fresh fruit and vegetables ripen quickly, so they need to be eaten within days of purchase. They'll usually last five days or so. A vegetable salad consisting of a full head of romaine lettuce, 4-5 carrots, and 4-5 stalks of broccoli will last just less than a week before you have eaten it all or have to throw it out. Frozen fruits and vegetables are a good option. Blueberries (for your oatmeal), asparagus, and green beans are all good options. The vitamin and mineral content is similar to fresh vegetables and they can be prepared more quickly than fresh.

To be prepared for a day of eating, you must know exactly what to eat each day. This includes what time each meal will take place and what each meal will consist of. Your nutrition plan must be thought out well in advance so that you know exactly how much protein, carbohydrate, fat, and calories you will consume each day. Once you have figured this out, you must look at your schedule to see where you will be for each meal. Someone who travels and is on the road all day will have to make different choices than someone who works from home or in an office. With your nutrition plan in hand, you can make sure everything is in place for the next day. There should be no guesswork when it comes to eating.

Protein drinks are invaluable if you must eat away from home. You can make them at home, then transport and store them in a drink container packed with ice. If you work in an office with a refrigerator and microwave, you can pack meals in plastic containers. This allows you to eat food that is part of your nutrition plan instead of making due with food from a restaurant or a vending machine.

Bodybuilders who eat on the road have the toughest time eating their own food, but it is still possible. Protein drinks are a must, but you can't live on protein drinks alone. Real food is necessary for proper nutrition. Therefore, you must get a cooler and ice or an ice pack. Unfortunately, in most cases, if you are eating out of your car you will have to eat your food cold.

If you must travel out of town, you will have to make even more sacrifices. To avoid eating in restaurants, bring food with you. Good choices are dry, nonperishable foods such as oatmeal, protein powders, and canned or frozen goods. If you have access to a grocery store and to a refrigerator in your hotel room, you can eat animal protein and fresh fruits or vegetables. You will also have to bring cooking appliances, unless you're staying in a kitchenette. A hot plate is ideal for warming up or cooking most foods, but if you plan to eat animal protein while away from home, a portable mini grill is necessary. Of course, you can't forget the pots and pans. You may have to pack an additional suitcase just for your cooking needs when traveling on a diet. If you're going to be away, packing your food the night before saves time in the morning. It also keeps you from rushing through the packing process, which inevitably leads to forgetting something.

Many bodybuilders pick one day of the week to prepare the majority of their food for the rest of the week. They go grocery shopping; pack the beef, chicken, fish, and turkey in the freezer; and make salads, rice, and other foods that will last a week. This is an excellent method for ensuring that the food will be ready when you need it for a full week.

Consistency in training and nutrition is one of the secrets to achieving your bodybuilding goals. Eating the right foods on schedule every day will make a big difference in the gains you make.

Sample shopping list

Eggs
Steak
Chicken
Extra lean ground turkey
Fish
Vegetables, fresh and frozen
Fruit, fresh and frozen
Water
Brown rice
Sweet potatoes
Oatmeal
Oat bran
Low-fat cheese

Nutrition Diary: Charting Your Success

One method for making sure that you eat the number of calories and the essential macronutrients required to reach your bodybuilding goals is to write down everything you eat each day. In addition to recording the amount of each food you consume, you can also calculate the number of calories and the grams of protein, carbohydrate, and fat that you take in. This valuable information provides you important feedback that will help you make the gains you are looking for.

For example, if you are unsuccessfully trying to gain weight, a nutrition diary shows you how many calories you are taking in each day. You may think you're eating a lot, but after counting the calories, you might see that your caloric intake is inconsistent. Perhaps you're eating 3,000 calories one day, 2,400 the next day, and 2,700 the next. If your body needs a minimum of 3,000 calories to gain body weight, your current caloric intake is not sufficient. Once you begin charting your daily intake, you can make sure that you eat the right number of calories. After a week or two of consistent eating, you should begin to see progress. Writing down everything you eat instead of guessing is a more foolproof route to success.

The nutrition diary helps track other pertinent data. If you are trying to eat at least 250 grams of protein per day, you can look in your diary to see if you are meeting this goal. If you find that you are only eating 220 grams, you can add another meal to your daily diet.

In addition to the food you eat every day, you can also record other statistics such as your waist size and body weight. This is particularly useful when you are dieting to lose body fat. If the diet is working, your waist size should gradually decrease as your body weight slowly drops. If your body weight drops and your waist size remains constant, you need to examine your nutrition diary as well as your training to determine what is wrong.

Table 4.3 provides a sample page from a nutrition diary. This page breaks down the number of calories consumed in addition to the grams of protein, carbohydrate, and fat, letting the bodybuilder know if he's eating what he needs to. Using this example, a person with a lean body weight of 225 pounds should eat 281 to 337 grams of protein each day (225 pounds × 1.25 to 1.5 grams per pound). Therefore, the 319 grams of protein consumed on this particular day were sufficient.

This example also breaks down the macronutrients into percentage of the total caloric intake. In this case, the percentages illustrated are ideal for adding muscle tissue. However, if the bodybuilder were on a precontest diet to lose body fat while maintaining muscle tissue, he should probably shift the percentages slightly to 45 percent protein, 40 percent carbohydrate, and 15 percent fat. In bodybuilding, knowledge about your training and nutrition is power for making progress, and the nutrition diary is a valuable tool for providing that knowledge.

Eating for Your Body Type

Even more so than the training, a nutrition program must be tailored to the individual. The following guidelines will allow you to make smart choices for your body type.

TABLE 4.3 Sample Bodybuilding Diet From a Nutrition Diary

	Calories	Grams of protein	Grams of carbohydrate	Grams of fat
1 X-large egg	77	7	1	5
9 X-large egg whites	173	39	5	0
1 cup oatmeal	310	10	54	6
½ cup frozen blueberries	53	0	13	0
2 servings protein powder	226	45	6	2
110 grams banana	71	.71	16	.27
1 tbs flaxseed oil	99	0	0	11
4.25 oz extra-lean turkey	112	26	0	.85
½ cup brown rice	99	2	21	.65
3 tbs salsa	15	0	4	0
3 oz broccoli	47	4	7	.45
5.5 oz salmon	260	39	0	11
1 cup frozen green beans	30	1	6	0
Meal replacement drink	307	40	12	11
100 grams banana	65	.65	15	.25
½ cup oat bran	155	7	25	3
½ cup frozen blueberries	53	0	13	0
1 serving whey protein	106	23	2	.5
1 serving creatine	136	0	34	0
Postworkout drink	440	40	60	4
7 X-large egg whites	135	30	4	0
2 tbs salsa	10	0	2	0
½ cup oatmeal	155	5	27	3
½ cup frozen blueberries	53	0	13	0
Totals	3,168	319	340	59
Percentage of calories		40%	43%	17%

Ectomorphs

Because of their extremely fast metabolisms, ectomorphs must consume more calories than the other body types. In addition to eating six meals a day, ectomorphs probably need to increase the number of calories per meal to gain the muscle size they desire. One way to increase caloric intake is to add protein drinks to the diet. It is much easier to finish off a protein drink than to consume lots of solid food. And it is easy to add calories to the drink itself by adding ingredients such as fruit, ice cream, protein powder, and flaxseed oil.

Most bodybuilders are well aware of the importance of eating enough protein to build muscle mass. However, too many ectomorphs forget that carbohydrate also plays a critical role. Without enough carbohydrate, all the protein in the world will not help ectomorphs add size. If an ectomorph eats 1.25 to 1.5 grams of protein for each pound of body weight, he should also eat 2 to 4 grams of carbohydrate per pound of body weight. Therefore, a 150-pound ectomorphic bodybuilder needs to eat 190 to 225 grams of protein and 300 to 600 grams of carbohydrate per day to gain size. If this bodybuilder were eating 500 grams of carbohydrate a day, he should get 400 grams from complex, slow-digesting foods such as oatmeal, brown rice, sweet potatoes, whole-wheat pasta, or corn. The remaining 100 grams could be from a simple carbohydrate such as cold cereals, bread, muffins, fruit preserves, or honey.

The nutritional breakdown for an ectomorph working to gain size is approximately 35 percent protein, 50 percent carbohydrate, and 15 percent fat. This breakdown allows a bodybuilder to eat more than enough protein, sufficient essential fat, and high amounts of carbohydrate to add muscle mass. Table 4.4 shows a sample diet for a 150-pound ectomorph who wants to gain muscular body weight.

Mesomorphs

A mesomorph is a naturally muscular person perfect for the sport of bodybuilding. Typically, mesomorphs' metabolic rate allows them to add muscle mass without adding too much body fat. Mesomorphs have it much easier than ectomorphs or endomorphs when it comes to building muscle mass.

Because of their efficient metabolism, a mesomorph can eat a diet similar to an ectomorph's: a moderately high amount of protein, a high amount of carbohydrate, and a low amount of fat. Plenty of carbohydrate allows the mesomorph to build muscle mass without the fear of adding body fat. If your metabolism allows you to eat lots of carbohydrate, do it, because the extra carbohydrate will help you build muscle mass. Mesomorphs also need a moderately high amount of protein, 1.25 to 1.5 grams of protein for each pound of bodyweight. And mesomorphs should eat more carbohydrate than protein when eating to add muscle mass.

Because mesomorphs' relatively fast metabolism allows them to eat lots of carbohydrate, they should keep their fat intake low. There is no reason to eat a high amount of fat in addition to the carbohydrate. Of course, they must get enough essential fatty acids to maintain good health, but after taking care of that requirement, they should not consume additional fat.

The nutritional breakdown for a mesomorph is approximately 35 to 40 percent protein, 45 to 50 percent carbohydrate, and 15 percent fat. These ratios are very similar to those of an ectomorph. A diet that includes high amounts of carbohydrate and protein is perfect for a mesomorph whose metabolism is geared toward adding muscle.

TABLE 4.4 Sample Mass-Building Diet for Ectomorphic Body Types

	Calories	Grams of protein	Grams of carbohydrate	Grams of fat
3 whole eggs	242	18	2	18
5 egg whites	97	21	3	0
½ oz Muenster cheese	52	3	.16	4
1 cup oatmeal	310	10	54	6
1 banana	130	1	30	.5
2 cups 2% milk	242	16	23	9
1 medium banana	130	1	30	.5
2 servings protein powder	226	45	6	2
1 tbs flaxseed oil	99	0	0	11
6 oz lean beef	203	36	0	7
2 slices whole-wheat bread	153	8	28	1
200 grams baked potato	155	4	34	.27
2 cups broccoli	63	5	9	.6
Meal replacement powder	307	40	12	11
2 cups 2% milk	242	16	23	9
1 medium banana	130	1	30	.5
1 cup oatmeal	310	10	54	6
1 cup blueberries	108	0	27	0
6 oz chicken	187	40	0	3
2 cups brown rice	198	4	43	1
2 cups corn	304	10	58	3
2 cups 2% milk	242	16	23	9
Meal replacement powder	307	40	12	11
1 medium banana	130	1.3	30	.5
½ cup oat bran	155	7	25	3
½ cup blueberries	53	0	13	0
Totals	4,754	353	369	118

Endomorphs

Endomorphs have no problem adding weight to their frames, but they do have trouble making sure that the added weight is muscle and not fat. Endomorphs' slower metabolism allows them to gain fat easily. They can add muscle quickly, but they are better off adding weight slowly so that most of that gain will be muscle.

Just as ectomorphs should write down everything they eat to ensure they are eating enough, endomorphs should also track their calories daily. If an endomorph notices that he is adding fat too quickly, he should reduce the total number of calories he eats. A nutrition journal will help an endomorph determine the exact number of calories he can consume to reach his size goals.

In addition to keeping an accurate diet journal, an endomorph should also keep track of his waist measurement and body weight in the off-season and precontest. These two values are easy to track daily. During the off-season, these measurements help the endomorph see if he's adding body fat or not.

Although it's true that an endomorph's slower metabolism presents challenges, it also makes adding muscle mass easier for them than for an ectomorph. To succeed in bodybuilding, endomorphs must eat a very clean diet and avoid most processed foods. Their diet is more strict than that for bodybuilders with faster metabolisms, but their discipline will pay off in greater progress and less body fat.

When breaking down the percentage of macronutrients, endomorphs need to eat more protein and a medium to low amount of carbohydrate. Because endomorphs tend to be more insulin sensitive than other body types, they must be very careful about the amount and type of carbohydrate they consume and carefully manage their insulin levels. They should obtain the majority of their carbohydrate from low-glycemic, fibrous foods. Starchy carbohydrate sources such as bread, rice, and potatoes, which have no negative effects on other body types, may add body fat to an endomorph. All simple sugars and processed foods should be eliminated or eaten only on rare occasions. Because of an endomorph's slow metabolism, these foods will most likely end up as body fat.

Because endomorphs eat less carbohydrate than other body types do, they must balance their diet with more protein. Although protein is not as efficient at producing energy as carbohydrate is, protein's additional amino acids will help maintain a stable blood sugar level. The additional protein will also help fill the calorie gap created by cutting down on carbohydrate.

The nutritional breakdown for a mesomorph is approximately 50 percent protein, 30 percent carbohydrate, and 20 percent fat. For example, a 200-pound endomorph could eat 2,900 calories consisting of 370 grams of protein, 220 grams of carbohydrate, and 60 grams of fat.

Another option for endomorphic bodybuilders limiting their carbohydrate intake is to cycle their diet. Eating a low-carbohydrate diet every day lowers the glycogen level in the muscle cells, leaving them with insufficient fuel for hard and heavy sessions in the gym. Therefore, even though reducing carbohydrate intake keeps body-fat levels under control, it can be detrimental for training and building muscle mass. Cycling carbohydrate intake, where the bodybuilder eats limited carbohydrate most of the time, but increases calories from carbohydrate every two to four days, allows them to restore glycogen levels in the muscle cells. This one day of increased carbohydrate should fully restore glycogen levels.

A typical schedule for cycling carbohydrate is to consume approximately 1 gram of carbohydrate for each pound of body weight for two or three days, followed by a day of eating 2 grams of carbohydrate for each pound of body weight. For example, a 200-pound endomorphic bodybuilder would eat only 200 grams of carbohydrate on his low-carbohydrate days, then increase the intake to 400 grams for one day before repeating the cycle.

The carbohydrate cycling process is a good method for controlling fat deposition while preventing muscle loss. You may have to experiment before determining the optimum number of low-carbohydrate days, but once the process is perfected, it can be very effective.

Table 4.5 shows a sample diet for a 175-pound endomorphic bodybuilder trying to add muscle but keep fat deposition to a minimum.

TABLE 4.5 Sample Mass-Building Diet for Endomorphic Body Types

	Calories	Grams of protein	Grams of carbohydrate	Grams of fat
2 whole eggs	154	14	2	10
6 egg whites	116	26	3	0
1 cup oatmeal	310	10	54	6
2 servings protein powder	222	45	6	2
1 tbs flaxseed oil	99	0	0	11
5 oz ground turkey	133	31	0	1
½ cup brown rice	99	2	21.3	.65
3 oz broccoli	48	4	7	.45
Meal replacement powder	307	40	12	11
½ banana	65	.65	15	.25
Postworkout drink	436	40	60	4
5 oz salmon	230	35	0	10
3 oz vegetable salad	34	1	7	.18
2 tbs olive oil	243	0	0	27
2 servings protein powder	226	45	6	2.5
Totals	2,721	294	193	86

Essential Bodybuilding Supplements

Bodybuilding supplementation is very important to the natural bodybuilder. The science and technology of nutritional supplements have improved dramatically since the early 1990s. Drug-free bodybuilders can now make much better gains than they could with food and training alone. Not taking advantage of advanced supplementation puts you at a distinct disadvantage.

The supplement industry is growing year by year. New products are introduced all the time, each promising to be the most incredible supplement ever produced. It's difficult to distinguish the truly effective supplements from those that are overly hyped through excessive advertising.

The world of bodybuilding supplements is so extensive that a full book could be written on this subject alone, and in fact, several have. This chapter covers the basics of bodybuilding supplementation as of this writing. However, because new products are being developed all the time, some of this material may become outdated in a year or two.

Bodybuilding supplements can be divided into the following categories: Protein, creatine, workout, amino acid, fat burning, testosterone boosting, and vitamins and minerals.

Protein Supplements

These are the supplements most often used by bodybuilders. Protein supplements help bodybuilders get enough grams of protein per day by adding protein drinks between regular-food meals. They also provide the opportunity to consume high quality protein as most of the protein powders available now are made of the best ingredients. The early protein powder supplements were often made with soy protein, which is not as productive at building muscle mass as milk, egg, or whey protein. This is because soy protein is protein derived from plants and not a complete protein food that comes from the dairy or meat groups. There is also less sugar in today's protein supplements than in previous years.

Many forms of protein powders are available. The most popular is whey protein. Whey is a by-product of cheese production.

Whey protein isolate is the purest form and contains 90 to 95 percent protein. It contains very little fat or lactose, which is ideal if you are lactose intolerant. The other form of whey protein is whey protein concentrate. It is not as pure as whey protein isolate, and the protein content can range from 25 to 89 percent pure protein. It contains some lactose, fat, and minerals. As the protein level increases, the amount of lactose decreases. Whey protein concentrate with 80 percent protein content is the form most readily available as a protein powder supplement.

Whey protein can be either hydrolyzed, where the protein chains have been broken into smaller segments called peptides, or nonhydrolyzed. Both forms provide high-quality protein. Hydrolyzed whey protein is more easily digested and presents less potential for allergic reactions than nonhydrolyzed whey protein because the process of hydrolysis breaks the protein chains down into smaller segments called peptides. The quality of the protein, however, remains very high.

It is this easy digestibility that is the one drawback of whey protein. Because whey protein is digested so quickly, the amino acids from the protein are rapidly absorbed. This fast-acting protein does not allow for a slow and steady release of amino acids into the bloodstream. As a result, muscle breakdown could occur from the lack of the essential amino acids available for growth.

The other popular form of protein is casein (milk) protein. Casein is also a high-quality form of protein that contains all the essential amino acids. Unlike whey protein, casein protein powder is digested much more slowly and provides a steady stream of amino acids to the muscles. However, the casein protein can cause problems for those who are lactose intolerant. If the protein is not properly digested, it will not benefit the user. Many adults become more lactose intolerant as they get older.

I prefer to use protein powders that combine fast-and-slow acting proteins such as whey protein and milk protein. These protein powders are the best absorbed and provide the best results.

I specifically use whey protein after my workouts since whey protein is a faster acting protein powder. I need to get those important amino acids into my muscle cells immediately after training. Whey protein is also a great form of protein to use prior to doing cardio or immediately upon arising. Since it is absorbed so quickly into the muscles, it is ideal for feeding the muscles with a fast form of protein to raise the blood sugar level when the body has been in a fasting state for some time.

Egg protein is another form of protein powder. Before whey protein was introduced to the marketplace, egg protein was considered the top of the line in protein supplements. Now it ranks right below whey protein.

Milk protein by itself is a cheaper form of protein. It can be effective if you are not lactose intolerant, but both egg and whey protein are better absorbed. A better alternative to milk protein by itself is a powder that combines whey, milk, and egg protein for the best absorption and assimilation.

Soy protein is the cheapest form. Because soy protein is derived from a plant and not from an animal source, it is an incomplete protein. Many people have difficulty digesting soy protein because it lacks essential amino acids. However, if you take soy protein with a complete protein food such as milk, the lack of essential amino acids is no longer an issue.

In addition to protein powders, many bodybuilders use meal replacement supplements. These are protein powders with carbohydrate, fat, vitamins, and minerals added. The first meal replacement powder, Met-Rx, was introduced in the early 1990s. Today many meal replacement powders are available. Some are lower in carbohydrate than others. Others contain ingredients such as glutamine and other important amino acids. The types of fat contained in a meal replacement supplement are usually essential fatty acids that are important to the muscle-building process.

Look for a meal replacement powder with the highest-quality protein you can find. Demand as much from your meal replacement powder as you do your protein powder. Also look for extra ingredients such as glutamine peptides (10 grams is a good amount), essential fatty acids, and a full spectrum of vitamins and minerals.

Creatine Supplements

Creatine is one of the most effective supplements introduced to the bodybuilding world in decades. After its emergence in the early 1990s, it rapidly caught on as one of the few supplements that actually works and makes a noticeable difference in a short time.

Creatine is a natural substance stored in muscle cells and is a part of the anaerobic energy system (ATP-CP). Muscles use adenosine triphosphate (ATP) as an energy source to contract the muscle fibers during exercise. During this process, ATP is broken into adenosine diphosphate (ADP) and inorganic phosphate. Unfortunately, ATP is depleted in 10 to 15 seconds. The creatine stored in the muscle cells then bonds with the abundant phosphorus stores to create more creatine phosphate (CP). The creatine phosphate combines with the useless ADP to create more ATP, which provides energy to the muscles.

By supplementing with creatine, you can provide muscle cells the means to produce more energy during exercise. This energy translates into more power during your weight training workouts. If you are able to bench press 200 pounds for three repetitions before reaching muscle failure, you may be able to do as many as eight repetitions with the same weight after supplementing with creatine.

Creatine can be obtained through food. Red meat is an excellent source. However, as the advertisements for creatine constantly remind us, it takes an enormous amount of meat to equal the same amount of creatine in one small tablespoon of creatine monohydrate. Creatine supplements come in several forms, but most bodybuilders prefer the powder mixed with simple sugar because the sugar helps raise insulin levels, which transports the creatine monohydrate directly into the muscle cells.

In addition to providing more power for workouts, creatine also increases muscle volume. During volumization, creatine pulls water from the body into the muscle cells, and this fluid buildup makes the muscles look bigger. This swelling also creates more strength during the workouts.

Most people have no trouble taking creatine. However, a few have trouble digesting it, which can cause stomach upset. Creatine supplements can also cause muscle cramps if the user is dehydrated. Because the supplement pulls water into the muscle cells, you must make sure you're drinking enough water. However, most bodybuilders drink approximately a gallon a day in the off season and two gallons a day when dieting or to lose fat, so consuming enough water should not be a problem for most people.

If you use a creatine supplement, take it in cycles. After using creatine monohydrate for several weeks, the body does not respond to it as dramatically as it did in the beginning. The initial benefits of greater strength and muscle fullness fade. Stay on creatine for six to eight weeks before taking a two-week break. This method of cycling is more effective than using it continuously. When starting creatine supplementation, take twice the recommended amount for the first five days to saturate the muscle cells. After this loading phase, a maintenance dose is 5 to 10 grams for the rest of the creatine cycle.

Workout Supplements

Many supplements are available to promote workout intensity and recovery. These range from carbohydrate drinks to give you more energy to recovery drinks to help you feed depleted muscles during the short window of opportunity immediately after a workout.

Carbohydrate drinks Carbohydrates are the preferred energy source for anaerobic exercise. During intense, short-duration training such as lifting heavy resistance for a limited number of reps, the body gets its energy from the glycogen stored in the muscles. This glycogen comes from the carbohydrate you eat. If you are low in carbohydrate, you will have trouble completing a heavy, intense workout before running out of energy.

Some carbohydrate drinks contain complex carbohydrate that breaks down slowly and provides energy over several hours. Many of the carbohydrate drinks, however, contain simple sugar for quick energy. A carbohydrate drink or powder made of complex carbohydrate such as corn or maltodextrin is ideal for a preworkout drink as long as you have enough time to digest it properly. If you drink it immediately before training, your body will try to digest it while it is also trying to force blood into your muscles during the workout. Therefore, give yourself 45 to 60 minutes to digest the complex carbohydrate drink before beginning your workout.

A carbohydrate drink containing mostly simple sugar provides immediate energy and can be consumed during a workout or immediately after a training session to begin replenishing glycogen stores. Research shows that simple carbohydrate ingested during a workout helps build up glycogen in the muscles more effectively than consuming the carbohydrate after a workout.

Postworkout recovery drinks In addition to the carbohydrate drinks, a new category of supplements has been designed specifically for postworkout recovery. These drinks contain not only simple carbohydrate to restore depleted glycogen, but also whey protein, which is transported directly to the muscle cells with the help of the insulin-raising properties of the simple sugar. The combination of simple sugar and fast-acting whey protein is exactly what the muscles crave immediately after a workout. Look for a postrecovery drink that contains at least 40 grams of protein and 60 grams of carbohydrate. Or you could mix two scoops of whey protein with a simple carb drink.

Glucosamine chondroitin An exciting recent nutritional find for bodybuilders is a supplement containing glucosamine sulfate combined with chondroitin sulfate. Originally developed as an aid for arthritis patients, glucosamine helps repair and lubricate the cartilage around damaged joints. Because it is composed of small molecules, glucosamine is absorbed quickly and efficiently when ingested.

Bodybuilders and other strength athletes who have trained heavy for many years tend to experience joint pain in the elbows and knees. The combination of glucosamine with chondroitin helps alleviate joint pain by providing lubrication. I can attest to the benefits of using this supplement after suffering with pain in my knees for years. Now my knees and elbows feel better than they have in a long time. If you experience joint pain, you owe it to yourself to give this effective supplement a try.

Phosphatidylserine Another supplement that many bodybuilders use before workouts is phosphatidylserine (PS). PS is a phospholipid, a type of fat found in every cell in the body. It is particularly concentrated in the brain, where it has the important task of keeping cell membranes fluid, flexible, and primed for nutrient absorption. PS also plays a critical role in supporting nerve tissue; it aids proper release and reception of neurotransmitters in the brain, for example.

For bodybuilders, PS is valuable because it can reduce cortisol levels. Cortisol is the hormone released by the adrenal glands during times of stress. Too much cortisol breaks down muscle tissue and blocks protein synthesis. Cortisol output also increases during periods of intense exercise. Any supplement that helps to lower cortisol production helps in the muscle-building process. Taking 200 to 400 milligrams of phosphatidylserine per day before a workout helps suppress cortisol levels.

Amino Acid Supplements

Amino acids are the building blocks of protein. Twenty amino acids may be taken individually or together to help build muscle tissue. The advantage of taking amino acids as a supplement rather than eating whole protein foods is that the amino acids have already been broken down and, therefore, can be absorbed more easily into the bloodstream. Food, on the other hand, needs to be broken down and digested before the amino acids from the protein can be assimilated. Remember: It's not what you eat that is important, but what you eat, digest, and assimilate. It's very possible that you will not use all of the protein you consume from whole-food sources. Therefore amino acid supplements can also increase a bodybuilder's protein intake.

An effective way to take amino acid supplements is to include them with every meal. Consume one tablet for each 10 pounds of body weight. A 200-pound bodybuilder would therefore swallow 20 amino acid pills per day. If this bodybuilder eats the standard five or six meals per day, he takes approximately four amino acid tablets with each meal.

In addition to amino acid supplements that contain all 20 amino acids, there are also supplements for the branched-chain amino acids (BCAA). The BCAAs are the three amino acids (L-isoleucine, L-leucine, and L-valine) that are metabolized in the muscles instead of the liver, unlike the other 17 amino acids. The BCAAs can be used to build new protein or be burned as fuel for energy.

The BCAAs are often taken before and after a workout because these specific amino acids are burned up in a training session. If the muscles are low in branched-chain amino acids, muscle tissue may be sacrificed during the workout. It's important to keep the muscles saturated with the BCAAs before and after the workout to prevent muscle tissue breakdown. Remember, a bodybuilder is trying to tear down muscle tissue during a training session but wants to prevent the body from dipping into the muscle cells to use these branched chain amino acids. That is why supplementing with BCAAs is a good idea because you don't want to take anything from the muscle cells themselves.

One of the most important supplements a bodybuilder can take is the amino acid L-glutamine. Sixty percent of the free-form amino acids contained in the skeletal muscle cells is glutamine. The body uses glutamine in the gut and the immune system to maintain peak performance. When extra glutamine is taken through supplementation, it helps prevent muscle tissue breakdown by preserving the glutamine stored in the muscles. Studies show that an intense weight training workout can reduce glutamine stores by as much as 50 percent. Because the body relies on glutamine to fuel the immune system, a glutamine supplement can prevent muscle tissue breakdown and help with protein metabolism.

Bodybuilders should use approximately 10 grams of glutamine in supplement form. It is best absorbed on an empty stomach. Some bodybuilders also take a 5 to 10-gram serving right before a weight training workout and another immediately after. Many meal replacement powders also include glutamine.

Fat-Burning Supplements

In addition to controlling their diet, many bodybuilders like to utilize fat-burning supplements to help speed up the fat loss during their preparation for a competition. The diet and training (including cardio training) is crucial for losing fat but if certain supplements can be utilized to help speed up or further the fat-loss process, it is certainly wise to make use of these supplements.

Ephedra In the 1990s, a new supplement hit the bodybuilding world with the force of a hurricane. It was designed to help a bodybuilder lose body fat while simultaneously retaining muscle mass. Soon, other companies began to market the same formula this supplement was based on, and a new era of fat-burning supplements was born.

The formula for this revolutionary fat-burning supplement was based on the combination of ephedra, caffeine, and aspirin. Termed the ECA stack for its three ingredients, this supplement gained widespread popularity and became a must-have for all bodybuilders preparing for a competition or just trying to get leaner.

Ephedra (also known as ma huang) is a plant and is the source for most ephedrine products. The ephedrine alkaloids in ephedra act as a mild stimulant. When used in conjunction with caffeine and aspirin, the ECA stack stimulates metabolism and enhances the effects of dieting. Most combinations of the ECA stack use a 10:1 ratio between caffeine and ephedrine; 20 milligrams of ephedrine are stacked with 200 milligrams of caffeine. Some products used the herbal equivalent of caffeine and ephedrine (guarana or kola nut for caffeine and ma huang for ephedrine). Besides burning fat and increasing metabolism, the ECA stack preserves muscle tissue and suppresses the appetite. It was an ideal supplement for bodybuilders trying to get contest ready.

Although many health professionals have documented ephedra as a safe supplement, the ephedra-based supplements have come under fire recently. Because ephedrine stimulates the central nervous system as well as metabolism, it is not advised for people who have heart problems or high blood pressure. After several deaths traced to inappropriate use of ephedra-based supplements, the government banned supplements using ephedrine as of March, 2004. All companies marketing supplements based on the ECA stack either revised their formulas by excluding ephedrine and adding other ingredients or simply removed the supplement from their product lines. Other fat-burning supplements have arrived on the marketplace. Because fat loss is a big business, not only for bodybuilders but also for the general public, many supplement companies are striving to find a fat-loss supplement that will create the results that the ECA stack did.

L-Carnitine L-carnitine is an amino acid that was used for losing fat decades before the ECA stack was invented. L-carnitine works by breaking down fat floating in the blood. These smaller fat particles are then transported to the mitochondrial membrane where they are burned as energy. Many bodybuilders take L-carnitine before cardio workouts in an effort to burn fat more efficiently while training.

Conjugated linoleic acid Conjugated linoleic acid (CLA) has been gaining popularity not only as an aid for losing fat, but also for maintaining or building lean muscle tissue while dieting. CLA is a naturally occurring free fatty acid found in small amounts in some meat and dairy products. When taken in supplement form, CLA helps regulate the body's growth-promoting hormones by offsetting the negative effects of linoleic acid and by regulating fat and protein metabolism. Research has shown that animals fed a diet high in CLA and lower in calories have increased their lean muscle tissue while losing body fat. CLA also enhances the immune system and increases the metabolism.

Green tea extract Green tea extract is highly regarded not only for its fat-loss potential, but also for the antioxidant and immune-enhancing properties it provides. Experts believe that the fat-loss benefits are derived from caffeine and polyphenols. Specifically, polyphenol epigallocatechin gallate (EGCG) has been shown to promote fat oxidation and thermogenesis. Taking 200 to 300 milligrams of a green tea extract containing at least 40 percent EGCG helps in the fat-loss process.

Guggulsterone Guggulsterone is a supplement designed to stimulate the thyroid. The thyroid regulates your metabolism and plays a big part in weight management. The two thyroid hormones important to a bodybuilder are the T3 (active thyroid) and T4 (inactive thyroid). T4 can be converted into T3 in the liver, which can help with fat loss by stimulating the thyroid.

Guggulsterone is an herb that has been used for hundreds of years in India. It is believed to be safe and nontoxic for humans and can help keep the thyroid functioning normally, which promotes fat loss. If you decide to use a guggulsterone product, make sure it is standardized, type E and Z from the plant Comminphora mukul. A good dose is 25 milligrams taken three times a day.

Forskolin Forskolin is an herb added to many fat-loss supplements. It provides many benefits by activating an enzyme called adenylate cyclase. These benefits include enhanced insulin secretion and increased thyroid hormone function. In addition, forskolin has been shown to enhance lipolysis (fat burning), and it may inhibit fat storage.

Testosterone-Boosting Supplements

In 1998, the sports world was rocked with controversy over a supplement used by baseball superstar Mark McGwire as he was closing in on the record set by Roger Maris of 62 home runs in a single season. A sports reporter interviewing McGwire in the locker room noticed a supplement in the baseball player's locker that he had never heard of: androstenedione, or andro for short.

It wasn't long before the media brought this supplement into the limelight and created a controversy. Was McGwire assisted through the use of this supplement? Many fans and sportswriters felt that McGwire was taking a substance very similar to steroids to help him power those home runs out of the park.

Androstenedione is not a steroid, but it is converted into testosterone by the liver. Similar in structure to the supplement DHEA (dehydroepiandrosterone), andro is only one step away from being converted into testosterone instead of DHEA's two steps from testosterone conversion. Androstenedione is identical to testosterone except that it is missing a hydrogen atom in the 17th position. When the liver processes the supplement, it adds a hydrogen atom to complete the testosterone.

Androstenedione was a popular supplement for several years, but many users were unhappy with their results. For one, the increased testosterone levels often lasted only a few hours. Second, many bodybuilders reported negative side effects including acne, receding hairlines, and gynecomastia (excessive breast development in men), all common side effects of the steroid testosterone.

Another problem with andro is that it slows the natural production of testosterone. Many bodybuilders have found their testosterone production to be far lower than normal after finishing a cycle (normally six weeks) of androstenedione. In addition, the conversion rate for androstenedione can be as low as 5 percent.

Since the introduction of androstenedione to the supplement world, newer products called prohormones have found their way to the marketplace. The first was called 19-norandrostenediol. Instead of converting to testosterone, 19-norandro converts to nortestosterone, a more anabolic process without the androgenic (secondary sex characteristics such as hair loss, acne, and estrogen conversion) side effects exhibited by the use of the androstenedione.

The difference between androstenedione and 19-norandrostenediol is that 19-norandro is missing a molecule that prevents it from converting directly into estrogen like the androstenedione does. It also has a conversion rate of 15 percent compared to androstenedione's 5 percent. However, the risk of side effects such as acne and prostate enlargement are also greater with the 19-norandro.

The prohormones are being upgraded and improved every year in an attempt to deliver a safer and more effective version for bodybuilders who do not want to take illegal steroids. Newer versions of some of the prohormones such as 1-AD have changed the compounds of the supplement into 17-alkylated so that most of the supplement is not wasted by the liver. They have also made changes so that the conversion rate is higher with less toxicity to the liver.

If you are thinking of trying any of the prohormones currently on the market, thoroughly research the product before using it. Check out any laboratory studies that may have been conducted on the supplements you are considering using. Another option would be to read the bodybuilding magazines for the latest objective information (make sure you are not reading an ad for a product) on any new supplements on the market. It is also a good idea to consult your physician to get his opinion before using them. The line between anabolic steroids and legal supplements is getting fuzzier as the supplement industry attempts to create more powerful prohormones.

Also, if you plan to compete as a natural bodybuilder, check the rules of each particular organization to see what is allowed and what is forbidden. Many natural bodybuilding federations do not allow supplements such as ephedrine and prohormones for their athletes.

Vitamin and Mineral Supplements

Vitamins and minerals are essential to a well-functioning body. Because you can never be sure of the quality of the food you eat, it's a good idea to take vitamin and mineral supplements to make sure your body gets the nutrients it requires to perform optimally.

Because you stress your body through physical exercise and tear down muscle tissue before building it back up, you need greater quantities of vitamins and minerals than the average couch potato. At the very least you should take a multivitamin every day to make sure you're providing your body the basic vitamins. This multivitamin should include 10,000 IU of vitamin A and 100 milligrams each of vitamins B_1, B_2 (riboflavin), B_3 (niacin), B_5 (pantothenic acid), B_6 (pyridoxine), B_{12}, and biotin. It should also contain 400 micrograms of folic acid, at least 500 milligrams of vitamin C and vitamin D, and 200 IU of vitamin E. Additionally it should include choline, inositol, and bioflavonoids.

I take multivitamins twice a day with my two biggest meals, normally breakfast and dinner. In addition to multivitamins, I also take extra vitamin C and vitamin E. Vitamin C is water soluble so any excess is excreted from the body on a continuous basis. It is an antioxidant and helps protect the body from oxidation caused by free radicals. It is also critical in the formation of collagen, the connective tissue of the body. I normally take 2,000 to 4,000 milligrams per day.

Vitamin E is another antioxidant and protects vitamin A and essential fatty acids from oxidation in the bloodstream. Because vitamin E is fat soluble, stored in the fat tissues, taking too much can be toxic. However, because it fights off free radicals and the fact that most vitamin E in food is destroyed by processing, I take in an extra 800 IU per day.

The B vitamins are useful in combating stress, including the stress of heavy weight training. The B vitamins, like vitamin C, are water soluble, so they need to be replaced constantly. Complex carbohydrate foods like bread, oatmeal, pasta, and rice, as well as meat, eggs, milk, fish, and green leafy vegetables are good sources of B vitamins.

Because minerals are not as abundant in the diet as vitamins are, supplementing these critical nutrients is important. Calcium, magnesium, phosphorus, and potassium are just as important as vitamins for building a strong, healthy body. Calcium, in addition to making up teeth and bones (99 percent of the calcium in your body is stored in your teeth and bones), also controls the conduction of impulses in nerves, the contraction of muscles, and many other functions. Calcium is found in abundance in milk and other dairy products such as cheese and yogurt. Dark green leafy vegetables are also a good source of calcium. Hard-training bodybuilders should supplement with 1,000 to 1,500 milligrams per day of calcium for optimum performance.

Food processing destroys magnesium; therefore, people who eat lots of refined foods are often deficient in this mineral. About half of your body's magnesium stores are located inside the cells of body tissues and organs. The other half is combined with calcium and phosphorus in the bones. This mineral is needed for more than 300 biochemical reactions in the body. It is important in normal nerve and muscle function as well as protein synthesis and energy metabolism. Spinach, nuts, and some whole grains are good sources of magnesium. Four hundred milligrams of magnesium per day is appropriate for the amount of calcium you should be supplementing.

Potassium is another important mineral. It works in opposition to sodium for proper conduction of nerve impulses and many other vital functions of the body. Unfortunately, because of the excessive sodium in refined and processed foods, potassium and sodium are often out of balance. Potassium is found abundantly in bananas and green leafy vegetables. Potassium levels are low in people who take in excessive sodium and those who lose lots of fluid through diuretics or too much coffee and tea. If your muscles are prone to cramping, lack of potassium is usually the culprit.

Zinc is another essential mineral often lost to the evils of food processing and refining. The body does not store zinc in high amounts, so it must be replaced continually. Zinc is important for cell growth and immunity, testosterone production, and sperm formation. A product called ZMA combines zinc monomethionine (zinc and magnesium together) with extra vitamin B_6. Calcium interferes with zinc absorption; therefore, it is best to take zinc at bedtime without calcium or calcium-related products.

Proper nutrition is essential to achieving success in bodybuilding. Understanding how the macronutrients work together to provide the building blocks for developing your physique is critical. Next let's look at the how to train each muscle group for maximal results.

PART II

Mastering the Exercises

The second part of this book deals with the exercises that train each area of the body. Because there are hundreds of exercises to choose from, many beginners are confused about which exercises to include in their training routine. Over the years, bodybuilders have recognized key exercises as the best and most effective movements for training individual muscles. These are the focus of this part of this book.

Chest, Back, and Shoulders

The muscles of the torso include the chest, back, and shoulders. Developing these three muscle groups is essential to an impressive physique. Well-defined pectoral muscles and a deep rib cage provide a look of power and ruggedness from the front. Well-developed lats, traps, and spinal erectors create an impressive back. And the deltoid muscles are vital in showcasing a wide, thick upper body. Finding the best exercises to develop these key areas is the first step in developing a contest-winning physique.

Chest

Next to the biceps, the pectorals are most bodybuilders' favorite muscle group. Everyone wants huge pecs like Arnold Schwarzenegger's or Lee Haney's. A body-builder wants his chest to stretch his shirt to the bursting point and command attention from everyone when he walks into a room. More than any other part of the body, the chest represents masculinity, and a bodybuilder with a sunken, flat chest is akin to a peacock without his feathers.

The main exercise for developing the pecs is, without a doubt, the most popular exercise in gyms all over the country. The bench press is a comfortable exercise compared to gut-busting exercises like squats and deadlifts, and it is the universal indicator of how strong you are. When someone unfamiliar with bodybuilding engages you in conversation, one of the first questions he inevitably asks is "How much do you bench?" Most bodybuilders do not need outside motivation to train the chest, unlike other target areas.

The pectoral muscles respond best to the basic exercises performed with heavy barbells and dumbbells. The free-weight movements force your body to balance and coordinate the resistance, a process missing from machine exercises. This extra work is effective in developing muscle strength and size. If you're new to the sport, or have poorly developed pecs, concentrate on these. Leave the fancy machines and cable crossovers to the bodybuilders who already have huge, thick pecs or to those who are interested only in toning up the chest and not in building pectorals you could rest a glass of water on while hitting a side chest pose. The following exercises are the most beneficial at developing the pectoral muscles, and table 5.1 on page 127 shows effective sample chest routines.

Barbell Bench Press

PRIMARY MUSCLES WORKED: **Chest • Anterior Deltoids • Triceps**

This king of the upper-body exercises is the best movement for adding inches to the pectorals, triceps, and anterior deltoids. The bench press exercise develops the middle and outer parts of the pecs, the belly of the muscle. Developing this central area of the muscle will greatly enhance its overall mass.

Although the bench press is one of the premier exercises for developing the central part of the pectorals, it can also build other areas of the chest depending on how you execute the movement. If your grip on the bar is wider than shoulder width, the outer pectorals and front deltoids will be most affected. If the hands are positioned more narrowly, the central area of the pecs and the triceps will be more stimulated. If the bar is lowered to the collarbone instead of farther down on the chest, the upper pecs will be affected more than the lower pecs.

After lying on the bench with the feet firmly planted on the floor, grip the bar slightly wider than shoulder width. Many bodybuilders mistakenly assume that they will gain more strength with a closer grip. Although a narrow grip may feel more powerful, the truth is that this grip activates the triceps more than the targeted muscle, making this less of a chest movement than you intended. For maximum stimulation of the chest, use a grip slightly wider than shoulder width.

After taking the bar off the bench press rack, slightly arch the low back and stick the chest out *(a)*. This positions the pecs at the forefront of the action and reduces the impact on the front deltoids. Many people do just the opposite. They let their chests cave in and overextend their arms at the completion of the movement. This turns one of the best chest movements into a great anterior deltoid builder. To build the pecs, expand the rib cage and keep the pecs high.

As you lower the bar, be aware of where the arms are during the movement. Pull the elbows back as the bar descends to stretch the pectorals and keep the triceps involvement to a minimum *(b)*. Allowing the elbows to drift forward will turn the bench press into more of an upper-arm exercise than the chest mass builder it was designed to be.

Perform a full range of motion on the bench press and watch your pecs develop. Many people who say that the bench press does nothing to build the pecs probably use too much weight and have sacrificed form for ego. Slowly develop your strength on the bench press as you maintain proper form and your pecs will respond. They won't have a choice.

Advanced bodybuilders should do four or five sets. Warm up with a set of 12 to 15 repetitions, then gradually add weight to each set, reaching your heaviest weight on the last set. Perform the second set at a weight that allows 10 repetitions, the third set 8 reps, and the fourth and fifth sets 5 or 6 repetitions. Pyramiding the weight each set allows you to acquaint the muscles and tendons with the increasing weight and forces the muscles to work harder each set. This results in more mass in the pectorals.

b

Incline Barbell Press

PRIMARY MUSCLES WORKED: Upper Pectorals • Anterior Deltoids • Triceps

The incline press is a mass-building exercise very similar to the bench press, except that the angle of the bench focuses more of the movement on the upper pectorals. Therefore, it is the primary movement for developing the upper pecs. Because the lower pecs tend to develop much more quickly than the upper, it is necessary to work the upper pecs just as hard as the lower pecs to keep both areas of the chest in proportion. Using the right amount of resistance in the incline barbell press will build size into the upper pecs, the front deltoids, and the triceps.

To properly perform the incline press, position yourself on an incline bench set at a 35- to 45-degree angle. Grab the bar with a slightly wider-than-shoulder-width grip *(a)*. Slowly lower the bar to the clavicles making sure to keep the elbows pulled back for a maximum stretch in the upper pecs. It's also important to hold the chest high with the low back arched. This places stress on the pecs and not the front delts. It's easy to let the hips sink down in the incline position. This reduces the arch in the back and places more stress on the anterior delts than on the pecs. For this reason, it is important to concentrate on form.

From the bottom position, push the bar back to the top keeping the elbows pulled back *(b)*. This elbow position focuses all of the stress on the upper pecs. Allowing the bar to drift lower on the chest takes the focus off the upper chest and puts more stress on the lower pecs and the front deltoids. Because the incline press is an important mass builder, many bodybuilders do it in place of or before the bench press. This is wise if the upper pectorals are less developed than the lower pecs.

a

b

Dumbbell Bench Press

PRIMARY MUSCLES WORKED: **Outer Pectorals • Anterior Deltoids • Triceps**

Using dumbbells instead of a barbell in the bench press provides several advantages. First, you can lower the dumbbells several inches deeper at the bottom of the movement than a barbell. This longer range of motion provides greater stretch.

The bench press performed with dumbbells also allows more freedom of motion. You can bring the dumbbells together on the top of the exercise. This contracts the pecs more than using a barbell. The dumbbells also seem to affect the deltoids less than a barbell. Therefore, if you have shoulder problems and can't do the standard barbell bench press without pain, you may be able to perform the bench press using dumbbells.

To perform this exercise, lie on a flat bench holding a pair of dumbbells *(a)*. Keeping the low back arched and the chest high, concentrate on pulling the elbows back in order to stress the pecs and to keep the involvement of the triceps and front delts to a minimum. Lower the dumbbells as far as possible, tilting the dumbbells at the bottom for a great stretch in the outer pecs *(b)*.

At the bottom position, keep the elbows pulled back and push the dumbbells back to the top. Visualize an upside-down V as you push the weights together and squeeze the pecs on top. Utilizing a full movement on this exercise is essential. The dumbbells allow a great stretch and contraction that barbell exercises do not permit.

Do three or four sets of the dumbbell bench press. Increase the weight on the second and third sets, aiming for six to eight reps each set. The first two sets should be moderately heavy so you can establish a correct pathway for the dumbbells to follow. Keeping the elbows pulled back, tilting the dumbbells at the bottom position, and squeezing the pecs on top are all important for correctly performing this exercise.

b

Incline Dumbbell Press

PRIMARY MUSCLES WORKED: **Upper Pectorals • Anterior Deltoids • Triceps**

Dumbbells can also be used for the incline press exercise. The incline dumbbell press combines heavy weights with the stretch and contraction of a typical isolation movement. The combination makes this exercise a real mass builder.

Position the incline bench at a 30-degree angle. If you can find a specially designed bench with a hump at the low back, you are in luck. This bench forces you to arch your back and stick your chest out, keeping the shoulders out of the movement and focusing on the pecs instead.

Begin the exercise with the palms facing forward and the elbows pulled back at shoulder level *(a)*. Arch the low back with the rib cage expanded and feel the stretch in the upper pecs before pressing the dumbbells back overhead. Don't push the dumbbells up in a straight line, instead bring them together at the top of the movement to peak-contract the upper pecs *(b)*.

As you lower the dumbbells, attempt to touch the anterior deltoids with the inside plates of the dumbbell. The arc of the movement should resemble an upside-down V. Professional bodybuilder Rich Gaspari tilted the dumbbell at the bottom portion of the exercise to achieve an exaggerated stretch, which resulted in an even greater contraction when he pushed the dumbbells to the top.

Do three sets on the incline dumbbell press. The first set should be moderately heavy and allow you to get into the groove of the movement. This set usually consists of 10 to 12 reps. Increase the weight of the next two sets to allow 5 to 7 reps. These last two sets are the real mass builders.

a

b

Dumbbell Flys

PRIMARY MUSCLES WORKED: **Outer Pectorals • Anterior Deltoids**

After performing the basic mass builders for the chest (barbell or dumbbell bench press and barbell or dumbbell incline press), add several sets of dumbbell flys. Dumbbell flys allow a full stretch and contraction of the pectorals while still using heavy weights. However, because this exercise does not use the triceps, it isolates the chest.

To properly perform the flat dumbbell fly, lie on a flat bench with the feet off the floor. Some prefer to bend the knees and cross the legs at the ankles. Elevating the feet focuses the tension on the pecs, not the legs. Hold the dumbbells overhead with the palms facing each other, expand the rib cage, and keep the chest high throughout the exercise *(a)*. Keeping the elbows slightly bent, slowly lower the arms in a wide arc so that the dumbbells travel down and out *(b)*. Maintaining the arm position, squeeze the dumbbells back to their starting point directly over the chest. To maintain constant tension on the outer pectoral muscles, stop the movement about 10 inches before the dumbbells touch. Think of the analogy that Arnold used in the book *Pumping Iron* when performing this exercise. He equated this movement with hugging a tree. Keep the arms bent, but be sure to arc the arms out as they descend to the bottom of the exercise to really stretch the pectorals.

To perform the movement properly, be sure not to bend the arms too much during the movement and press the weight back up with the triceps. Don't turn this exercise into a flat dumbbell press; it is a fly movement. Do three sets of this exercise. In the first set use a weight that allows you to do 10 reps to get the feel of the movement. Increase the weight over the next two sets, aiming for 6 to 8 reps each.

a

b

Incline Dumbbell Flys

PRIMARY MUSCLES WORKED: **Upper Pectorals • Anterior Deltoids**

Incline flys target the important upper chest in a way that the incline press cannot. Just like flat flys, incline flys isolate the pectoral muscles while allowing you to use heavy weights.

To perform incline flys, lie on an incline bench set at a 30-degree angle holding the dumbbells overhead *(a)*. Keep the elbows slightly bent with the palms facing each other and slowly lower the dumbbells for a full stretch *(b)*. Maintain this arm position throughout the exercise.

The movement for the incline fly arcs down and out. As the dumbbells are lowered for a full stretch, it's important to keep the arms semistraight so that the weights descend out in a half circle. If the elbows bend too much, the triceps will push the weights up, eliminating the effectiveness of the fly movement.

As you raise the dumbbells back to the top position, use the power of the upper pecs to squeeze the weights up. For the last one-third of the movement, twist the dumbbells to isolate the pecs. You can do this by touching the front-facing plates of the dumbbells together. Some bodybuilders do the opposite, touching the dumbbells together so they are in the same position as an incline dumbbell press. However, this involves the front deltoids too much and takes the upper pecs out of the movement. Bringing the opposite plates together isolates the upper inner pecs.

Do three sets of incline flys. Start with a moderately heavy weight for 10 full, deep reps and increase the weight for 6 to 8 reps in the next two sets.

a

b

Dumbbell Pullovers

PRIMARY MUSCLES WORKED: **Upper & Inner Pectorals • Latissimus Dorsi • Serratus**

Dumbbell pullovers involve not only the upper pecs but also the lats and the serratus magnus muscles. Doing this exercise at the end of your chest routine will pump up the upper, inner pecs. Because the movement is over the head, the upper pecs receive the majority of the tension, and the close grip affects the inner pecs.

Dumbbell pullovers also affect the rib cage and are often recommended for teenage bodybuilders to expand the rib cage. I can attest to their effectiveness. I began training at 14 and used the dumbbell pullover exercise with each chest workout. Today, my rib cage is very full and wide. This is an asset in bodybuilding competitions when performing the side chest pose, front double biceps, and front lat spread. Bodybuilders with small rib cages often appear narrow when viewed from the front or side positions.

To perform the dumbbell pullover, lie sideways on an exercise bench with only the upper back in contact with the bench. By placing the palms on the underside of the plates, hold a single dumbbell overhead with both hands *(a).*

Keeping the hips low throughout the movement, take a deep breath and expand the rib cage while simultaneously lowering the dumbbell until it is parallel with the head *(b).* Keep the elbows slightly bent while maintaining the arms in the same position during the exercise.

Do two or three sets at the end of your chest routine. The first set is with a moderately heavy dumbbell for 12 deep reps followed by a heavier dumbbell for 8 to 10 reps for the second and third set. This exercise is much more effective when you use a full arc (from overhead to parallel with the bench). Good form is important.

b

Decline Barbell Press

PRIMARY MUSCLES WORKED: Lower Pectorals • Anterior Deltoids • Triceps

The decline barbell press is a good substitute for the regular barbell press if the lower pectorals are a weak point. By performing this movement on a decline bench, more mass will be developed in the lower pecs, the anterior deltoids and the triceps.

Begin by grabbing the bar with a slightly wider-than-shoulder-width grip *(a)*. Keep the elbows pulled back and lower the bar to the lower pecs *(b)*. Pause for a second and push the bar back to the starting position. For safety, be sure to grab the bar with the thumb around the bar as opposed to the false grip with the thumb under the bar. If the bar slips from the hand while using a false grip, the results could be disastrous.

Be careful to lower the bar only to the lower-chest area. Bringing the bar higher on the chest can place too much stress on the shoulders. Performing a bench press exercise on a decline bench requires more concentration than the standard bench press due to the angle of the movement.

a

b

Decline Dumbbell Press

PRIMARY MUSCLES WORKED: **Lower Pectorals • Anterior Deltoids • Triceps**

Performing the dumbbell press on a decline bench targets the lower pectorals. Most bodybuilders have no problem building the lower pectorals because the standard bench press effectively develops this area. However, if you need more mass in the lower pecs, dumbbell presses on a decline bench direct the stress to that area of the muscle.

To perform this exercise, lie on a decline bench set at a 45-degree angle. Grab a dumbbell in each hand, pull the elbows back and lower the dumbbells to the outer edge of the lower pecs *(a)*. Press the dumbbells straight up and together at the top position to complete the exercise *(b)*. Controlling the weights is very important because the body is in a precarious position. The shoulders, in particular, are vulnerable to injury if the dumbbells go in the wrong direction on the way down.

Use the upside-down V angle when performing the decline dumbbell press. Press the dumbbells to the full extension to peak-contract the lower pectorals. Lower the weights very slowly to control the movement when pressing the dumbbells back to the top.

Do two or three sets of this exercise at the end of your chest training session if the lower pecs are a weak area. Because you are already warmed up, you can use a moderately heavy weight for the first set and increase the weight for the second and third.

a

b

Dips

PRIMARY MUSCLES WORKED: **Lower Pectorals • Anterior Deltoids • Triceps**

Dips are a great movement for building the lower pecs. They also build the triceps, but altering your body position can direct the stress of the movement toward the chest.

A set of dip bars that are narrow at one end and wide at the other are best. To properly perform dips for the chest, grab the dipping bars in their widest position and slightly bend your upper body at the waist so that you face the floor *(a)*. Slowly dip by bending the elbows and keep the upper body in the same bent-over position. Go as low as possible to stretch the lower pecs, keeping the elbows flared out to the sides as you descend *(b)*. Push back up to the starting position using the pecs. Aim for a full movement, but concentrate more on the bottom half of the motion; this is where the pectorals work the hardest.

a

b

Cable Crossovers

PRIMARY MUSCLES WORKED: Lower Pectorals • Anterior Deltoids • Triceps

Cable crossovers are more of a refining movement than a mass builder. However, prior to a competition, many bodybuilders like using cable exercises as a means of keeping constant tension on the pectorals and developing more striations in the muscle.

Cable crossovers can be performed from a variety of positions but the most common one is performed standing with the cables in front of the body. This exercise is best executed utilizing a weight that is moderate so the contraction can be felt in the pecs during the movement. Start the exercise with the arms extended out to the side grabbing each handle on a cable crossover attachment. Bend slightly at the waist and bring the handles down in front of the body until they touch in front of the body. Squeeze the pecs in the bottom position before slowly bringing the handles back to the starting position.

Perform cable crossovers at the end of the chest training session. This is not an exercise to use in the off-season, but it's a good finishing-off exercise during a pre-contest training routine. Use a moderate weight and aim for 10-12 reps for 2-3 sets.

TABLE 5.1 Sample Chest Routines

Basic mass-building routine		
Exercise	**Sets**	**Reps**
Barbell bench press	3	6-10
Incline barbell press	3	6-10
Dumbbell pullovers	2	10-12
Advanced mass-building routine		
Barbell bench press	5	6-12
Incline dumbbell press	3	6-8
Flat dumbbell flys	3	6-10
Dumbbell pullovers	2	10-12
Advanced mass-building routine: Alternate		
Incline barbell press	5	6-12
Dumbbell bench press	3	6-8
Incline dumbbell flys	3	6-10
Dips	2	8-10
Emphasis on the upper chest		
Incline barbell press	4	6-10
Incline dumbbell flys	3	6-8
Dumbbell pullovers	3	10-12
Emphasis on the lower chest		
Decline barbell press	4	6-10
Decline dumbbell press	3	6-8
Dips	2	8-10
Decline dumbbell flys	2	8-10
Cable crossovers	2	10-12
Emphasis on the outer chest		
Decline dumbbell press	4	6-10
Incline dumbbell press	4	6-10
Flat dumbbell flys	3	6-10
Dips (using a wide grip)	2	10-12

Back

The back is one of the most critical areas of the body for a competitive bodybuilder. It is one of the biggest muscle groups and is important in any pose from the front or back. Its development is important to creating a contest-winning physique.

Despite its importance, it is also one of the most neglected areas. Perhaps this is because you can't see it (out of sight, out of mind), and some bodybuilders focus more on muscle groups such as the chest and arms that they can see.

Poor exercise selection also contributes to the lack of well-developed backs among bodybuilders. Legends such as Arnold Schwarzenegger, Franco Columbu, and Robby Robinson favored basic exercises with barbells and dumbbells, the tools of the trade for that generation of bodybuilders. However, since then, machine manufacturers have flooded the gyms with their own variations of back-building equipment. But despite the glittering new machines that promise to develop lats like Lee Haney's, the most effective way to develop an outstanding back is still with good, old-fashioned barbells and dumbbells. Basic exercises for the back performed with free weights are extremely difficult movements, but they work. Arnold knew it, Franco knew it, and Robby knew it, too.

The first back training article I ever read was written by Arnold Schwarzenegger. Arnold explained that each back exercise works a different area of the back. The exercises you choose depend on what you are trying to accomplish. Arnold broke it down into exercises for:

1. Lat width
2. Lat thickness
3. Lower-lat development
4. Low back and spinal erector thickness

After years of training, I determined which exercises were most effective. And through years of trial and error, I also figured out how to perform each exercise to get the most out of each movement. The following exercises are those I've found to be most effective, and table 5.2 on page 139 provides sample back routines.

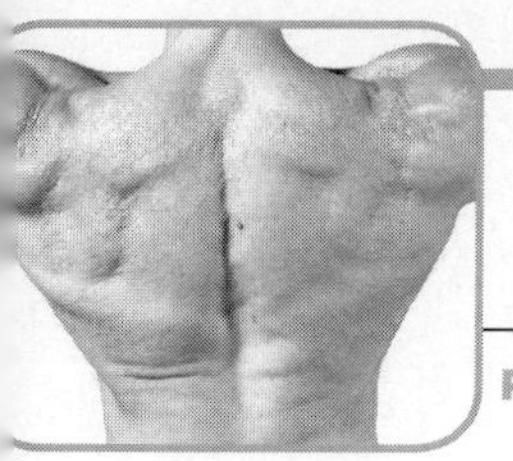

Wide-Grip Chins

PRIMARY MUSCLES WORKED: Upper Latissimus • Rear Deltoids • Biceps • Forearms

Chin-ups with a wide grip (slightly wider than shoulder width) are the number-one exercise for developing width in the upper lats. Wide lats are a bodybuilder's trademark. Wide lats improve a bodybuilder's symmetry and create a three-dimensional look when he hits his poses.

To perform wide-grip chins properly, grab the chinning bar with the hands slightly wider than shoulder width *(a)*. The area just beyond where most chinning bars are bent is the perfect grip for most bodybuilders. To keep the tension on the lats, avoid locking the elbows. Arch the low back in the starting position and tilt the head back so you're looking at the ceiling. Maintaining that position, pull yourself up to the chinning bar, and touch the clavicle to the bar *(b)*. With the low back arched, the elbows are pulled back, which forces the upper lats to contract.

As you return to the starting position, don't lose the arch in your low back and don't lock the elbows at the bottom. Instead, keep looking at the ceiling, a position that maintains the tension on the lats and sets you up for the next rep. Dorian Yates believes that the key to building lats is to arch the low back during each exercise. Arching leads to a greater contraction and builds more muscle.

When you have the strength to do 10 to 12 repetitions of wide-grip chins with your own body weight, you can add a weight belt to make the exercise more difficult. This added resistance will develop more inches of muscle in the upper lats, increasing the width of your back and your whole upper body.

b

Lat Pull-Downs

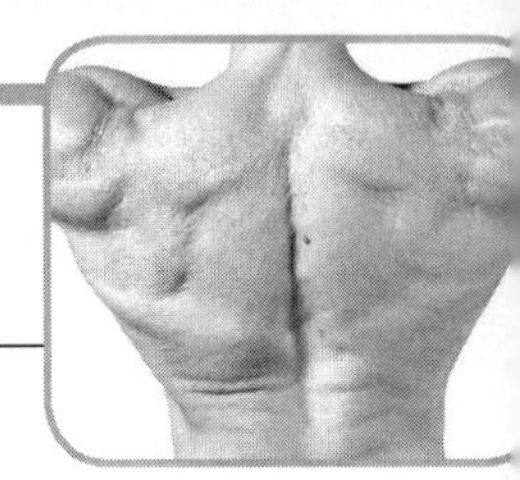

PRIMARY MUSCLES WORKED: **Upper & Outer Latissimus • Rear Deltoids • Biceps • Forearms**

As an alternative to chins, lat pull-downs work the upper back. Perform this exercise on a lat machine, pulling the weight down to the chest rather than pulling your own body weight up to a chinning bar.

To perform lat pull-downs to the front, position yourself on a lat machine with the thighs secure under the bars and use a long bar to target the upper lats. Grab the bar with the same hand position you use for chins, just slightly wider than shoulder width *(a)*. Arch the low back and tilt the head toward the ceiling. Pull the bar down to the clavicle, keeping the elbows back to stimulate the upper-back muscles *(b)*. Slowly return the bar to the starting position, but avoid locking the elbows at the top. This will remove the tension from the lats.

Lat pull-downs performed behind the neck have a different effect on the upper-back muscles. Position yourself on the lat machine either facing the machine or facing away from it. Grab the bar with a grip slightly wider than shoulder width. Pull the bar down to the base of the neck while tucking the chin into the chest. Squeeze the upper back muscles at the bottom position. Slowly return the bar to the starting position aiming for a good stretch in the upper lats.

Pull-downs behind the neck stimulate the upper, inner lats more than the front lat pull-downs do, which works the upper, outer lats more. Perform the lat pull-downs to the rear when you are trying to build the smaller, "cookie-cutter" muscles of the upper back rather than trying to build more lat width.

a

b

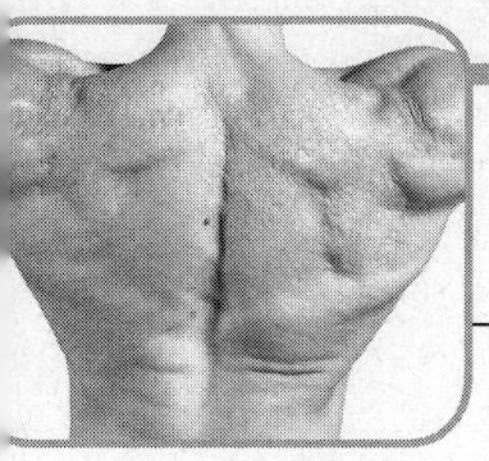

Close-Grip Chins

PRIMARY MUSCLES WORKED: **Lower Latissimus • Rear Deltoids • Biceps • Forearms**

When it comes to developing the lower lats, the close-grip chin is king. Most bodybuilders prefer working this area with close-grip lat pull-downs on a machine. Close-grip pull-downs are effective as an alternate, but working this muscle on the chinning bar with your own body weight provides superior results. Don't neglect this exercise if you want to add inches to the lower lats for complete back development.

Use a V-bar handle and place it over a regular chinning bar. Some gyms have an attachment for the V-bar that makes the movement easier to perform. Begin by grabbing the V-bar and hang with the low back arched *(a)*. Keep the arms slightly flexed so that the elbows aren't locked. From this position, slowly pull the body up to the V-bar until the chest touches the handle *(b)*. Hold this position for a second for the ultimate peak contraction in the lower lats.

Lower slowly for a good stretch, but be careful not to lock the elbows. As you come up, the elbows and arms should be held in, not flared outward as they are when performing wide-grip chins. You want the elbows to be in front of the torso until the finished position where they'll be pointed toward the floor. If you're doing it right, you'll feel the contraction in the lower lats.

To some, this may seem like an insignificant exercise, but the lower lats are very important to a quality back. Lower-lat development is noticeable in the rear double biceps pose and rear lat spread. Roy Callendar, Ronnie Coleman, and Lee Haney have fantastic lower-lat development, and they all look great in the rear double biceps pose.

a

b

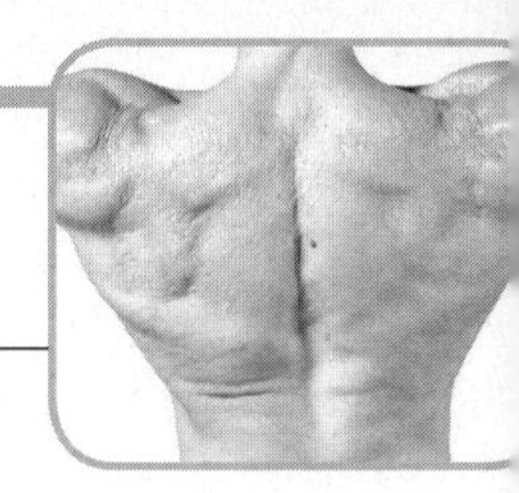

Close-Grip Pull-Downs

PRIMARY MUSCLES WORKED: **Lower Latissimus • Rear Deltoids • Biceps • Forearms**

Close-grip pull-downs target the same area as close-grip chins. To perform this exercise correctly, attach the V-bar handle to the lat pull-down machine and assume the same position as described for close-grip chins, looking upward with the low back arched and the arms slightly flexible *(a)*. Keeping the elbows close to the torso, pull the handle to the chest until you feel the lower lats contract *(b)*.

Slowly return the handle to the starting position, being careful not to lock the elbows. This technique maintains the tension on the lats throughout the movement. Make sure the low back stays arched, which also maintains the tension.

a

b

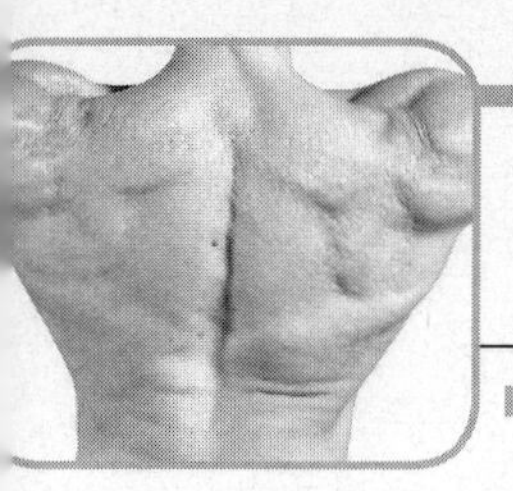

Bent-Over Barbell Rows

PRIMARY MUSCLES WORKED: **Middle & Outer Latissimus • Rear Deltoids • Biceps • Lower Back • Forearms**

This is the bread-and-butter exercise for developing big, thick lats. It is to lats what squats are to the thighs or barbell bench presses are to the chest. If you do not perform it regularly, it's no mystery why you don't have thick lats. Done correctly, bent-over barbell rows stimulate growth—not only in the lats but also in the biceps, forearms, low back, hamstrings, rear delts, inner traps, teres major, and infraspinatus. Talk about a basic exercise!

Many modern-day bodybuilders prefer the Dorian Yates version of bent-over barbell rows. This version tilts the upper body at a 70-degree angle to the floor and uses an underhand grip. It is probably the most poorly executed exercise used in gyms around the country by bodybuilders incorrectly copying his version. Bodybuilders tilt their upper bodies so high, they're nearly standing up. At this angle, they have no choice but to pull the barbell into their hips instead of their rib cage. The result is an incorrectly executed movement and no lat development.

To perform bent-over rows the old-fashioned way, take an overhand, slightly wider-than-shoulder-width grip on the barbell and position the hands in the same position as a barbell bench press *(a)*. In fact, think of a barbell row as a bench press turned upside down.

With the correct grip on the bar, stand on a block of wood. The extra height allows the barbell to lower a few inches farther. This gives the lats a good stretch before the barbell makes contact with the floor. Keeping the knees bent and the low back arched, forcefully pull the barbell into the solar plexus (the area right between the lower pecs and the upper abs) *(b)*. As the bar comes up, keep the elbows flared to the sides.

Slowly lower the bar for a good stretch, but don't let it touch the floor. Keeping the back arched and the knees bent throughout the movement, forcefully pull the bar back to the solar plexus with the elbows flared to the sides. This is a basic power movement, so don't be afraid to pile on the plates. Using heavy weights with good form develops massive, thick lats that will balance the width you're developing from the wide-grip chins.

The bent-over barbell row is a true basic exercise involving many muscle groups; therefore, you must perform it with great care to prevent low back injuries or shifting the stress to the biceps instead of the lats. Avoid these common mistakes: using a grip that is too narrow, letting the elbows squeeze in too close to the body instead of flaring out, finishing the exercise with the upper body above parallel to the floor, not arching the low back, and locking the knees.

b

One-Arm Dumbbell Rows

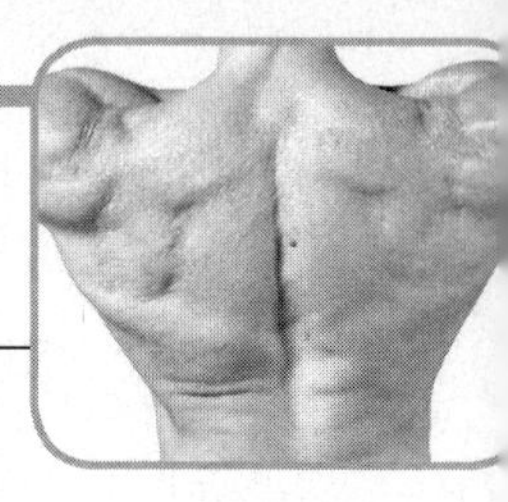

PRIMARY MUSCLES WORKED: **Middle & Outer Latissimus • Rear Deltoids • Biceps • Forearms**

As an alternative to barbell rows, substitute this exercise, which develops lat thickness. One-arm dumbbell rows work the same part of the muscle that barbell rows do, the belly of the muscle. They also allow the use of heavy weights, which makes them even better for building muscle.

The standard procedure for executing this exercise is to put one knee on a bench and the other leg on the floor. However, this position causes you to use the muscles of the waist when the upper body torques while pulling up the dumbbell. A better position plants both feet firmly on the ground while rowing the dumbbell up to the waist.

Support yourself on a bench with the free arm and lift the dumbbell with the other *(a).* Keeping the low back flat, pull the dumbbell up with the elbow tucked in to the side *(b).* Don't let the elbow flare out to the side and don't complicate the movement by swinging the dumbbell. Instead, forcefully pull the dumbbell up and contract the middle portion of the lats.

a

b

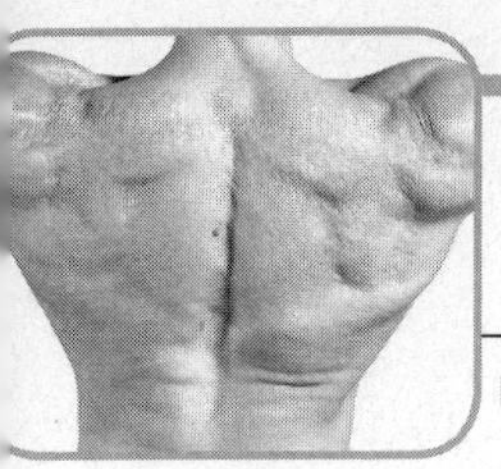

Seated Cable Rows

PRIMARY MUSCLES WORKED: **Middle & Outer Latissimus • Rear Deltoids • Biceps • Lower Back • Forearms**

Although this exercise uses cables instead of barbells or dumbbells, it's still considered a basic exercise for building size and thickness because it involves the lats, low back, biceps, forearms, and even the hamstrings to a lesser extent. It's the perfect exercise to follow a heavy barbell movement like bent-over rows.

With the knees bent and the low back arched, grab the handle attached to the cable *(a)*. To develop more width in the lats use a wide-grip attachment. Pull the attachment in toward the belly button as you bring the upper body back until it is perpendicular to the floor *(b)*. Keep the elbows close to the body throughout the movement. They should brush against the ribs as you bring them back to the finished position. It's important to keep the low back arched with the chest out in the finished position.

To return to the beginning of the movement, keep the low back arched and slowly lower the weight, stretching the lats. It's acceptable to lean the upper body forward as long as you keep the low back arched and flexed. Because the low back is the weak link, it's important to keep this area tight. As with the wide-grip chins, avoid locking the elbows in the starting position. Keep a slight bend in the elbows to maintain the tension on the latissimus muscles.

a

b

T-Bar Rows

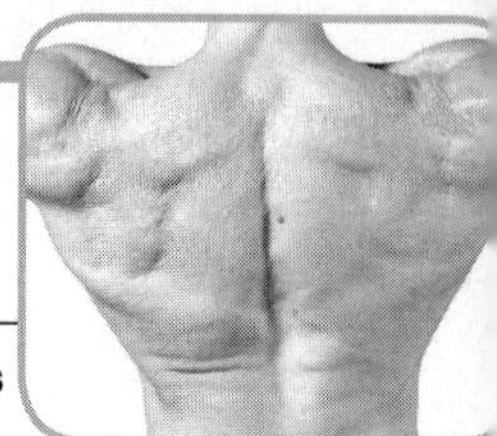

PRIMARY MUSCLES WORKED: **Middle & Outer Latissimus • Rear Deltoids • Biceps • Lower Back • Forearms**

T-bar rows are an excellent alternative to seated cable rows and are a true power movement that stimulates many of the same muscle groups. Old magazine photos show Franco Columbu, who had incredible cobralike lats that were thick, powerful, and wide, performing T-bar rows with as many as seven 45-pound plates loaded on one end of a barbell.

To perform this exercise in the old-fashioned method, place an empty 45-pound Olympic bar in a corner or have someone place his foot on one end of the bar. Load the other end with weight and place the triangle-shaped handle directly behind the plates. The shape of the handle allows a close grip that targets the outer lats to develop a wide, thick upper back.

Because this exercise places a disproportionate amount of stress on the low back, it is extremely important to maintain proper form. Keeping the low back arched and the knees flexed, grab the handle *(a)*. Pull the loaded bar into the chest with the elbows brushing against the rib cage, similar to the form employed for seated cable rows *(b)*. The narrow grip keeps the elbows from extending as far back as they do in bent-over barbell rows. The shorter range of motion lets you use heavier weights, which will build more thickness.

Control the descent when lowering the weight. Dropping the bar too quickly puts the low back muscles at risk for injury. Maintaining tension while lowering the bar achieves a greater contraction when executing the next rep. It takes a strong low back to perform this exercise properly but, if you can master it, you'll develop thick, shirt-expanding lats.

a

b

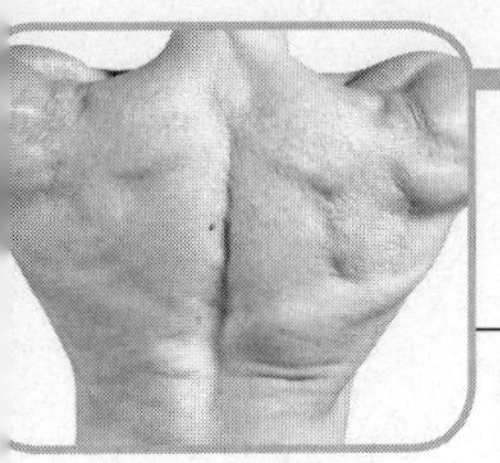

Deadlifts

PRIMARY MUSCLES WORKED: **Lower back • Spinal Erectors • Trapezius • Gluteus Maximus**

A superior power movement for building strength in the low back as well as developing impressive spinal erectors (the long muscles that extend down the length of the spine), this exercise is often dismissed by bodybuilders as a powerlifting movement. That's a mistake. Deadlifts not only develop an important area of the physique, but they also build the strength and power in the low back that are critical in exercises such as squats, bent-over barbell rows, military presses, and T-bar rows.

Developing the spinal erectors requires heavy power movements. You can always pick out the bodybuilders who regularly perform heavy deadlifts by the thick development of the spinal erector muscles. Bodybuilders such as Franco Columbu and Mike Francois included deadlifts in their regular training program, and they had the rugged back development to show for it.

To perform deadlifts properly, keep the low back slightly arched while bending the knees and grabbing the barbell with a shoulder-width grip *(a)*. You can grab the bar with an overhand grip and use wrist straps as the weight gets heavier, or you can use the over–under grip that many powerlifters use. In this grip you grab the bar overhand with one hand and underhand with the other. This grip prevents the bar from slipping out of the hands when using heavy weights.

While grabbing the bar with a firm grip, keep the hips down, the knees bent, and the arms locked. Keep the head up, looking straight ahead. This head position helps keep the low back arched and prevents the back from rounding out, which can open the vertebrae to injury. In the starting position the shoulders are lined up right over the bar.

Slowly stand up while pulling the bar with the legs and back *(b)*. Continue pulling until you are standing straight with the low back arched and the shoulders pulled back. Let the bar descend until the plates lightly touch the floor, then pull the bar back up to the finished position. Some lifters prefer to rest the weight on the floor between each rep. This method may be better for strength development, but to build the muscles of the low back and spinal erectors, pull the bar back up immediately after the plates touch the floor. This provides continuous tension, which builds the muscles more effectively. To prevent injury, maintain the arch and flexion in the low back.

b

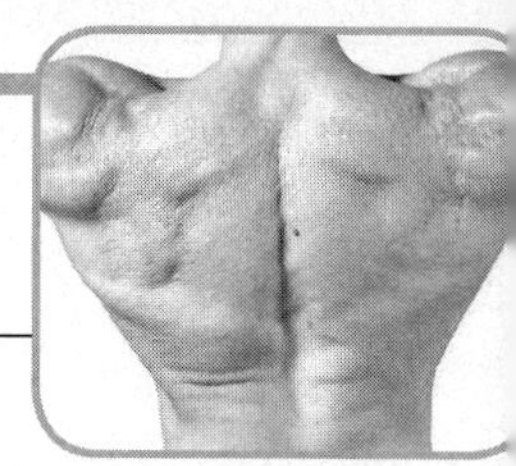

Hyperextensions

PRIMARY MUSCLES WORKED: **Lower back • Spinal Erectors • Hamstrings**

Hyperextensions for the low back are an alternative to the deadlift exercise. Hyperextensions are more of an isolation movement and do not place as much stress on the low back as the deadlift does.

To perform this exercise, position yourself on a hyperextension bench. Hook the feet under the pads and rest the top of the thighs and hipbones on the bench *(a)*. The upper body should be free to extend down for a full stretch without interference from the bench *(b)*.

Keeping the head up and the low back arched, cross the arms over the chest or interlock the fingers behind the head with the elbows out. The exercise is more difficult with the hands behind the head. Maintain tension in the low back throughout the exercise.

To make hyperextensions more difficult, hold a plate or two against the chest and do as many repetitions as you can. After you reach failure, drop the plates and continue with just your body weight. Because of the isolated nature of this exercise and the higher number of repetitions, the low back muscles get more of a pump with hyperextensions than with deadlifts.

a

b

TABLE 5.2 Sample Back Routines

Exercise	Sets	Reps
Basic back routine		
Wide-grip chins	3	10-12
Bent-over barbell rows	3	8-10
Deadlifts	3	6-10
Advanced mass-building routine		
Close-grip pull-downs	2-3	10-12
Wide-grip chins	4	10-12
Bent-over barbell rows	4	6-10
Seated cable rows	3	6-8
Deadlifts	3	6-8
Advanced mass-building routine: Alternate		
Wide-grip chins	4	10-12
T-bar rows	4	6-10
One-arm dumbbell rows	3	6-8
Close-grip chins	2-3	10-12
Hyperextensions	3	12-15
Emphasis on back width		
Wide-grip chins	4	10-12
Bent-over barbell rows	3	6-10
Wide-grip seated cable rows	3	6-10
Lat pull-downs	3	8-10
Emphasis on back thickness		
Barbell rows	4	6-10
T-bar rows	4	6-10
One-arm dumbbell rows	3	6-8
Wide-grip chins	3	8-10

Shoulders

Ask any qualified bodybuilding judge which three muscle groups contribute most to the symmetry of a physique, and he will tell you abs, calves, and delts. If you don't believe how important the deltoids are to the overall look of the body, just picture bodybuilders known for outstanding symmetry: Steve Reeves, Frank Zane, Lenda Murray, Dennis Newman, Lee Haney, Flex Wheeler, and Bob Paris. What do these legends have in common? You got it, they all possess incredible delts. The deltoids are also an important component of a great physique because they can be viewed from all angles. A bodybuilder with underdeveloped deltoids will never win a championship.

Deltoid development is important for bodybuilders who are not blessed with naturally wide clavicles. Bodybuilders such as Larry Scott, Rich Gaspari, and Nasser el Sonbaty created the illusion of width by developing inches of raw muscle on their shoulders to achieve a more symmetrical look. However, even if you were born with naturally wide shoulders, you'll need to focus on your delts. You must develop thick, round muscles to balance your broad clavicles.

The deltoids are made up of three distinct areas: the anterior (front) head, the medial (side) head, and the posterior (rear) head. Developing all three heads of the delts proportionately is the key to success in building this important muscle. In addition to training each head of the deltoids, shoulder training also involves the trapezius muscles of the upper back. Because you use the traps when you raise your arms overhead or out to the side, most bodybuilders train the traps and the delts in the same workout.

The following exercises are the most effective in training the deltoids and traps. It's important to know which exercise affects which area of the delts, so the exercises are divided into those for the front, the side, and the rear deltoid. The trapezius exercises are listed after the deltoid exercises in this section, and table 5.3 at the end of the chapter (page 153) provides sample shoulder routines to guide your training.

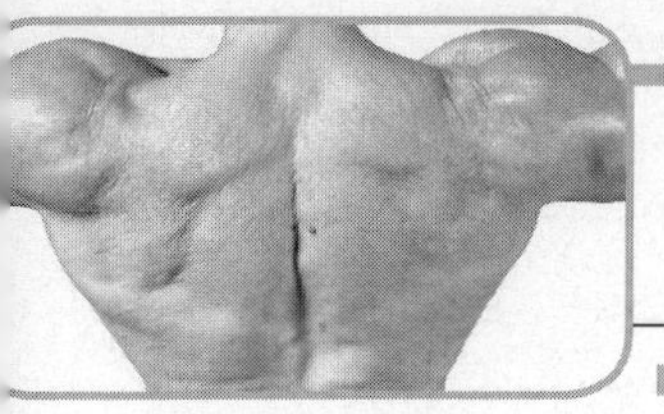

Clean and Press

PRIMARY MUSCLES WORKED: **Anterior Deltoids • Trapezius • Triceps • Biceps • Forearms**

The standing clean and press is the most basic exercise for training the deltoids. You perform it by standing over a barbell and cleaning it, or lifting it from the floor to the collarbone in one smooth movement, then pressing it overhead.

To begin the clean and press, grab the barbell with a slightly wider-than-shoulder-width grip while bending the knees and keeping the head and shoulders up with the back flat *(a)*. From this position, stand up and clean the bar to the collarbone *(b)*. From here, press the barbell overhead while keeping the elbows under the bar *(c)*. Be very careful to keep the upper body straight while pressing the barbell and avoid bending back, which could injure the low back.

The standing clean and press involves the deltoids, particularly the front deltoids. Because this is a pressing movement, it also works the triceps. Cleaning the barbell off the floor works the traps and the biceps as well. Because so many muscle groups are involved in one exercise, the standing clean and press is ideal for the beginning bodybuilder who wants to increase his muscle mass and strength.

b

c

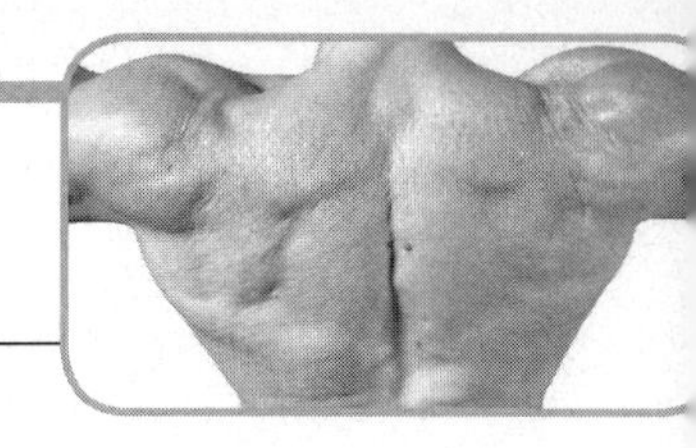

Military Press

PRIMARY MUSCLES WORKED: **Anterior Deltoids • Triceps • Upper Pectorals**

Pressing a barbell overhead affects all three heads of the deltoid. Although pressing movements target the front delts, the side and rear delts are used to complete the exercise. The traps stabilize the movement and balance the weight. The triceps and upper pecs also help press the barbell overhead.

You can perform the military press while sitting or standing. Beginners or those looking to pack mass onto the whole body should stand. (In fact, performing the clean and press, which includes more muscle groups, is a better option.) Sitting takes stress off the low back. Both positions begin the exercise with the barbell resting on the upper chest *(a)*. Press the barbell straight toward the ceiling while keeping the elbows back underneath the weight *(b)*. Keep the upper body tight as you press the bar overhead, and do not bend backward as you complete the motion. To focus the movement on the delts, concentrate on proper form throughout the body. The coordinated involvement of so many muscle groups makes the military press a superior mass builder.

Do at least four sets of the military press. After warming up with rotator cuff exercises, pump some blood into the delts by pressing a light barbell to the front and the back (a combination of standing barbell presses and standing presses behind the neck) for a total of 20 reps. Then you're ready to begin the military press.

a

b

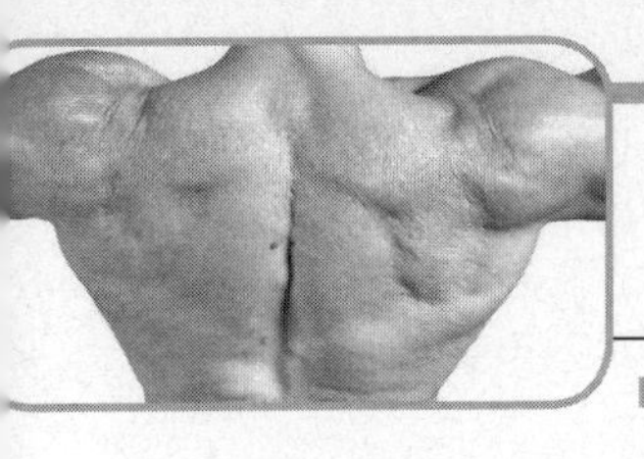

Press Behind the Neck

PRIMARY MUSCLES WORKED: Anterior Deltoids • Medial Deltoid • Trapezius

You can also perform the military press by pressing the bar behind the neck instead of in front of it. This pulls the elbows back, which involves the side deltoids more than if the bar is pressed in front. However, this is still primarily a front deltoid movement.

You can perform this exercise either standing or sitting. Sitting puts less stress on the low back. Grab the bar with a slightly wider-than-shoulder-width grip. Begin the exercise at the top with the arms straight *(a)*. Slowly lower the bar to a position just behind the neck before pressing it back to the top *(b)*. Keep the elbows pulled back.

Because the press behind the neck can be stressful to the rotator cuff, take extra care when performing this movement. Do not bring the bar down too low, especially when using a heavy weight. Also, control the weight when lowering the bar and never bounce the weight at the bottom. If you have problems with your rotator cuff, use dumbbells for a pressing movement rather than the press behind the neck.

a

b

Seated Dumbbell Press

PRIMARY MUSCLES WORKED: **Anterior Deltoids • Medial Deltoids • Triceps**

You can also perform pressing movements for the front deltoids with dumbbells. This allows freer movements and demands more coordination and balance.

To perform the seated dumbbell press, sit on a bench and hold the dumbbells at shoulder level *(a)*. Keeping the elbows pulled back, press the dumbbells up and together with an arcing motion *(b)*. Keeping the elbows pulled to the rear stimulates the medial head of the deltoids in addition to the anterior head. To involve more muscles, sit on a bench without back support so that the low back muscles must stabilize the upper body during the exercise.

a

b

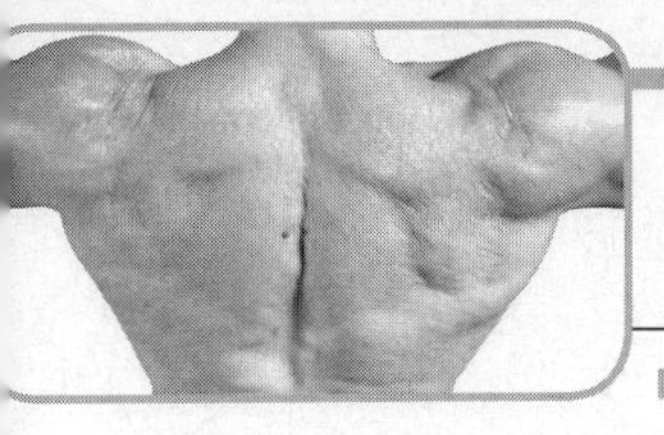

Arnold Press

PRIMARY MUSCLES WORKED: **Medial Deltoid • Anterior Deltoid • Trapezius • Triceps**

The legendary Arnold Schwarzenegger came up with this exercise as a means to develop more size in his deltoids. It's a combination pressing and lateral raise movement. It lets you use heavy weights while training the medial head of the delts.

Begin this exercise in the completed position of the standing dumbbell curl *(a)*. Press the dumbbells up in a circular motion by rotating the hands out until the arms are at the midpoint of the dumbbell press exercise *(b)*. This portion of the movement is similar to the lateral raise exercise in which the lateral delts position the arms for the rest of the movement. From this point, keep the elbows pulled back and press the dumbbells overhead and together *(c)*. The second part of the exercise trains the anterior delts.

Four sets of the Arnold press should pump your delts to the max. Unlike regular dumbbell or barbell presses, the Arnold press pumps up the side delts just as much as the front delts. Start with a weight that allows 12 reps for the first set and increase the weight each set aiming for 10, 8, and 6 reps respectively.

b

c

Standing Side Lateral Raises

PRIMARY MUSCLES WORKED: **Medial Deltoids • Trapezius**

Lateral raises is the primary exercise for building the side deltoids. Although this exercise could be classified as an isolation movement because it targets only a specific area of the muscle, there is no better movement for adding inches of muscle to the side delts.

The key to success for lateral raises is proper form. Too many bodybuilders swing the dumbbells up to shoulder level without focusing on the area of the muscle they should be working. For this exercise to be effective, the wrists and the elbows must be aligned perfectly as the dumbbells are raised to shoulder height. Too often, the dumbbells are flung out to the side, leaving the elbows to drift behind the wrists.

Start the standing lateral raise exercise with the dumbbells in front of the thighs instead of at the sides *(a)*. This position allows you to "cheat" the dumbbells past the sticking point, which occurs at the very beginning of the exercise. If you were to start the movement with the dumbbells at the sides of the thighs, you would reach failure before the delts were completely exhausted. The key is to just nudge the weight at the start in order to get the dumbbells moving before the side delts take over and do their job.

To fully involve the side delts, raise the arms to the side in a semistraight position, but don't lock the elbows; this places too much stress on the joint. Keeping the arms in this position, raise the arms up and out in a wide arc until the arms are at shoulder height *(b)*. In the finished position, the elbows should be at the same height as the wrists and dumbbells with the palms facing the floor. The natural tendency is to raise the dumbbell higher than the rest of the arm, twisting the arm at an awkward angle in order to get the weight up to the required position. It takes concentration and discipline to keep the elbow and wrist level throughout the movement. Concentrate on keeping the upper body straight and don't bend over too much as you lower the dumbbells to the starting position.

Drop sets work wonders in developing the side delts. In some cases, going heavier and heavier on the side lateral raise exercise does not automatically translate into bigger side delts. To completely exhaust the muscle, extend the set after reaching failure by grabbing a lighter pair of dumbbells and continuing the movement. After two or three drop sets, your delts should be on fire.

Perform four sets of the standing lateral raise exercise. For example, you could begin with 40-pound dumbbells for 12 reps followed by the 45s for 10 reps on the second. The third and fourth sets are your heaviest sets and include the drop sets. Start out with either the 50- or 55-pound dumbbells and force out 8 reps, then immediately grab the 45-pound dumbbells and pump out at least another 6 reps followed by one final torture set with the 35-pound dumbbells for 6 more reps. Two sets like this should leave your deltoids with no choice but to grow. You can also perform side lateral raises from a seated position.

a

b

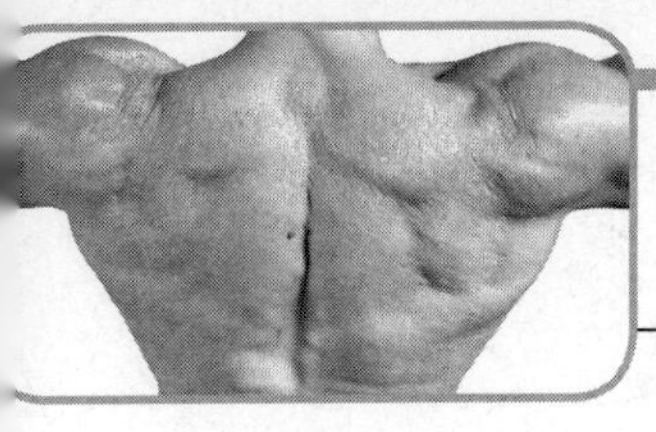

Seated Side Lateral Raises

PRIMARY MUSCLES WORKED: **Medial Deltoids • Trapezius**

Now that your medial delts are fully pumped, continue the assault on this area by performing side lateral raises in a seated position. This version is stricter than the standing version.

Start the exercise by sitting at the end of a bench with the arms extended downward, holding the dumbbells just below the thighs *(a)*. Keep the torso upright during the exercise and slowly raise the arms out to the side until they reach shoulder height *(b)*.

Control the negative portion of the lift as the dumbbells descend to the bottom position. Allow the dumbbells to go beneath the bench before bringing them back up for another rep. This exaggerated range of motion serves two purposes: It allows a greater stretch in the deltoids, thus setting it up for a more intense contraction, and it helps you get the dumbbells moving again for the next rep without hitting a sticking point.

Even though your delts will be fully pumped before beginning this exercise, do four sets. Begin with a moderate weight that allows 12 reps for the first set. Increase the weight for the second set and shoot for 10 reps. For the third and fourth sets, increase the weight one more time and attempt 8 reps with each set while maintaining textbook form.

b

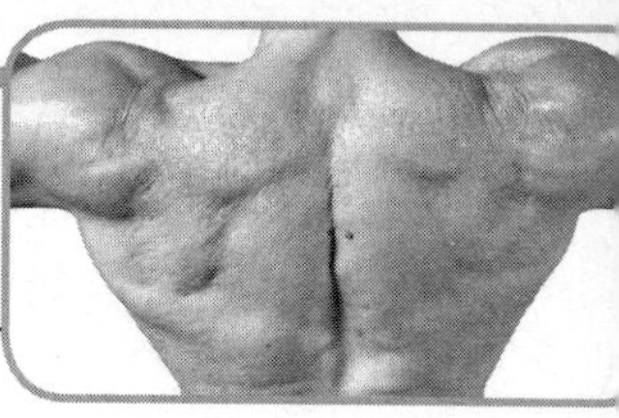

Upright Rows

PRIMARY MUSCLES WORKED: **Medial Deltoids • Anterior Deltoids • Trapezius • Biceps • Forearms**

To continue working the side delts, perform upright rows. Grab the bar with a medium grip *(a)*. If using an Olympic bar, position your hand so that two fingers are on the smooth part of the bar and the other two are on the knurled part. This grip involves the side deltoids as well as the traps. Pull the barbell to the chin while keeping the elbows flared to the sides *(b)*. The elbows should lead as you pull the bar up. The upright row is especially effective after performing the side lateral raise exercise because the side delts should already be pumped to the limit.

Do three sets of upright rows after the side lateral raises. Begin with a weight that allows 10 reps and increase the weight over the next two sets. Attempt 8 reps on the second set and 6 to 8 reps on the third.

a

b

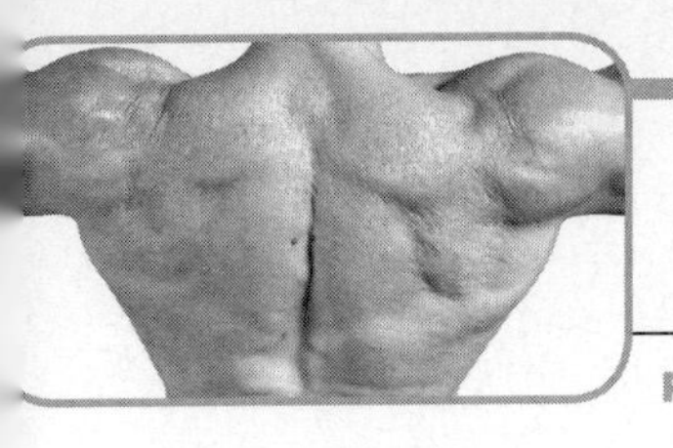

Bent-Over Lateral Raises

PRIMARY MUSCLES WORKED: **Posterior Deltoids • Trapezius**

Nothing beats the bent-over lateral raise with dumbbells for developing the rear delts, probably the most neglected portion of the deltoids. Many bodybuilders rely on machines to develop their rear delts, but machines are a poor substitute for the real thing—free weights.

To start the exercise, bend at the waist with the low back arched and the knees bent *(a)*. Grab the dumbbells so that the palms face the legs and the elbows point outward. Raise the dumbbells up and out in a wide arc until the arms are level with your upper body *(b)*. Lead the exercise with the elbows. Try to feel the contraction in the rear delts at the top of the movement.

If you don't feel this exercise in the rear delts, use a lighter weight and do the exercise more slowly to feel the pump in the right area. Do not let the dumbbells touch in the bottom position. This accentuates the negative portion of each rep and keeps the tension on the rear deltoids constant.

Do three or four sets of 8 to 12 reps of this exercise. Franco Columbu, who had incredibly thick delts, did this exercise first in his deltoid routine when he was competing. He routinely performed six sets, which shows you the importance he placed on rear deltoid development.

b

Lying Side Lateral Raises

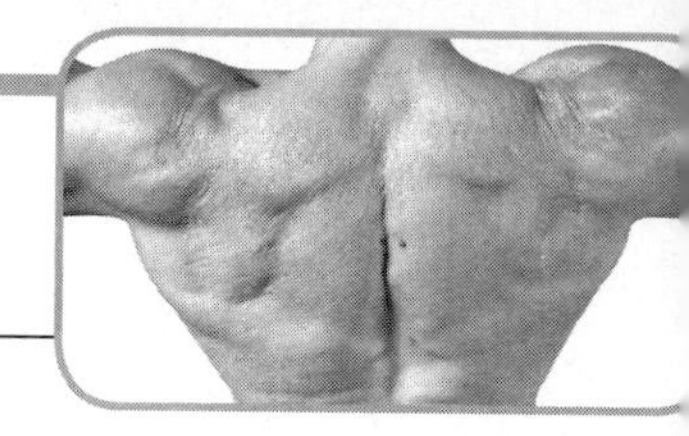

PRIMARY MUSCLES WORKED: **Posterior Deltoids • Trapezius • Forearms**

This little-known exercise is especially effective for isolating and building the rear delts. It was a favorite of Serge Nubret and Arnold Schwarzenegger in the '70s, but it is rarely performed today.

Begin by lying on your side on a flat bench at a slight incline. Prop yourself on one arm and grab a dumbbell with the hand of the other *(a)*. Keeping the arm straight, raise the arm up in a wide arc until the knuckles face the ceiling *(b)*. You should feel the contraction in the rear delts at the top position. Slowly return the arm to the start position to accentuate the negative portion of the exercise. Aim for an exaggerated stretch at the bottom to provide a greater contraction on the next rep.

This exercise, which isolates the rear delts, is superior to the typical exercises on rear delt machines. Although it takes a great deal of concentration to perform the movement correctly, the reward is rear deltoids that jut out from the side.

Because form is essential in this exercise, use moderate weight. Perform three sets: 12 reps in the first set and 10 in the second and third. Increase the weight for the second set and keep it the same for the third. This is not a power movement so concentrate on your form and the pump.

a

b

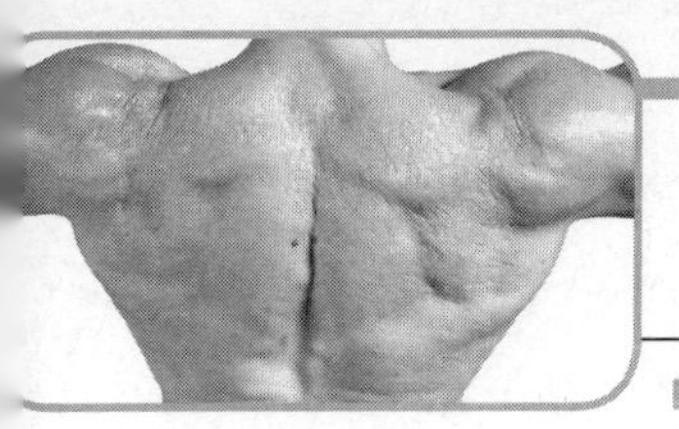

Barbell Shrugs

PRIMARY MUSCLES WORKED: **Trapezius**

The barbell shrug is the most basic exercise for building the trapezius muscle. Because this movement allows you to use heavy weights, it is one of the most effective exercises for building big, thick traps.

To begin, grab a barbell and hold it with straight arms in front of the thighs *(a)*. Keeping the arms straight, shrug the barbell up by contracting the traps *(b)*. Try to touch the delts to the ears to achieve a full contraction. Try to shrug the shoulders slightly back as you raise the weight to the top. The slightly backward angle involves more of the trapezius muscle than just shrugging straight up. Lower the bar slowly and let the traps relax at the bottom position so that the muscles get a full stretch. This allows an even greater contraction on the next rep.

You can also do barbell shrugs holding the weight behind the thighs. This angle isolates the lower, inner traps. Some gyms have specially designed bars that are bent out in the middle so you can comfortably shrug the bar from the back without interference from overly developed glutes. Behind-the-back barbell shrugs were a favorite of Mr. Olympia Lee Haney, who was renowned for his huge traps.

Do at least four sets of barbell shrugs. Warm up with a moderate weight, then add a plate to each side of the barbell each succeeding set. Because the traps are a powerful muscle that responds best to heavy weights (a heavy weight traditionally limits reps to six, while a moderate weight limits reps to 12), finish with a heavy set for six to eight reps. Occasionally begin your shoulder workout with barbell shrugs before moving onto the other deltoid exercises so that you can use heavier weights than you can at the end of the workout.

b

Dumbbell Shrugs

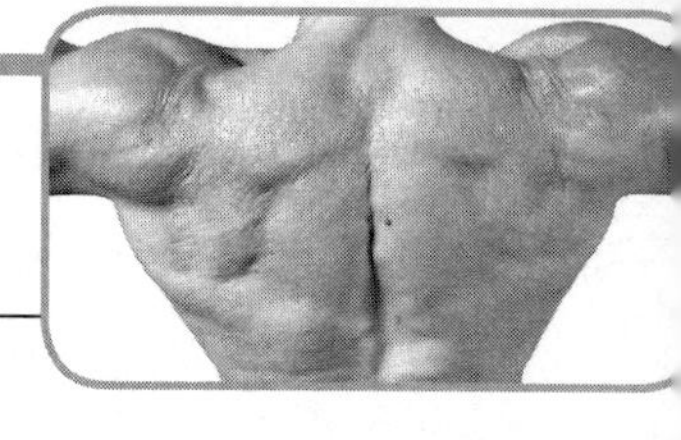

PRIMARY MUSCLES WORKED: Trapezius

To finish off your second deltoid workout, work your traps with heavy dumbbell shrugs. Because you are already very pumped at this stage, grab a heavy pair of dumbbells, keep the arms straight at your sides, and shrug your shoulders as far as possible.

The dumbbells allow you to hold the weight at the sides of your thighs instead of in the front, like you do with a barbell *(a)*. Shrug your shoulders up and slightly back and attempt to hold that position for a count of two before slowly returning to the starting position *(b)*. Let your shoulders drop as far as possible at the bottom for the maximum stretch before bringing them back up for another rep.

Perform four sets of 8 to 12 reps; the traps seem to respond better to slightly higher repetitions. Begin with a weight that lets you easily do 12 reps, then add weight over the next three sets, finishing with a fairly heavy weight.

a

b

TABLE 5.3 Sample Shoulder Routines

Exercise	Sets	Reps
Basic shoulder routine		
Clean and press	3	10
Upright rows	3	8-10
Bent-over lateral raises	3	8-10
Intermediate shoulder routine		
Standing military press	3 or 4	6-10
Standing side lateral raises	3	6-10
Bent-over lateral raises	3	8-10
Barbell shrugs	3	6-10
Advanced shoulder routine		
Military press or press behind the neck	4	6-10
Standing side lateral raises	4	6-10
Upright rows	3	8-10
Bent-over lateral raises	3	8-10
Barbell shrugs	4	6-10
Advanced shoulder routine: Alternate		
Seated dumbbell press or Arnold press	4	6-10
Seated side lateral raises	4	6-10
Lying side lateral raises	3	8-10
Dumbbell shrugs	3	6-10

Make your deltoids a priority in your training. Many bodybuilders spend more time on the showpiece muscles such as the chest and arms, but thick, round deltoids will add symmetry and impressiveness to your physique in a way that few muscle groups can. Concentrate on feeling each movement in the specific part of the muscle you are trying to build and gradually increase the weights as you progress, then watch those shoulders grow. Remember, to build a championship physique, you need a pair of championship shoulders. Now let's move on to the arms, most bodybuilders' favorite area.

Biceps, Triceps, and Forearms

The biceps, triceps and forearms are usually a high priority for bodybuilders. Nearly everyone who picks up a weight is interested in developing big arms. Well-developed biceps, triceps, and forearms can be displayed in any short-sleeved shirt, and a pair of "big guns" will win the admiration and awe of men, women, and children. Here are the exercises and routines that will deliver the greatest gains.

Biceps

Whenever someone asks you to "make a muscle," he or she is asking you to flex your biceps. It is the universal symbol for muscles and is usually one of the first muscles a beginning bodybuilder focuses on.

The popularity of the biceps is not based on its size, however. It is one of the smallest muscles bodybuilders regularly train. And compared to the much bigger target areas like the chest, back, or thighs, the biceps don't require a lot of sets. Therefore, in their quest for bigger guns, many beginners do too many sets for their arms in an effort to speed up the building process. Instead, perform a limited number of sets of the following exercises with the most effective form to build this muscle. Table 6.1 on page 164 provides sample biceps routines based on this guideline.

Standing Barbell Curls

PRIMARY MUSCLES WORKED: **Biceps**

The best exercise for building overall mass is the standing barbell curl. The basic exercises are effective because they target the belly of the muscle, which is the major contributor to the size of the muscle.

To properly perform the barbell curl, grab the bar with an underhand grip *(a)*. Position the hands so that they are just outside the thighs when standing. Keep the elbows tucked into the sides with the rib cage expanded and the shoulders held back and down. Maintaining this starting position throughout the exercise puts all of the stress on the biceps muscle and keeps the shoulders from contributing.

Curl the barbell up while keeping the elbows tight against the sides *(b)*. Feel the biceps contract at the top position before slowly lowering the barbell to the starting position. Don't be tempted to pull the elbows away from the sides as the weight gets heavier. Keep the chest expanded and the low back arched, which will help keep the elbows in position.

"Cheating" is permissible on this exercise and lets you work the muscle longer than you could using perfect form and stopping when the biceps reach failure. To properly cheat, use the low back to nudge the bar past the sticking point, which normally occurs at the beginning of the exercise. After the bar is past the sticking point, use only the biceps for the remainder of the movement. Swinging the bar with excessive momentum makes the exercise easier not harder, which is the primary goal of "cheating" the weight up.

a

b

E-Z Bar Curls

PRIMARY MUSCLES WORKED: Biceps

Barbell curls can also be performed with an E-Z curl bar which places less stress on the wrists due to a more pronated grip than a standard straight bar. This modified version of barbell curls also stresses the brachialis muscle underneath the bicep more so than when using a supinated grip. The brachialis muscle is very important in the overall development of the upper arm as it helps to actually push the bicep muscle up and make the arm bigger. It also adds to the detail of the upper arm when viewed from the back, making the arm look like it has muscles popping out all over the arm.

To perform barbell curls using an E-Z curl bar, grab the bar with a wide grip so the thumbs are slightly higher than the rest of the hand *(a)*. Keep the elbows tight near the sides of the waist and the lower back arched. Curl the barbell up focusing on the outer head of the biceps muscle *(b)*. You will feel much more stress on this area of the muscle due to the position of the hands.

b

Incline Curls

PRIMARY MUSCLES WORKED: Biceps

Incline curls are another great movement for building size. They produce a great stretch in the biceps and build mass into the belly of the muscle.

To perform incline curls, lie on an incline bench. A high incline keeps the tension on the biceps, but you can use a lower incline to produce a different feel to the muscle. To achieve a greater stretch in the bottom position, keep the knees bent as you lean back, but avoid sitting down *(a)*. Keeping the head and shoulders back, use an underhand grip and curl the dumbbells up to the shoulders while keeping the elbows pulled in at the waist *(b)*. Letting the elbows float out calls the front delts into action, taking the stress off the biceps muscles. At the top position, squeeze the biceps before lowering the weight to the starting position. Feel the stretch at the bottom but do not extend the arms until the elbows are locked. Keeping the elbows slightly bent maintains constant tension on the biceps and results in a greater contraction on the next rep.

a

b

Preacher Curls

PRIMARY MUSCLES WORKED: Biceps

Preacher curls develop the lower area of the biceps. More mass in the lower part of the muscle creates big biceps when the arm is flexed and makes the arm look more massive when it is relaxed.

Preacher curls can be performed with a barbell (both arms) or a dumbbell (one arm) in a standing or sitting position. Many bodybuilders tuck the bench right under their underarms, but positioning your arms on the bench so that only the elbows rest on the pad puts the biceps under greater tension *(a)*.

When the elbows are positioned on the bench, slowly lower the weight until the arms are extended on the bottom *(b)*. Don't let the weight drop at the bottom. This could injure the elbow joint or the tendons of the biceps. Maintain the tension on the muscle by resisting the weight on the way down. When the biceps muscle is fully stretched, curl the weight back up for a full contraction. The exaggerated stretch on the bottom of the movement builds up the lower biceps area.

b

Seated Dumbbell Curls

PRIMARY MUSCLES WORKED: Biceps

Seated dumbbell curls build up the belly of the biceps muscle. Using dumbbells instead of a barbell allows more freedom of movement and a greater range of motion in the exercise.

Grab the dumbbells with an underhand grip and keep the low back arched, the chest expanded, and the elbows in at the waist *(a)*. This elbow position ensures that you use the biceps and not the deltoids as you curl the weight for a full contraction of the biceps *(b)*.

It is permissible to cheat on seated dumbbell curls. Ask a training partner to hold your knees to help keep your feet on the floor. When the biceps reach failure, use the upper body to cheat past the sticking point and get the dumbbells moving. After you overcome the sticking point, use only biceps power to complete the movement.

a

b

Alternate Dumbbell Curls

PRIMARY MUSCLES WORKED: **Biceps • Brachialis**

Dumbbells can be used to build a better peak on the biceps. One of the best exercises for this is the alternate dumbbell curl. This exercise lets you concentrate completely because you perform the repetitions one at a time for each arm. This exercise also develops the inner head of the biceps.

To begin, grab a dumbbell in each hand and stand with the palms facing the thighs. Grip the dumbbell with the outside of the hand touching the inside plates of the dumbbell. This tends to throw the grip slightly off balance, which puts more stress on the inner head of the biceps.

Tuck the elbow in at the waist and keep it there so that you are contracting the biceps to create the movement. Curl one arm up and twist the wrist as the weight ascends to the finished position with the inside plates of the dumbbell in line with the front deltoid *(a)*. Squeeze the bicep at the top of the movement and slowly lower the dumbbell before curling the other arm up. Repeat the movement with the other arm *(b)*.

This exercise requires perfect form for maximum benefit, and it may be necessary to start with lighter-than-normal weights until you perfect the form. Famous pro bodybuilder Tom Platz had a difficult time building his biceps when he started training. He couldn't feel the muscle working like he could his other muscles. To perfect his form on this exercise, Tom reduced the weight until he was working with 10-pound dumbbells. This extremely light weight allowed him finally to feel the muscle work. After mastering this exercise with the lighter weights, he increased the weight and developed biceps in proportion to the rest of his physique.

b

Concentration Curls

PRIMARY MUSCLES WORKED: Biceps

The concentration curl is the premier exercise for developing the peak on the biceps. Properly done, it adds inches of muscle to the outside head of the biceps, which increases the peak of the muscle.

Concentration curls can be performed seated or in a bent-over position while standing. To perform the method Arnold dramatically demonstrated in the film *Pumping Iron,* bend at the waist and support your body weight with one hand on the knee and grab a dumbbell with the other hand *(a).* Keep the upper arm vertical to the floor, and slowly curl the dumbbell up to the shoulder without moving the elbow or the upper arm *(b).* When the arm is hanging down, the knuckles are toward the floor. Keep the wrist in this position throughout the movement to provide constant stress on the muscle. The forearm should travel in a wide arc as the dumbbell curls to the shoulder. It becomes tempting to move the upper arm and elbow as the exercise becomes more difficult; therefore, it requires a lot of concentration (hence the name) to perform the exercise correctly.

You can also perform seated concentration curls, supporting the curling arm on the knee. This position locks the elbow into place and allows heavier weights and a more relaxed form. It is possible to lean back to help curl the weight up as the exercise progresses. Both methods are effective. However, the first version places more stress on the outside head of the biceps, which is responsible for an impressively peaked arm.

a

b

Hammer Curls

PRIMARY MUSCLES WORKED: **Brachialis Major • Biceps**

Hammer curls with dumbbells develop the brachialis muscle. To begin this exercise, hold a pair of dumbbells at your sides with the thumbs facing forward *(a)*. Keeping the elbows in tight, curl each dumbbell up while maintaining this wrist position *(b)*. The movement is similar to pounding a hammer, which is where the exercise derives its name.

You should feel the stress of this movement in the outer head of the biceps and in the brachialis muscle. Hold the top position for a second and squeeze the muscle hard before lowering the weight to the start position. You can alternate each arm or curl them simultaneously. For a variation of the hammer curl, curl each dumbbell across the chest, trying to touch the opposite shoulder. This also works the outer biceps muscle and the brachialis.

a

b

TABLE 6.1 Sample Biceps Routines

Exercise	Sets	Reps
Basic biceps routine		
Standing barbell curls	3	6-10
Intermediate biceps routine		
E-Z bar curls	3	6-10
Incline curls	2	8-10
Advanced biceps routine		
Alternate dumbbell curls	3	6-10
Barbell preacher curls	2	6-8
Hammer curls	2	8-10
Biceps routine: Specializing in mass		
Standing barbell curls	3	6-10
Incline curls	2	8-10
Seated dumbbell curls	2	6-8
Biceps routine: Specializing in peak		
Alternate dumbbell curls	3	6-10
One-arm dumbbell preacher curls	2	8-10
Concentration curls	2	8-10

Triceps

Although most bodybuilders concentrate on the biceps when working to build big guns, it is the triceps muscle on the back of the arm that accounts for most of the mass. The biceps muscle has two heads, while the triceps has three. Adding it all up, 60 percent of your upper arm mass comes from the triceps and not the biceps.

The triceps are heavily involved in many exercises for the deltoids and chest because all pushing movements use the triceps to some extent. For this reason, you must limit the total number of sets for the triceps. This makes it especially important to use only the most effective exercises. A well-planned triceps routine should focus on all three heads: lateral (outer), medial, and long (inner).

Because the location of attachments for and the shape of the triceps varies from individual to individual, each bodybuilder must know which exercises target which head. For example, a bodybuilder with a naturally well-developed outer head but a lagging long head should use a specific exercise to develop this area of the muscle.

The following exercises are the most effective for developing the triceps muscle. Each description includes instructions for performing the exercise and which head of the triceps muscle it specifically develops. Table 6.2 on page 173 provides sample triceps routines to guide your workouts.

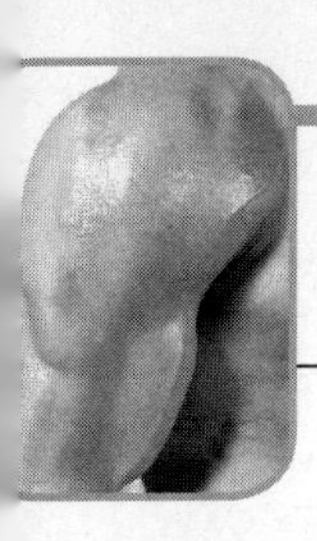

Close-Grip Bench Press

PRIMARY MUSCLES WORKED: **Medial Head of the Triceps • Anterior Deltoids • Inner Pectoralis**

This is a primary exercise for building mass in the triceps. It is a true basic movement that uses the chest and deltoids in addition to the triceps. The narrow grip on the bar places more stress on the triceps than the standard bench press does.

You can perform the close-grip bench press with an E-Z curl bar, which alleviates stress on the wrists and works the outer head, or a regular Olympic bar, which works the medial head. To perform this exercise with an E-Z curl bar, grab the bar with a close grip and outside of the hand angled higher than the thumb *(a)*. Keeping the elbows out, slowly lower the bar to the middle of the chest *(b)*. Push the bar back to the top keeping the elbows out to place the stress on the outer head of the triceps.

To perform the close-grip bench press with an Olympic bar, grab it with a slightly wider grip. I like to place at least two fingers on the knurled area of the bar and two fingers on the smooth area. This hand position places less stress on the wrists than a closer grip would. Lower the bar to the low chest, pointing the elbows to the feet instead of out to the sides. Keep the stress on the triceps by slowly lowering the bar to the chest before forcefully pushing it back to the top. Keeping the shoulders back and the chest up during the exercise places most of the stress on the triceps, not the shoulders. This version of the exercise develops the medial head of the triceps, which is considered the belly of the muscle. And building the belly of a muscle greatly increases the mass of any target area.

a

b

Dips

PRIMARY MUSCLES WORKED: **Medial Head of the Triceps • Anterior Deltoids**

This basic exercise develops the chest or the medial head of the triceps, depending on how you perform it. To target the triceps, keep the upper body straight so that the arms do all the work. Keep the head up and point the elbows behind you during the exercise. Bending at the waist brings the chest into the exercise, so it's important that the upper body remain vertical throughout the movement.

Begin the exercise by setting a pair of dipping bars in a narrow position. This narrow grip stresses the triceps more than the chest. Start with the elbows locked at the top. Slowly lower the upper body until the upper arms are parallel to the floor *(a)*. Dipping lower than horizontal puts more stress on the shoulders. Push the upper body to the top using the power of the triceps *(b)*. Lock the arms at the top for a maximum contraction of the triceps. If you can do more than 12 reps on this exercise, strap on extra weight in a weight belt.

Dips are a great movement for developing the belly, or medial head, of the muscle. Mike Mentzer, known for some of the most massive triceps in the sport, called dips "squats for the upper body," claiming that they are as effective for building the upper body as squats are for developing the legs.

a

b

Triceps Push-Downs

PRIMARY MUSCLES WORKED: Triceps

This exercise is one of the most popular exercises for developing the triceps. This movement develops all three heads of the muscle with particular emphasis on the medial head in the fully contracted position.

To perform the triceps push-down, attach a short bar to an overhead-pulley machine. Grab the bar with an overhand grip, keeping the elbows tight at the sides *(a)*. Push the bar down until the arms are straight and the elbows locked *(b)*. Feel the contraction in the triceps muscle before slowly returning the bar to the top for a full stretch in the muscle. Keep the elbows at the sides during the exercise.

There are many variations of the triceps push-down exercise. Many bodybuilders use a rope attachment, which lets the hands and wrists move with more freedom. Because the hands are in a pronated position, this stresses the lateral head of the triceps more than when using a straight bar. The rope also allows a greater contraction because the arms move down and out before completing the movement.

You can also perform the triceps push-down with an underhand grip. This variation places more stress on the long head of the triceps. Perform this with the elbows locked at the sides, but using an underhand grip, which provides a greater stretch in the starting position.

a

b

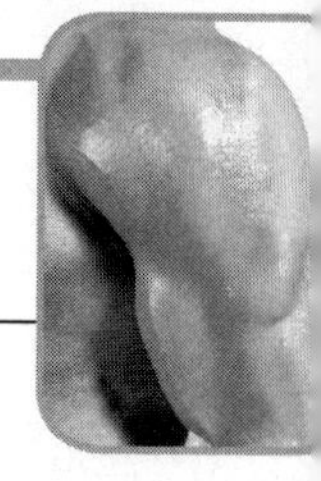

Lying Triceps Extensions

PRIMARY MUSCLES WORKED: Medial Head of the Triceps (flat bench) • Long Head of the Triceps (decline bench)

Lying triceps extensions, also known as skull crushers, work the medial head to build mass. This exercise is similar to the close-grip bench press except that the triceps produces the movement with no help from the chest and delts.

To perform this exercise, lie on your back on a flat bench with your head at the end of the bench. Grab the bar with a close grip and slowly lower the bar to the forehead by bending the arms at the elbows *(a)*. Keep the upper arms vertical and the elbows pointed toward the ceiling. Touch the bar to the forehead (hence the nickname skull crusher) before pressing the bar back to the starting position using only the power of the triceps *(b)*.

Another technique is to let the bar go past the forehead on the way down. Instead of keeping the upper arms locked in the same position, this looser version uses the lats to help push the bar past the sticking point to the top position. This cheating method permits heavier weights because of the assistance of the lats in completing the exercise. Both methods are effective as long as you feel the movement in the triceps.

You can also perform this exercise on a decline bench to focus on the long head of the triceps muscle. Lying triceps extensions can stress the elbow, so perform them second or third in your triceps workout so that you are thoroughly warmed up.

a

b

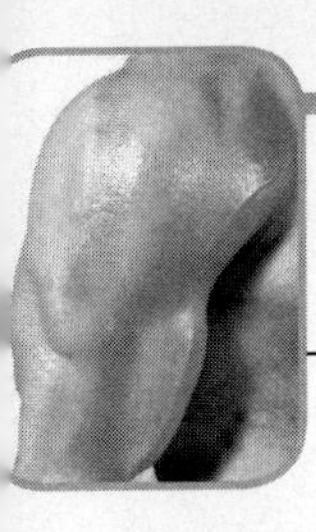

Seated Triceps Extensions

PRIMARY MUSCLES WORKED: **Long Head of the Triceps • Lateral Head of the Triceps**

This exercise develops the long head of the triceps, provides a great stretch, and can be performed with a barbell or a dumbbell. Using some type of back support, such as sitting backward on the preacher bench, during the seated triceps extensions lets you focus on the exercise and not on remaining upright. Using an E-Z curl bar places less stress on the wrists.

To perform the exercise, point the elbows toward the ceiling and slowly lower the bar to the back of the neck for a good stretch in the triceps. Keep the arms close to the head in the bottom position. Maintain the upper arm and elbow position and press the weight back up. Don't let the elbows flare out to the sides. This will make the exercise easier, but will take the stress off of the triceps where you want it.

You can also perform seated triceps extensions with a single dumbbell instead of a barbell. Place both hands on the inside plate of a dumbbell so it is positioned the same as a barbell would be. Keeping the elbows up, lower the dumbbell behind the neck before pressing it back to the starting position. Do not lock the elbows on top; this will take the stress off of the triceps.

Both versions of the seated triceps extension work the long head. However, if you want to shift the focus to the lateral head, use a straight bar and wider grip. Grab the bar with a shoulder-width grip and slowly lower the bar to the base of the neck. Be sure the space between the hands and the space between the elbows are the same. (With an E-Z curl bar or a single dumbbell the space between the hands is smaller than the space between the elbows.The wider grip, however, places more stress on the wrists than a closer grip.)

Lying Dumbbell Extensions

PRIMARY MUSCLES WORKED: **Lateral Head of the Triceps**

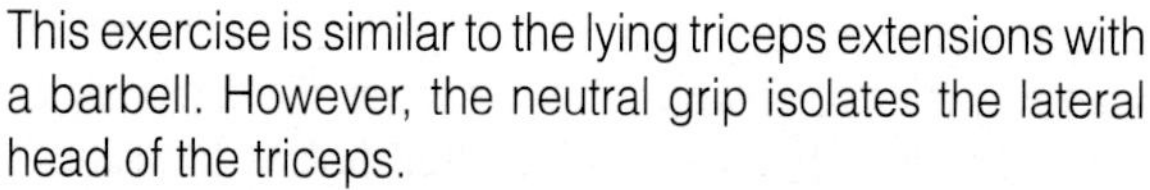

This exercise is similar to the lying triceps extensions with a barbell. However, the neutral grip isolates the lateral head of the triceps.

To perform lying dumbbell extensions, lie on a flat bench with the feet on the end of the bench. Begin by holding a dumbbell in each hand with the arms extended and perpendicular to the bench and the palms facing each other *(a)*. Maintain this hand position throughout the exercise. With the elbows pointing toward the ceiling, slowly lower the dumbbells to the ears *(b)*. Push the dumbbells back to the top keeping the elbows in the same position. Contract the triceps hard at the top of the movement before beginning the next rep.

The key to getting the most out of lying dumbbell extensions is to perform the movement slowly so that you can feel all the tension in the outside head of the triceps. Jerking the dumbbells up ruins the effectiveness of the exercise and takes the tension off the triceps.

a

b

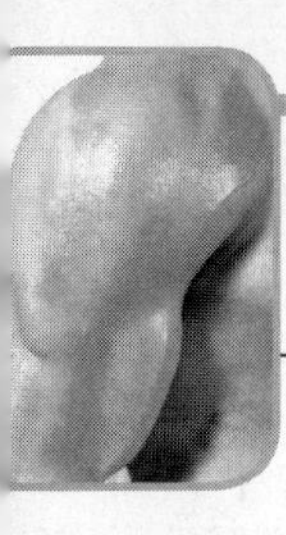

One-Arm Dumbbell Extensions

PRIMARY MUSCLES WORKED: Long Head of the Triceps • Anterior Deltoids

Dumbbell extensions can also be performed with one dumbbell instead of with two dumbbells or a barbell. This exercise also targets the long head of the triceps and provides a great stretch to the muscle. Because of the superior stretch, I've always found the one-arm dumbbell extensions excellent for developing more separation between the three heads of the triceps muscle.

To perform one-arm dumbbell extensions, grab a dumbbell with one hand and raise it overhead *(a)*. This exercise can be done either standing or seated. I prefer the seated version as it allows me to concentrate on the movement much more. Keep the arm tucked against the head (I like to have my bicep right next to my ear) and slowly lower the dumbbell down to the back of the neck *(b)*. The dumbbell should travel through a 180 degree arc from the top position to the bottom for a full stretch. Keep the arm tight throughout the exercise and raise it back to the top after the triceps is fully stretched at the bottom of the movement. Bring the dumbbell all the way back to the top for a full contraction of the muscle.

Using only one dumbbell will limit the amount of weight that can used during this exercise. For this reason, I consider one-arm dumbbell extensions better for developing separation in the triceps than building mass. It's a great pre-contest movement for refining massive triceps.

a

b

Bench Dips

PRIMARY MUSCLES WORKED: Long Head of the Triceps • Anterior Deltoids

Bench dips develop the long head of the triceps. This is not a power movement by any means, but as a final exercise in your triceps routine it will pump up the long head of this muscle.

To perform bench dips, position two long benches parallel to each other. Stand between the two benches with your back to one of them. Put both hands behind your hips and support yourself on the bench behind you. Place your feet on the other bench so that your legs are stretched out in front of you. Slowly lower your body between the two benches by bending your elbows *(a)*. This provides the triceps a great stretch at the bottom of the movement. Push back to the starting position using the power of the triceps *(b)*. Squeeze the triceps at the top before starting another repetition.

Because the only resistance on bench dips is your own body weight, you can increase the resistance by placing a weight on your lap. Some bodybuilders can do this exercise with several 45-pound plates. However, bench dips can place a lot of strain on the shoulders, so use this movement as a final pump exercise instead of a power movement with lots of weight stacked on. After all, this is a triceps exercise and not a shoulder exercise.

a

b

TABLE 6.2 Sample Triceps Routines

Exercise	Sets	Reps
Beginning routine		
Triceps push-downs or dips	3	8-10
Intermediate routine		
Close-grip bench press	3	6-10
Lying triceps extensions	3	6-8
Advanced mass-building routine		
Close-grip bench press	3	6-10
Decline triceps extensions	3	6-10
Dips	2	6-8
Advanced routine: Variation		
Triceps push-downs	3	6-10
Seated triceps extensions	3	6-10
Seated dumbbell extensions	3	6-8

Forearms

The muscles of the forearm are in many ways similar to the calf muscles. Both of these muscle groups are located at the end of the extremities, both are composed of dense muscle fibers accustomed to repetitive work (walking and grabbing), and both are often neglected by bodybuilders in favor of the showpiece muscles of the upper arms and chest. However, massive forearms contribute to a rugged look. Sergio Oliva, Casey Viator, Tim Belknap, and Mike Mentzer displayed great forearm development, which contributed to their impressive physiques.

Complete arm development is impossible without big forearms. Huge biceps and triceps are lacking if the forearms supporting these massive guns are thin and underdeveloped. Just as the calves contribute to great leg development, massive forearms make the arms look even more impressive.

The forearms can be divided into two parts: the upper and lower areas. The muscles on the top of the forearm are called extensor muscles, and they include the brachioradialis and the extensor carpi radialis. The muscles on the bottom of the forearm are the flexor muscles and they include the flexor carpi radialis, the flexor carpi ulnaris, and the palmaris longus.

A lot of forearm development is due to the indirect stimulation from other upper-body exercises. Exercises that require a strong grip build the strength and size of the forearm flexors. These include back exercises such as the deadlift, barbell rows, dumbbell rows, seated cable rows, chin-ups, and T-bar rows as well as bicep exercises such as barbell curls, dumbbell curls, and hammer curls. Similarly, the extensor muscles of the forearms are also indirectly stimulated by other upper-body exercises. Exercises for the delts and traps, such as standing or seated side lateral raises, upright rows, power cleans, and any type of shrug exercise affect the forearms.

The forearms respond best to slightly higher repetitions. This may be due to the dense muscle tissue in this muscle group. Therefore, use a weight that allows 12 to 15 repetitions for most of the sets in your forearm routine. The exercises on the following pages, used in combination with more repetitions, are effective for developing strong forearms, and table 6.3 on page 181 provides sample routines to guide your development.

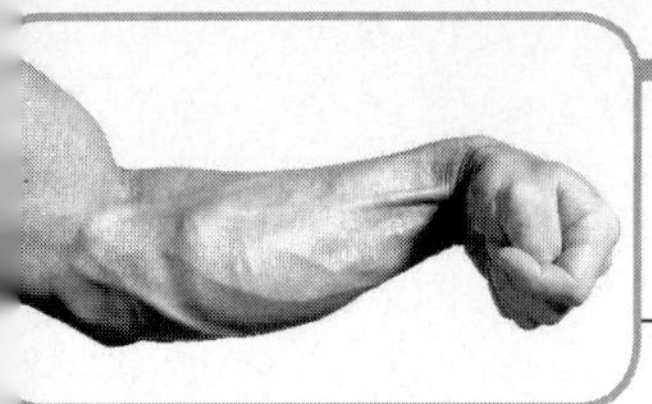

Reverse Curls

PRIMARY MUSCLES WORKED: **Extensor Muscles of the Forearm • Brachialis • Biceps**

This is the most basic exercise for developing the extensor muscles of the forearm. It is basically a barbell curl using an overhand grip rather than underhand. In addition to the extensor muscles, this exercise also affects the biceps and brachialis muscles of the upper arm.

To perform reverse curls, grab a barbell with a pronated grip (palms facing down) and keep the elbows tucked in at the sides *(a)*. You can use a straight bar or a curling bar. The curling bar is easier on the wrists. Curl the bar up while keeping the elbows in tight *(b)*. Bring the bar all the way to the top for a full contraction. Don't let the elbows move away from the sides at the top of the movement; this will bring the anterior delts into play and shift the focus away from the targeted muscles.

b

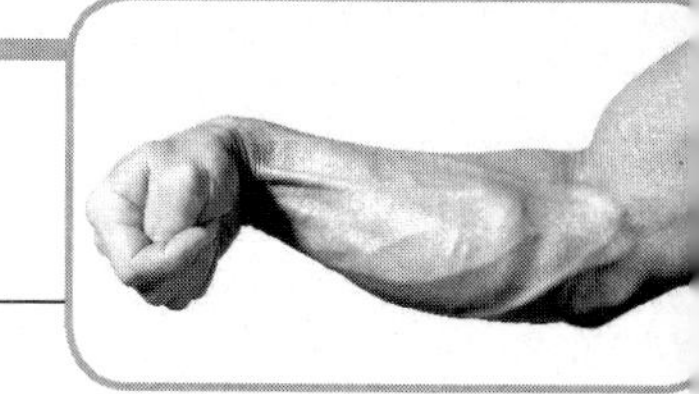

Hammer Curls

PRIMARY MUSCLES WORKED: **Extensor Muscles of the Forearm • Brachialis • Biceps**

This exercise was mentioned in the chapter on biceps as a movement used to develop the outer head of the biceps and the brachialis muscle. However, since it is very similar in execution to a reverse curl, it also affects the extensor muscles of the forearm.

To perform hammer curls, grab a pair of dumbbells while keeping the thumbs facing forward *(a).* Curl each dumbbell up (either alternately or together) maintaining the same grip position throughout the exercise *(b).* Concentrate on squeezing the forearm muscles at the top of each repetition to build the extensor muscles.

a

b

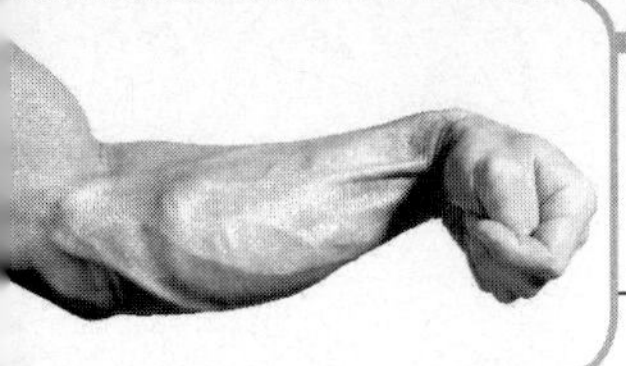

Reverse Wrist Curls

PRIMARY MUSCLES WORKED: **Extensor Muscles of the Forearm**

This exercise fully isolates the extensor muscles of the forearm. Because it is an isolation exercise, you must be sure the resistance is light enough that you can perform the exercise correctly.

To perform reverse wrist curls, sit at the edge of an exercise bench with the knees bent. Rest the forearms on the thighs and hold a straight bar with an overhand grip *(a)*. Keeping the forearms on the thighs, curl the bar up, moving only the wrists *(b)*. Fully contract and extend the muscles on each repetition.

b

Wrist Curls

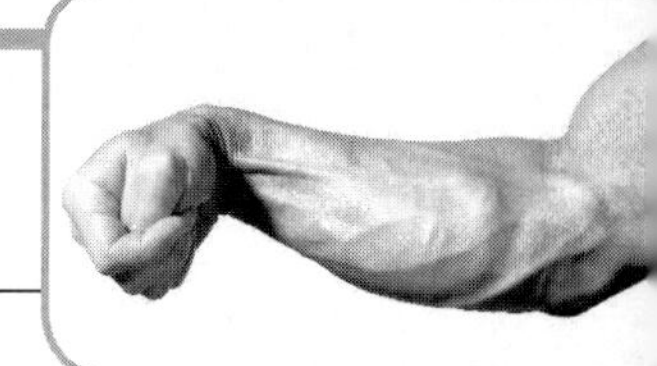

PRIMARY MUSCLES WORKED: Flexor Muscles of the Forearms

Wrist curls are the most direct movement for building up the underside of the forearms and building strength in the wrists and fingers.

To perform wrist curls, sit on a flat exercise bench and grab a straight bar with an underhand grip. Position the forearms on the bench so that the wrists are at the end of the bench and the hands are hanging off the edge *(a)*. Holding the barbell with an underhand grip, curl the wrists up until the flexor muscles of the forearm are fully contracted *(b)*. Slowly lower the barbell to the starting position. When the barbell reaches the bottom position, straighten the fingers until the barbell is hanging by the fingertips. Curl the barbell back up to the top position for the next repetition.

When the forearm muscles reach failure and you can't perform another repetition, continue the set by doing partial reps. Raise the barbell as far as you can (usually half reps) after it is impossible to do another full rep. Do as many half reps as possible until the flexor muscles of the forearm are burning. At this point, continue the set by straightening the fingers and rolling the barbell up with only the fingers. When you cannot move the barbell another inch, you have reached total failure. These "burns" at the end of a set of wrist curls promote more growth by taking the muscle to failure.

a

b

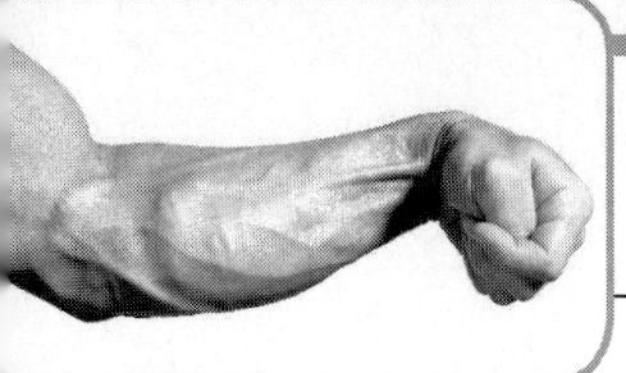

Standing Wrist Curls

PRIMARY MUSCLES WORKED: Flexor Muscles of the Forearm

Another exercise for the flexor muscles is the standing wrist curl. This exercise provides a great peak contraction in the area close to the elbow.

To perform standing wrist curls, stand straight and hold a barbell behind the legs with the palms facing away from you *(a)*. Keeping the arms straight, curl the barbell up by flexing the wrists until the forearms are fully contracted at the top of the repetition *(b)*. Lower the barbell to the starting position before beginning the next repetition. Properly done, you will feel this exercise in the lower part of the flexor muscles.

a

b

Dumbbell Wrist Curls

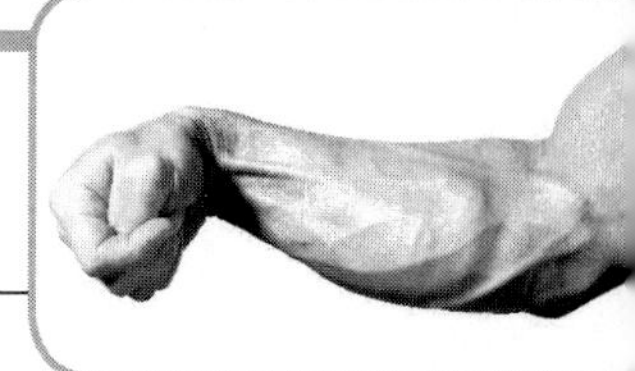

PRIMARY MUSCLES WORKED: Flexor Muscles of the Forearm

Wrist curls can also be performed using dumbbells instead of a barbell. The dumbbells allow for more isolation when working one forearm at a time instead of both arms simultaneously.

To perform dumbbell wrist curls, sit on the edge of a flat exercise bench or crouch down by bending both knees so the thighs are close to parallel to the floor *(a)*. Grab a dumbbell with one hand and position it on the inside of the thigh so the wrist is hanging off the leg. Holding the forearm in place with your free arm, slowly curl the dumbbell up until the flexor muscles of the forearm are fully contracted *(b)*. Slowly lower the weight back to the starting position before beginning the next rep. Doing one arm at a time requires more concentration but the result is a greater isolation of each forearm.

a

b

TABLE 6.3 Sample Forearm Routines

Exercise	Sets	Reps
Beginning routine		
Reverse curls	2	10-12
Wrist curls	2	12-15
Intermediate routine		
Reverse wrist curls	3	10-12
Wrist curls	3	12-15
Advanced routine		
Hammer curls	3	10-12
Reverse wrist curls	2	10-12
Dumbbell wrist curls	3	10-12
Standing wrist curls	2	12

Now that you know how to develop the arms, one of the most popular target areas, it's time to move onto a less popular area—the legs. Probably the most physically demanding of all the muscle groups, the legs are also the most neglected by many bodybuilders. However, if you want to be considered a "real" bodybuilder, you must build a pair of massive, muscular thighs and calves.

Thighs and Calves

Well-developed thighs (quadriceps, hamstrings) and calves in proportion to the upper body are vital for a complete physique. Everyone from experienced bodybuilding judges to the uninformed general public can spot weak legs.

Thighs

Developing the thighs is one of the most important tasks for the competitive bodybuilder. The natural tendency for most beginners is to concentrate on the showpiece muscles: the arms and chest. However, focusing on the upper body at the expense of the legs soon leads to a physique that is grossly out of proportion.

Any bodybuilder planning to compete (or even wear shorts) should work the legs from the very beginning of his or her training program. It is very difficult to bring up a part of the body you neglected for the first few years of training. A novice bodybuilder should focus on developing a proportionate physique from the very beginning.

The muscles of the thighs are some of the biggest muscles in the body. They can withstand a lot of work and are capable of lifting very heavy resistance. Exercises like squats and leg presses are some of the most physically demanding movements you can perform. Therefore, developing massive legs takes guts. Lifting extremely heavy weights and pushing yourself past the pain barrier with some of the biggest muscles in the body is anything but easy. When you see a bodybuilder with great legs, you know he busted his butt to obtain them.

Tom Platz is known for the most massive legs in the sport. Tom, coincidentally, is also revered as one the hardest training bodybuilders in the history of the sport. His overwhelmingly intense squat workouts are so legendary that they are still talked about decades after they occurred.

The following exercises are key to developing massive thighs.Table 7.1 on page 197 provides sample thigh routines to guide you.

Quadriceps Excercises

The quadriceps muscle on the front of the thigh consists of four separate heads with distinct names. The rectus femoris is the long portion in the center of the thigh. The vastus medialis is the teardrop-shaped head located near the knee on the inside of the thigh. The vastus lateralis is the long head on the outside of the thigh. It is responsible for the "sweep" of the quadriceps. The vastus intermedius is located at the top of the thigh near the rectus femoris. Also on the front of the thigh is the sartorius. This long, thin muscle is the longest in the body and angles from the outside of the hip to the inside of the thigh next to the knee.

The hamstrings are the muscles on the back of the thigh. These muscles consist of the biceps femoris, the semitendinosus, and the semimembranosus. Train these muscles just as hard as the muscles on the front of the thigh so that they are in proportion the same way that the biceps and triceps balance your arms.

The following exercises are the most effective for developing the thighs. Included are descriptions for variations that focus on different areas of the muscle. Sometimes it is necessary to bring up a weak area so that the muscle group is evenly developed and well shaped. Genetics, of course, plays a big role in the shape of any muscle group, but through intelligent training, you can change the shape of a muscle to conform to your ideal image.

Vertical Leg Press

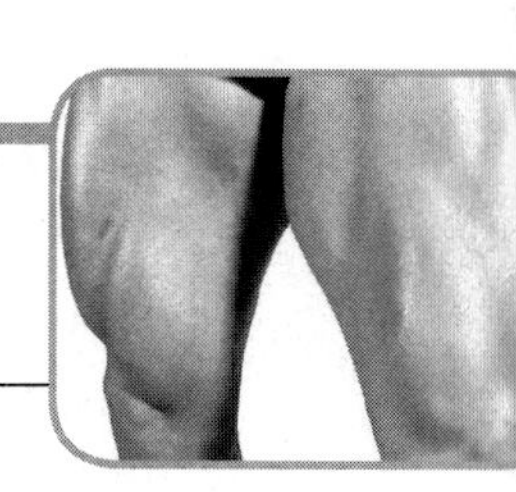

PRIMARY MUSCLES WORKED: Quadriceps • Hamstrings • Hips

This is an old school exercise that is great for developing mass into the quadriceps. Unfortunately, the vertical leg press machine in not available at most gyms anymore, having been replaced by the more popular angled leg press machine described in the next exercise. However, if the vertical leg press machine is available, it can be a valuable asset in any leg-building training routine.

To perform the vertical leg press, position yourself on the machine by lying on your back and placing your feet on the platform which should be located above you. Keep the feet slightly wider than normal with the toes pointed out. This is necessary so the knees descend in the direction of the armpits. If the feet are positioned too narrow, the legs will come down on the ribcage which could potentially crush the ribs if a substantial weight is being used.

When the feet are in position with the lower back firmly set against the back pad, straighten the legs and release the supporting bars. Slowly lower the legs as far as possible before pushing the weight back to the top. Do not lock the knees on top as this will remove the stress from the muscles to the tendons and ligaments of the knees.

The vertical leg press exercise is excellent for adding mass to the upper thigh. This exercise, more than the standard angled leg press, is the closest substitute for Squats. Be careful of the ribcage and the lower back during the course of the exercise and watch the quads respond from doing this exercise.

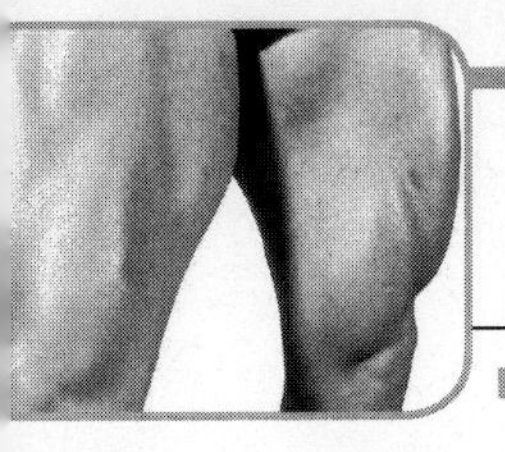

Leg Press

PRIMARY MUSCLES WORKED: Quadriceps • Hamstrings • Hips

The leg press is a popular exercise for developing massive thighs. It uses the same muscles of the thighs and hips as the squat, but because it does not require the coordination or balance that squats do, it is much easier to perform. Although you can use of a tremendous amount of weight with this exercise to build mass, it does not use the muscles of the low back or upper body, so it is not the superior mass builder that squats are.

To perform this exercise, sit in a leg press machine with your low back pressed against the back pad. Maintain this back position throughout the exercise. Allowing your low back to arch when the knees are bent can severely injure the muscles and vertebrae of the low back.

Center the feet on the platform about hip-width apart. Straighten the legs to push the platform and release the stop bars *(a)*. Keep the shoulders back and the low back pressed against the back pad. Do not lock the knees; this takes the tension off the quadriceps and puts it on the tendons and ligaments of the knees instead. Slowly return the platform to the start position by bending the knees until the thighs touch the rib cage *(b)*.

To build more mass in the inner thigh, position the feet wider than shoulder width and the toes pointed out. Just as with squats, the knees follow the direction of the toes as you return the platform to the start position.

To develop the outer quadriceps and a thigh sweep, position your feet closer than shoulder width and parallel to each other. As you lower the weights, the knees point straight ahead, following the position of the toes.

To focus on the hamstrings more than the quadriceps with this exercise, place the feet at the top of the platform and push the platform with the heels. Bring the knees to the armpits or as far as possible to achieve the ultimate hamstring stretch.

a

b

Squats

PRIMARY MUSCLES WORKED: **Quadriceps • Hamstrings • Gluteus Maximus • Lower Back • Hips**

Squats are considered the most difficult exercise. Bodybuilders recognize them as the premier movement for developing mass and power in the quadriceps, hamstrings, glutes, hips, and low back. Squats even affect the upper-body muscles, which play a major role in stabilization during the exercise.

You can perform squats with a barbell, on a Smith machine, or with dumbbells. Squatting with a barbell is the most popular and most effective method. Position yourself under a barbell and balance the bar evenly on the upper back (traps). When the bar is secure, hold it with both hands and step back from the rack *(a)*. You can take one big step back to prepare yourself to perform the movement. Position the feet at least a shoulder-width apart. You can use a variety of positions depending on which area of the quadriceps you want to target. For overall development, keep the feet slightly wider than shoulder width with the toes pointing out. Because the knees always follow the direction of the toes, pointing them out allows the knees to travel at the safest angle.

Begin the exercise by bending the knees and squatting with the weight *(b)*. Keep the upper body straight as you descend. The low back is the weak link, so it is important to keep it slightly arched and flexed and maintain a vertical position with the upper body. This will keep you from lurching forward and injuring the low back.

Keep the hips under the bar during the exercise. To focus on the quadriceps, squat until the thighs are slightly lower than parallel to the floor. Squatting lower puts more emphasis on the glutes and hamstrings. From the bottom position, push the weight back to the starting position using the power of the legs. The glutes should be the first area of your body to descend and the first to begin the push back to the top. Maintain a vertical back

a

b

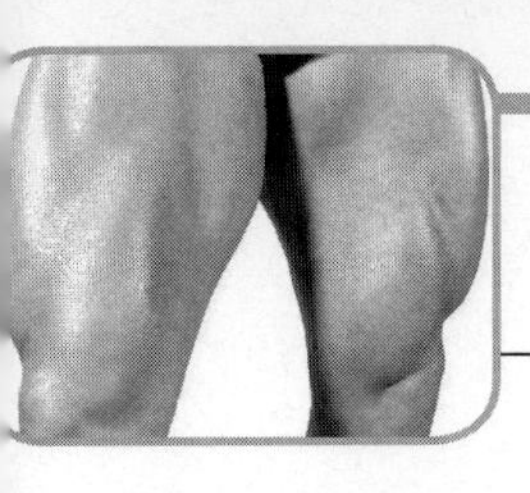

Squats, *continued*

to stress the legs, not the low back. Do not bounce out of the bottom position, which can injure the ligaments and tendons in the knees.

If you want to work the inner area of the thighs, keep the feet wider than shoulder width and point the toes out. This position allows the knees to flare out, which stresses the inner thighs. Keep the low back straight when the feet are positioned wider.

To work the outer area of the quadriceps and create a sweep to the quads, position the feet shoulder-width apart or less with the toes pointed forward and parallel with each other. The knees will point straight ahead during the descent.

Another variation on the squat is to pause at the bottom. Pause squats develop more power in the bottom position and put more stress on the quadriceps and less on the low back. This exercise is useful if you have a low back injury. You will be pleasantly surprised to discover you can perform this variation without pain in the low back.

To correctly perform pause squats, squat to the parallel position or lower and hold this position for two or three seconds before returning to the top. This pause makes it impossible to bounce out of the bottom, or cheat, on this exercise. Pushing from a complete stop stresses the quadriceps more than a traditional squat movement.

Squats stress the quadriceps primarily and the whole body to some degree or another. When performed properly, squats are extremely difficult. It takes guts to push this exercise to failure, but the results are undeniable.

Front Squats

PRIMARY MUSCLES WORKED: **Quadriceps • Hamstrings • Hips**

Another variation of squats is the front squat. This exercise is actually more difficult than the regular version of squats. It involves holding the bar in front of the body by balancing it on the shoulders while keeping the elbows held high. Properly performed, the front squat forces the upper body to remain vertical throughout the course of the exercise, which eliminates any assistance from the lower back.

To do the front squat exercise, position yourself under the bar and balance the bar on the front of the shoulders. Cross the hands in front so the right hand is by the left shoulder and vice versa. It's extremely important to keep the elbows high throughout the movement so the bar stays in place. If the elbows dip down during the performance of the exercise, the bar can slip off the shoulders and fall to the ground.

Keeping the head up and the elbows and arms in position, slowly squat down while maintaining a vertical position with the upper body. Squat down to parallel or slightly below before pushing back to the starting position. The front squat takes a lot of practice to get right, but it can be a great quadriceps builder when utilized correctly.

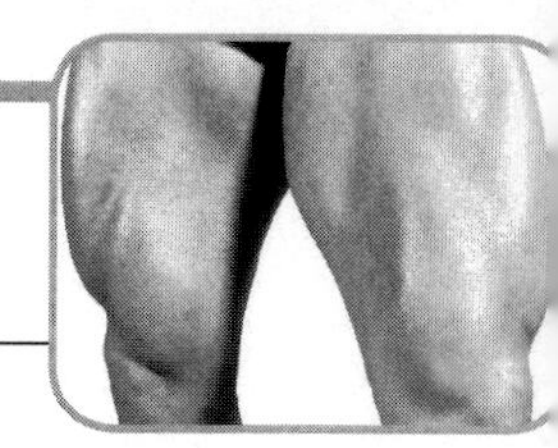

Hack Squats

PRIMARY MUSCLES WORKED: Quadriceps • Gluteus Maximus • Hamstrings

Hack squats are an effective exercise for the quadriceps. Unlike the traditional squat, this exercise is performed on a sled, so balance is not a factor. It isolates the thighs without involving the low back or upper body.

To perform the hack squat, position the shoulders under the pads, the upper body firmly against the back pad, and the feet toward the top of the foot platform *(a)*. Positioning the feet under the hips places too much strain on the knees. After releasing the stop bars, slowly descend to the bottom position by bending the knees and keeping the hips pressed against the back pad *(b)*. Don't bounce out of the bottom position (this can injure the knees); instead, push the weight back to the top.

To use the hack squat exercise to build a sweep to the outside of the quads, position the feet parallel to each other closer than shoulder width. This causes the knees to travel straight ahead and affect the vastus lateralis. To train the inner thighs with the hack squat exercise, point the toes out with the heels in.

The advantage of working the quads on a machine such as the leg press or hack squat is that you can focus on certain areas of the thigh without worrying about balancing a barbell. Also, the low back, which is often a weak link in barbell exercises, is not a factor in these machine exercises.

a

b

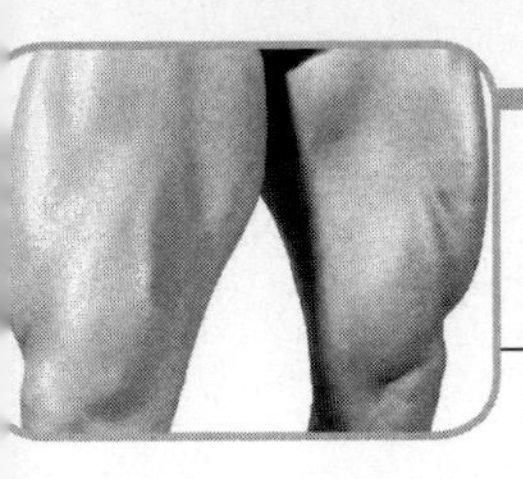

Leg Extensions

PRIMARY MUSCLES WORKED: Quadriceps

The leg extension exercise is an isolation movement for the quadriceps and does not receive assistance from the hips, glutes, or low back. Because it affects only the quads, you cannot use as much weight as you can in squats, leg presses, and hack squats. Therefore, this exercise does not have the same mass-building capabilities as the basic exercises. However, leg extensions create a good stretch and contraction during each repetition, which isolates and defines each head of the quadriceps.

To perform this exercise, sit on the leg extension machine with your back firmly against the back pad *(a).* Position the ankles behind the pads at the end of the leg attachment. Straighten the legs until the knees are locked at the top position *(b).* Hold this position for a second or two before slowly lowering the weight to the starting position. Aim for a maximum stretch in the quadriceps at the bottom before extending the legs for another repetition.

A variation of the leg extension exercise is to perform the movement while lying flat on the bench. This causes a greater stretch in the quadriceps muscles, which creates more separation between the heads. Lying on the bench also directs the stress more toward the upper quadriceps than the standard exercise does.

a

b

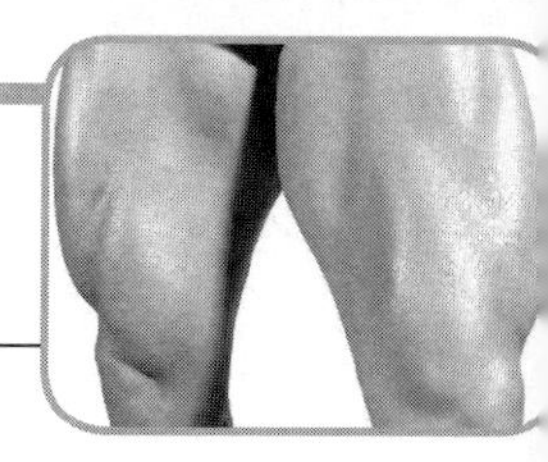

Lunges

PRIMARY MUSCLES WORKED: Quadriceps • Gluteus Maximus • Hamstrings

Lunges are a variation on the squat, but with slightly more emphasis on the glutes and hamstrings than on the quads. Lunging forward with one leg creates a superior stretch in the quadriceps and relies a great deal on the glutes to complete the movement. You can perform lunges with a barbell or a pair of dumbbells. You can stand in one spot or walk during the exercise.

To perform the barbell lunge, place a bar on your upper back as if you were going to do a barbell squat *(a)*. Step forward with one leg and plant the foot with the heel first and the toes second. This heel-to-toe motion helps you maintain balance and prevents missteps. After the foot is secure, keep the upper body straight and bend the knee of the forward leg until the thigh is parallel to the floor *(b)*. You should feel a significant stretch in the quads and glutes. Push back to the starting position before beginning the next repetition on the other leg.

If you want to stress the quadriceps in this exercise, take a shorter step so that the angle of the knee is greater. Pushing out from the bottom position at this angle is almost like performing a one-leg squat, which is effective for developing the quads. Taking a longer step stretches the hamstrings and glutes more.

Walking lunges create a slightly different effect. Instead of pushing back to the starting position, you pull your back leg forward to meet the front leg. To perform walking lunges, take a step forward with one leg as you would in the standard lunge. From the bottom position, continue moving forward and pull your back leg forward until you are standing in the beginning position. Repeat with the other leg.

a

b

Hamstring Exercises

Many bodybuilders make the mistake of focusing all of their energy on heavy quadriceps exercises like the squat and leg press, leaving little energy to train the hamstrings. However, the hamstrings are just as important as the quadriceps and are on display from the side and the rear. To develop hamstrings in proportion to the quadriceps, you must put forth as much effort as you do to develop the quadriceps.

Although many of the exercises that train the quadriceps affect the muscles of the hamstrings to some degree, you must also train the hams directly so that they stay in proportion to the quadriceps. Many bodybuilders prefer training the hamstrings at a different time or on a totally separate day from the quadriceps because exercises such as squats and leg presses are so physically demanding that it's difficult to keep the intensity up for the hamstring exercises.

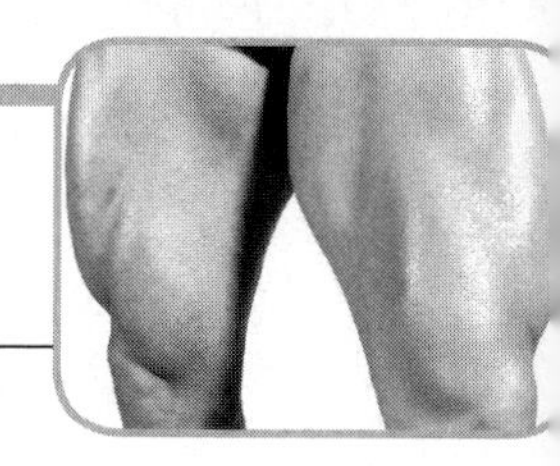

Leg Curls

PRIMARY MUSCLES WORKED: Hamstrings

The leg curl is the primary exercise for the hamstrings. It is performed on a leg curl machine that uses either a pulley attachment or free weights for resistance. Many leg curl machines have a hump in the bench at the hip position. This prevents you from arching your low back during the exercise, which can cause back injury.

To perform this exercise, lie face down on a leg curl bench with the knees off the bench and the ankles under the pads *(a)*. Grab the handles in front of you and slightly raise the shoulders off the bench before beginning the exercise. Keeping the shoulders high allows you to feel the contraction in the hamstrings more than if the shoulders are flat and relaxed on the bench.

Begin the exercise by slowly curling the legs up all the way to the top for a full contraction of the hamstrings *(b)*. Pause for a second on top before slowly lowering the legs to the starting position. The leg curl exercise is a great movement for emphasizing the negative portion of each repetition. The hamstrings respond best to heavy resistance and low reps, so they will be very strong on the eccentric part of the exercise. Tom Platz used to have his training partner push his legs down to emphasize the negative part of each repetition.

You can perform leg curls one leg at a time to isolate the hamstrings even more. It's possible to use the hips when trying to lift heavy resistance, which takes the stress off the hamstrings. Working one leg at a time takes the low back and hips out of the movement and focuses the movement completely on the hamstrings. You can do all the repetitions with one leg before moving on to the next, or you can alternate legs.

a

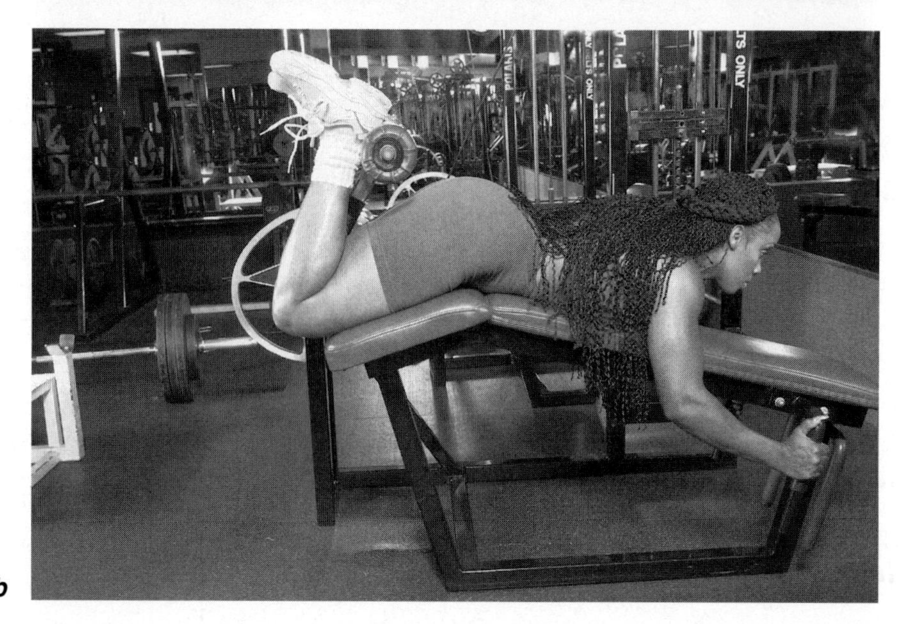

b

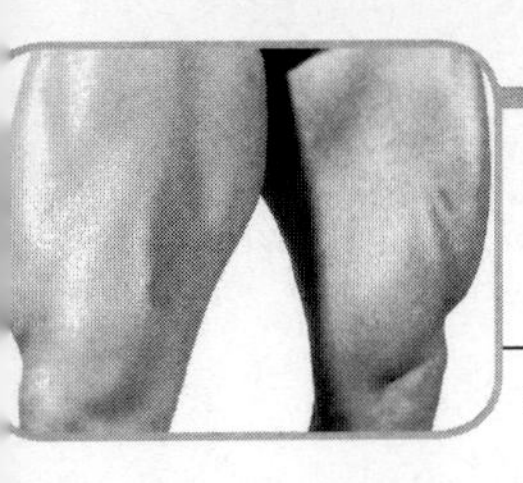

Dumbbell Leg Curls

PRIMARY MUSCLES WORKED: Hamstrings

You can also perform leg curls with a dumbbell instead of on a machine. This free-weight exercise provides a completely different feel than leg curls on a machine. Muscles in the hamstrings that are not used during the cable exercise are called on to balance and coordinate the weight.

To perform dumbbell leg curls, lie on a decline bench. Using a decline bench stresses the hamstrings through a greater range of motion than performing the exercise on a flat bench. Position the legs at the bottom of the bench with the knees just off the edge. Bend the knees and have a training partner place a single dumbbell between your feet *(a)*. Position the soles of the feet on the inside plate of the dumbbell. You must concentrate to keep the dumbbell in place throughout the exercise.

Slowly lower the dumbbell until the legs are straight *(b)*. Keep the tension on the hamstrings by not locking the knees in the bottom position. Curl the dumbbell back up with the power of the hamstrings. Bring the dumbbell all the way to the top to contract the hamstrings before beginning another repetition.

One trick to help balance the dumbbell throughout the exercise is to change the position of the feet during the movement. When the dumbbell is at the bottom position, point the feet so they are straight. This prevents the dumbbell from slipping and falling to the floor. As you return the dumbbell to the top position, curl the ankles up so that the dumbbell does not slip in the top position. It takes practice to master this exercise, but once you get it down, it is effective for building mass into the hamstrings.

a

b

Standing Leg Curls

PRIMARY MUSCLES WORKED: **Hamstrings**

Another variation on the leg curl exercise is the standing leg curl, which is performed on a machine that allows a full contraction of the hamstrings while training one leg at a time.

You can perform the standing leg curl two different ways. You can stand in the machine with both legs behind the pads, or you can stand to the side of the machine with just one leg behind a pad. One leg at a time allows you to concentrate on the movement.

To do this exercise, grab the support bars at the top of the machine, stand to the side of the machine, and place one leg behind the pad. Keep the upper body straight and curl the leg up and flex the hamstrings hard at the top of the movement. Slowly lower the weight during the eccentric portion of the rep and keep the knees slightly bent at the bottom to maintain tension on the hamstrings.

Because this exercise isolates the hamstrings to produce a superior contraction with each rep, it's important not to use too much resistance and compromise your form. Too much resistance can cause you to bend at the waist and use the hips to help lift the weight. This takes the focus off the hamstrings, which defeats the purpose of the exercise.

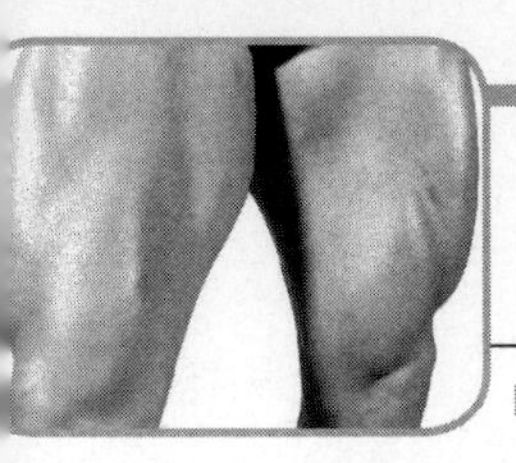

Seated Leg Curls

PRIMARY MUSCLES WORKED: Hamstrings

Another useful machine for training the hamstrings is the seated leg curl machine. In addition to isolating the hamstrings, it also provides a great peak contraction in the muscles.

To perform seated leg curls, position yourself so that the ankles are on the pads *(a)*. You may have to adjust the seat. Keeping the back against the back support, curl the weight down and squeeze the hamstrings at the bottom *(b)*. Hold this position for a second or two to peak contract the muscle before slowly returning the weight to the top. Avoid building up momentum and swinging the weight down. To isolate the hamstring and feel the muscle work, you must use proper form and a controlled tempo. This is not a power exercise.

a

b

Stiff-Leg Deadlifts

PRIMARY MUSCLES WORKED: **Hamstrings • Lower Back • Gluteus Maximus • Spinal Erectors**

This is the most basic movement to build the hamstrings. It involves not only the hams, but also the back, glutes, and the spinal erectors. Because this exercise uses several muscle groups, you can use more resistance than you can with exercises that isolate the hamstrings. And more resistance means more potential for building mass. As a result, the stiff-leg deadlift is one of the best mass-building exercises for the hamstrings.

To perform this exercise, stand with the feet about shoulder-width apart and grab a barbell with an over-hand grip. Keep the arms straight and the hands set on the bar so that they are just outside of the thighs. Begin the exercise by arching the low back with the shoulders back and the chest expanded. Keep the legs and arms straight and the low back arched as you slowly bend forward with the bar. Stop when the bar is about halfway down the shins. Pull the bar back up to the top keeping the low back arched throughout the movement.

The key to performing stiff-leg deadlifts correctly is to arch the low back to stabilize the torso and allow the hamstrings to do the work. If the back loses the arch, the stress shifts from the hamstrings to the low back. This position can cause serious injury. And even if you avoid injury, this position does not properly work the hamstrings.

You can also perform stiff-leg deadlifts by lowering the bar to the feet *(a)* and then raising it only to the middle of the thighs *(b)*. This keeps constant tension on the hamstrings without involving the low back as much as the other version. The only drawback to this method is that it requires much greater strength in the low back to arch the back while the upper body bends farther over. However, if the low back can stand it, this exercise provides a greater hamstring stretch, which will produce more growth.

a

b

TABLE 7.1 Sample Thigh Routines

Exercise	Sets	Reps
Beginning routine		
Squats	3	8-12
Leg curls	3	6-10
Intermediate routine		
Squats	4	6-12
Leg press	3	8-10
Leg curls	3	6-10
Stiff-leg deadlifts	2-3	6-8
Advanced routine		
Leg extensions	3	8-12
Squats	4	6-10
Hack squats	3	8-10
Dumbbell leg curls	3	6-10
Seated leg curls	3	6-10
Advanced routine: Alternate		
Leg press	4	6-12
Front squats	3	6-10
Lunges	3	10-12
Standing leg curls	3	6-10
Stiff-leg deadlifts	3	6-8

Calves

The contribution of the calves is as important to displaying great legs as that of the thighs. In fact, many bodybuilders know that if they have huge thighs but skinny calves, their legs will look thin no matter how big the thighs are. However, huge, diamond-shaped calves make the legs as a whole look bigger, even if the thighs are too thin. The illusion that big calves create cannot be overlooked.

The calves are also one of the few target areas (along with the deltoids and the abs) that contribute to the symmetry of your physique. These areas create what is known as an X-type physique. Wide deltoids at the top of the body form the beginning of the taper, the tight abdominals and midsection bring the physique to a narrow center, and the calves at the bottom of the physique help to create the flare at the bottom of the X. Impressive calves are important to the overall look of the physique.

In spite of their importance, the calves are one of the least-liked muscle groups among bodybuilders. They are the most stubborn muscle group and definitely are not as fun to train as the showpiece areas like the arms and chest.

There are several theories to explain why the calves are difficult to develop. The first is that the muscle fibers that make up the calves are extremely dense because of their constant activity during walking, standing, and running. Another theory states that because this muscle group is farthest from the heart, it is the most difficult to pump up, and this pump is an integral part of muscle development.

Another explanation, which is more mental than physiological, is that many bodybuilders are resigned to the idea that great calves are a matter of great genetics, so if you are not born with them, you will never get them. As a result, they do not train their calves as consistently or as hard as other muscle groups. This lack of dedicated, hard training leads to subpar results and weak calves. To build diamond-shaped, massive calves, you must train them just as hard as you would any other muscle group.

Train the calves twice a week using slightly higher repetitions than other muscle groups. Performing 15 to 30 repetitions for calf exercises results in a better pump and more growth.

The calves consist of two separate muscles. The gastrocnemius is the large, heart-shaped muscle that makes up the bulk of the calf area. The soleus muscle is the large, fan-shaped muscle that lies under the gastrocnemius. The soleus muscle, although somewhat hidden by the gastrocnemius, is the muscle responsible for the width of the calf that gives this muscle its renowned diamond shape.

The gastrocnemius muscle is composed of mostly white muscle fibers, so it responds best to explosive movements with heavy weights. However, because of the dense muscle fibers and limited blood supply, perform slightly more reps than the standard 6 to 8. Perform at least 10 reps of exercises for this muscle. The soleus muscle, on the other hand, is composed of mostly red muscle fibers. Because of this makeup, 15 to 20 reps are recommended for exercises that emphasize this muscle.

The following calf exercises are effective for developing this stubborn muscle group. Table 7.2 on page 203 provides sample calf routines for reference.

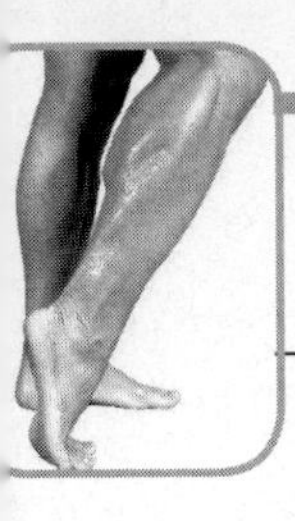

Standing Calf Raises

PRIMARY MUSCLES WORKED: Gastrocnemius Muscles of the Calves

The standing calf raise exercise is the fundamental movement for developing the calves. Raising the heels up and standing on the balls of the feet is the basic movement for activating the calf muscles. Unlike other more complex muscle groups, this movement is the same for every calf exercise.

You can perform this exercise with a barbell, on a Smith machine, or on a standing calf raise machine. In all of these exercises you stand with the balls of the feet on a block and the heels hanging off. Keep the upper body and legs straight and support the weight on the shoulders. Raise the heels of both feet so that the weight is on the balls of the feet. Hold this position for a second or two to contract the calf muscles before slowly lowering the heels past the block for a full stretch.

Keep the knees straight to maximally stress the gastrocnemius muscle. It's also critical to get a good stretch at the bottom of the movement and a good contraction at the top. Use as much weight as you can while maintaining good form for 12 to 15 repetitions. The calves can handle a lot of weight. In fact, Arnold Schwarzenegger performed standing calf raises with 1,000 pounds.

Seated Calf Raises

PRIMARY MUSCLES WORKED: Soleus Muscle of the Calves

The best exercise for the often forgotten soleus muscle is the seated calf raise on a machine. This equipment lets you perform calf raises with the legs bent, which is the only position that targets the soleus muscle.

Position the legs so that the knees are under the pads of the seated calf raise machine. Position the feet so that only the balls of the feet are in contact with the foot pads *(a).* This allows the heels to fully lower for a full stretch. From this full stretch, rise all the way to the top for a maximum contraction *(b).* The soleus muscles respond best to higher repetitions, so do at least 15 repetitions of this exercise.

a

b

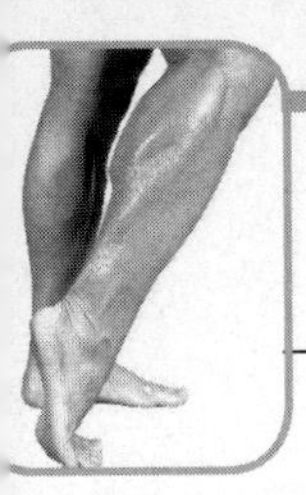

Donkey Calf Raises

PRIMARY MUSCLES WORKED: Gastrocnemius Muscles of the Calves

This old-school exercise is the best movement for developing massive calves. Although it is not as popular as the standing or seated calf raises, it is superior to both of these movements. This exercise is so effective because the resistance is located directly over the hips rather than on the shoulders. This leads to a greater stretch of the calf muscles and a more direct contraction.

To perform this exercise, you need the help of a partner or two. There are donkey calf raise machines that try to mimic the original exercise, but they are a poor substitute for the real thing. Use the original.

To begin, stand on a block of wood that allows your heels to descend for a full stretch. Bend over and support the weight of your upper body on the forearms. You can use the side of a squat rack that has safety bars on the side. Keep the knees semistraight while a training partner sits on your hips as if he were riding a horse. Make sure your partner is not sitting on your low back, but far enough back so that his weight is directly over your hips. Maintaining this position, raise the heels up and down to train the calf muscles. Hold the bottom and top positions for a second or two to feel the muscles working.

You can also use a weight belt that holds extra weight in addition to the weight of your partner. This allows you to do drop sets. After performing as many repetitions as possible, have your partner jump off, then continue with only the resistance on the weight belt.

For the ultimate drop set while doing donkey calf raises, use two partners on your back in addition to the weight belt. Perform at least 15 repetitions with the full load, then have the person sitting on your hips jump off. Continue the set aiming for another 12 to 15 repetitions with one partner and the weight belt. When you reach failure, have the second partner jump off and continue repetitions with the resistance on the weight belt. Try to pump out another 10 to 12 repetitions before concluding the set. This is a great method for developing the calves because it uses heavy resistance and a high number of repetitions.

Leg Press Calf Raises

PRIMARY MUSCLES WORKED: Gastrocnemius and Soleus Muscles of the Calves

This is another version of the calf raise movement. You can perform this exercise on a vertical or angled leg press machine. It is effective because it produces a superior stretch at the bottom of each repetition.

To perform calf raises on a leg press machine, position your feet so that only the balls of the feet are in contact with the bottom of the foot pad *(a)*. Extend the legs so that the knees are straight and release the safety latch. Push the weight up by pushing with the balls of the feet, contracting the calf muscles at the top position *(b)*. Slowly lower the weight, being careful to keep the feet on the foot pad. Stretch the calves at the bottom of each rep and hold that position for a second before pushing the weight back up to the top. Perform each repetition slowly to feel the calf muscles working on both the concentric and eccentric portions of the rep.

a

b

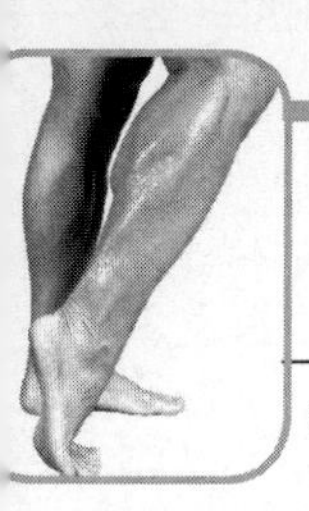

Standing Dumbbell Calf Raises

PRIMARY MUSCLES WORKED: **Gastrocnemius Muscles of the Calves**

Dumbbell calf raises are an excellent method of isolating each calf individually. They are performed one leg at a time which allows for greater concentration and focus on each leg. This is a great exercise for developing each calf so they are in proportion to each other.

To perform dumbbell calf raises, stand with one leg on a block and bend the knee of the other leg so all of your bodyweight is supported by the leg that is standing on the block. Holding a dumbbell with the same arm as the leg you are training, raise the heel up and down and isolating the calf muscle on that leg. Feel the contraction at the top of the movement before slowly lowering the heel down for a full stretch. Repeat the exercise with the opposite leg.

Standing dumbbell calf raises are also excellent for bringing up a calf that is smaller than the other one. A good method for bringing up a calf that is out of proportion is to superset dumbbell calf raises for the weaker calf with standing calf raises or leg press calf raises with both legs. The extra work performed by the weaker calf will help to eventually bring this muscle in proportion to the other calf.

TABLE 7.2 Sample Calf Routines

Beginning routine		
Exercise	**Sets**	**Reps**
Standing calf raises	3	12-15
Intermediate routine		
Standing calf raises	3	12-15
Seated calf raises	3	15-20
Advanced routine		
Donkey calf raises	4	15-25
Leg press calf raises	4	10-15
Standing dumbbell calf raises	2	10-12

Now that you have trained the chest, back, shoulders, arms, and legs, it's time to tie them all together and develop the abdominal muscles. Tight, well-developed abs are critical to a winning physique.

Standing Dumbbell Calf Raises

Sample Calf Routines

Chapter 8

Abs

The abdominal muscles are an extremely important muscle group for bodybuilders. Although bodybuilders train with heavy resistance to develop massive, proportionate physiques, their goal is much different than those of other iron athletes such as powerlifters and other weight-trained athletes. A bodybuilder is concerned primarily with developing a massive physique with shape and aesthetics. Well-developed abdominals are critical to attaining this goal.

Located in the center of the body, the abdominal muscles are the first area the eye is drawn to when viewing a bodybuilder. Well-developed abs coupled with very low body fat give the body a look of muscularity and refinement no other muscle group can duplicate. If you want to see if a bodybuilder is in top condition, check out his or her abs.

Of course, attaining contest-winning definition involves reducing body-fat levels to single-digit percentages. This is mostly a matter of following a diet that reduces body fat without sacrificing muscle tissue. However, developing the abdominal muscles themselves is a matter of training with the correct exercises to develop all areas of this muscle group.

When it comes to training the abs, there are many different training methods. Some people believe in hundreds of crunches every day to tighten their waistlines. Others recommend training the abs like any other muscle group, using heavy weights and low reps. Which is the right training method?

To completely develop the abdominal muscles, you must train all areas of the abdominal region with the right amount of intensity and resistance. These regions are the upper abs, lower abs, external obliques, and serratus magnus. Developing these areas will result in an outstanding six-pack.

Upper Abs

The upper abdominal muscles are trained with any type of crunch or sit-up movement. Pulling the torso up toward the legs primarily activates the muscles of the upper abs, developing thickness and muscularity in this area of the muscle. The thicker and more developed the upper abs become, the more they stand out on the physique, even when the body is completely relaxed.

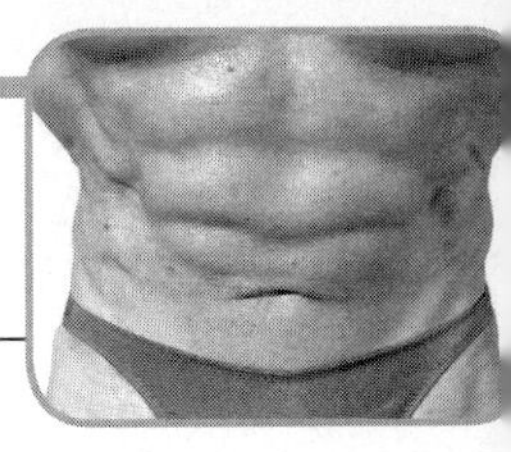

Incline Sit-Ups

PRIMARY MUSCLES WORKED: **Upper Abdominals • External Obliques**

This is an old-school exercise, and it's one of the best for developing the upper abs and external obliques. If you only perform crunches for your abs, you will be surprised at how difficult this exercise is.

Although the standard full sit-up can place a lot of stress on the waist and actually make the waistline bigger, you can modify this exercise to build only the abs and keep the waist nice and small. To emphasize the abs, perform the sit-up on an incline board (the higher the setting, the more difficult the exercise). Keep the knees sharply bent to take the strain off the low back.

Begin the exercise at the top with the elbows pointing forward and the hands at the side of the head *(a).* Holding the hands tightly behind the head can lead to strained neck muscles. Lower the upper body slowly, keeping the torso crunched forward *(b).* When the low back touches the incline board, return to the beginning position, contracting the abs and curling the body all the way up.

If you perform this exercise at a slow tempo, keeping continuous tension on the abs, you should find it difficult to do more than 50 reps per set. Don't hold extra weight during this exercise. This will causes the lower obliques to take over. It is better to keep constant tension on the abs by slowing the exercise and crunching each and every rep. Shoot for three sets of 30 to 50 reps.

a

b

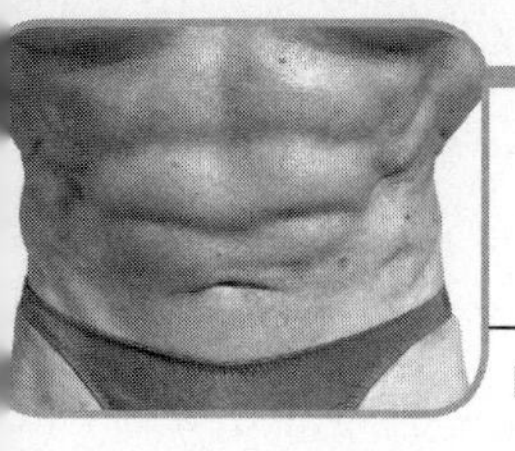

Crunches

PRIMARY MUSCLES WORKED: Upper Abdominals

This is the favorite ab exercise of today's generation. Perform crunches by lying on a bench *(a)* and lifting the shoulders off the bench toward the waist *(b)*. Think of this limited movement as a modified sit-up without sitting up. The short range of movement isolates the upper abdominals and develops this area without involving the obliques and thickening the waist.

Doing crunches on the floor with the feet flat on the ground may be an effective movement for a beginner, but other variations make it much more difficult. When you perform crunches lying on a bench, with your head and shoulders off the bench, you achieve a superior stretch by increasing the range of movement. Point the elbows forward and don't strain the muscles in the back of the neck by pulling on them. Keeping the feet in the air with the legs bent at a 45-degree angle keeps continuous tension on the abs.

When the crunch exercise becomes too easy, add resistance by holding a plate behind the head. Because this movement isolates the upper abs, added weight translates into thicker abdominals. Do as many reps as you can holding a 10- or 25-pound plate then dropping the weight and continuing the exercise until failure occurs.

a

b

Kneeling Cable Crunches

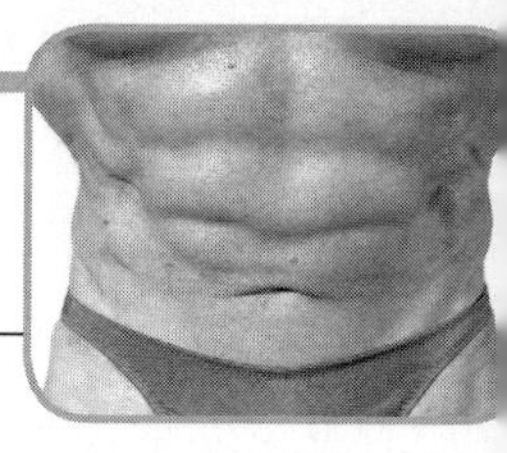

PRIMARY MUSCLES WORKED: Upper Abdominals • External Obliques

This is another exercise with a short range of motion perfect for thickening the upper abs. Kneel on the floor and grab a rope attachment connected to a cable *(a).* Keeping the chin on the chest and upper body crunched forward with the elbows close to the head and the rope overhead, bring the elbows to the floor, feeling the contraction in the abs and obliques *(b).* The added resistance from the weight machine thickens the upper abs.

The key to success with the kneeling cable crunches is to limit the range of motion so that you feel the tension only in the upper abs. Full extension risks thickening the waistline and not the upper abs. Do three sets with a weight that allows 15 to 20 reps.

a

b

Lower Abs

The lower abdominal muscles are sometimes neglected in favor of the upper abs. Many people only do crunches or sit-ups for the abs and these movements primarily develop and strengthen the upper abs. In order to hit the lower abs, the legs or knees must be pulled toward the chest. For complete abdominal development, the lower abs must be proportional to the upper abs.

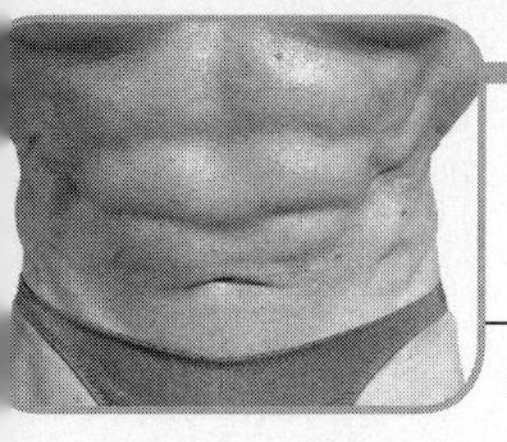

Hanging Knee Raises

PRIMARY MUSCLES WORKED: **Lower Abdominals • Upper Thighs**

This is the best exercise for the lower abs. Hang from a chin-up bar with the legs straight *(a)*. Slowly bring the knees to the chest and feel the contraction in the lower abs *(b)*. Lower the legs slowly, keeping the tension on the abs before bringing the knees back to the chest for the next rep. Avoid building momentum that causes the body to sway with each rep. Keep the upper body straight, raising only the knees during the movement.

The exaggerated stretch to the lower abdominal muscles in the bottom position is what makes this exercise such a great movement. You can also perform the hanging knee raises by keeping the legs straight as you raise them. This makes the exercise much more difficult and can be slightly more stressful to the low back, but it's very effective if you get the hang of it (no pun intended). Champion bodybuilders Jay Cutler and Milos Sarcev use the hanging leg raise exercise consistently. One look at their abdominal development verifies the effectiveness of the exercise. Perform three sets of 30 to 40 reps.

b

Incline Knee Raises

PRIMARY MUSCLES WORKED: **Lower Abdominals • Upper Thighs**

Another great exercise targeting the lower abs is the incline knee raises. To perform this exercise, set an incline bench at a steep angle and position yourself so that your head is at the top of the incline *(a)*. Hold on to to the top of the bench and raise the knees to the chest, squeezing the lower abs at the top *(b)*. Lower the legs slowly and extend them until they are straight at the bottom before immediately bringing them up for the next repetition.

Unlike the hanging knee raises, which you can occasionally do with the legs straight for variety, always perform the incline knee raises with the legs bent. Straight legs put too much stress on the low back. Do three sets of 25 to 35 reps.

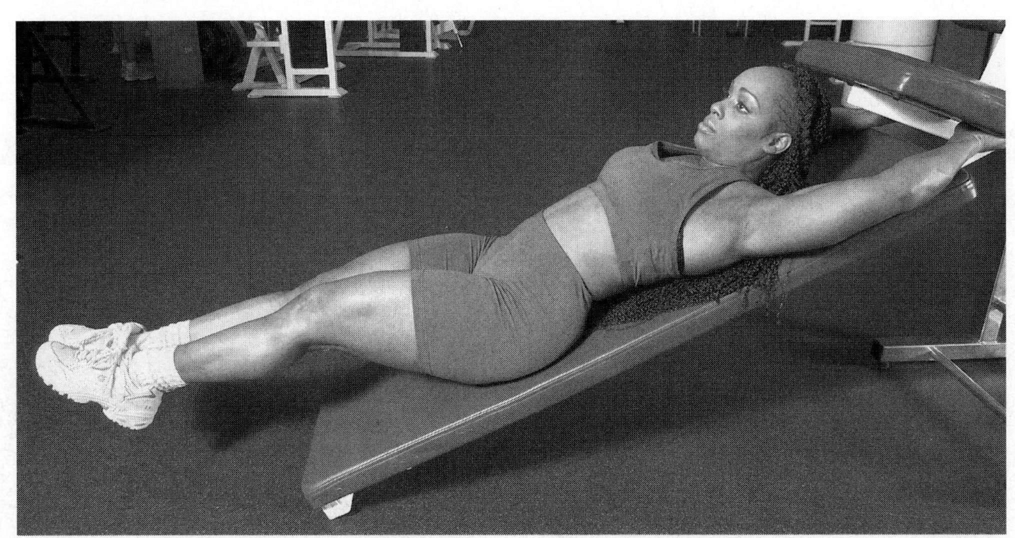

a

b

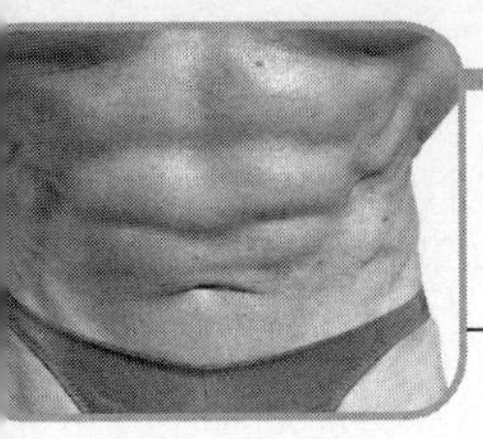

Vertical Leg Raises

PRIMARY MUSCLES WORKED: **Lower Abdominals • Upper Thighs**

This exercise is similar to the hanging knee raises, but instead of hanging off a chinning bar, you use a vertical leg raise chair. This piece of equipment, which is available at most gyms and fitness centers, allows you to support the upper body by resting your forearms on arm pads and your upper body on a back support *(a)*. From here, raise the legs to waist level before slowly lowering them back to the starting position *(b)*. Keep the legs nearly straight when performing vertical leg raises.

This exercise is somewhat easier than the hanging knee raises because the equipment supports the upper body. However, the added support allows more focus on the lower abdominals. Use this movement at the end of your ab routine when the muscles are already exhausted. Perform three sets of 20 to 30 reps.

b

Reverse Crunches

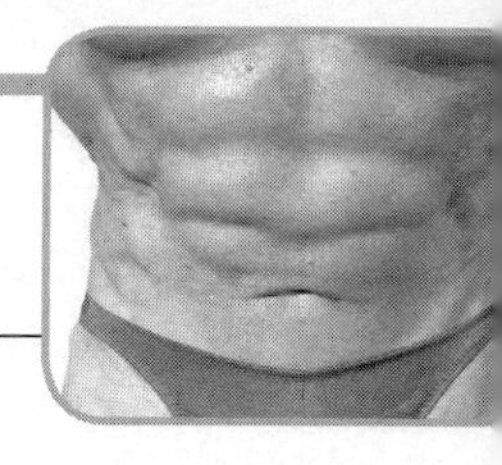

PRIMARY MUSCLES WORKED: Lower Abdominals

This exercise is rarely used by bodybuilders but was a favorite of Mr. Olympia Dorian Yates. It isolates and develops the lower abs, although it requires strong abs and lots of concentration to perform it correctly.

Lie on an exercise bench and bend the hips and knees at 45-degree angles *(a)*. Hold the bench near the head to support the body and focus the movement on the lower abs. From this position, raise the hips off the bench while keeping the upper body stabilized *(b)*. The hips should rise up and slightly toward the shoulders to fully contract the lower area of the abdominals. Slowly lower the hips to the bench before performing another repetition. Keep the abs flexed until the set is completed to keep constant tension on the lower abs. If you have a bad low back, don't use this movement because it requires a lot of low back strength. Do two to three sets of 25 to 30 reps.

a

b

External Obliques

The external obliques are the muscles that cover the ribs. They are located on each side of the abdominal wall, and when fully developed, they add dimension and muscularity to the overall "six-pack." Robby Robinson and Shawn Ray have outstanding external obliques, which contribute greatly to their abdominal development.

Although the development of the upper external obliques contributes immensely to the look of your overall abdominals, you must be careful not to overdevelop the lower obliques, which tie into the waistline. Building these muscles will make your waist bigger and ruin the V-taper that bodybuilders aspire to.

Many of the exercises for the upper and lower abs also affect the external obliques. In particular, you feel the external obliques working while doing incline sit-ups, kneeling cable crunches, and incline knee raises. However, a few exercises target the external obliques directly.

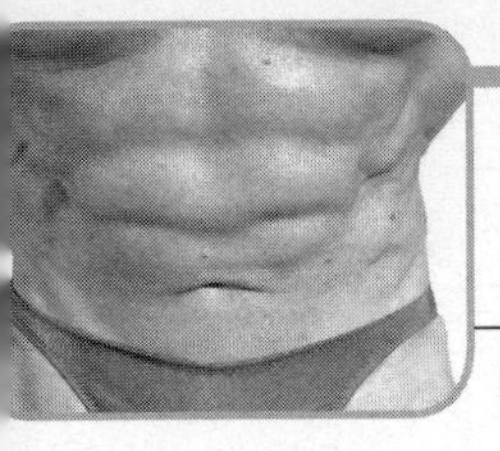

Alternate Crunches

PRIMARY MUSCLES WORKED: External Obliques

This exercise directly hits the external obliques because of the angle of the movement. To perform alternate crunches, lie on the floor with the legs draped over a bench to stabilize the upper body. Place one hand behind the head and the other hand over the area of the muscle you are working *(a)*. Curl up and pull the elbow toward the opposite knee *(b)*. If you are raising the right elbow to the left knee, you should feel the contraction in the right, upper obliques.

Complete all the repetitions for one side before moving on to the other. Raise slowly and hold the contracted position for a second or two before lowering. Although you are raising the elbow toward the opposite knee, the upper body does not actually come off the ground except for a small area of the shoulder and upper back. Most of the effectiveness of the exercise comes from twisting the torso in just the right way to target the upper obliques. Because this is a crunch exercise, there is no need for concern about developing the obliques around the waist because this part of the body is stabilized on the floor. Perform two or three sets of 25 reps.

a

b

Twisting Hanging Knee Raises

PRIMARY MUSCLES WORKED: External Obliques

To hit the obliques from another angle, try this exercise. Hang from a chinning bar as you would for standard hanging knee raises, but twist the knees to one side to contract the obliques *(a).* Bring the knees back to the starting position, then bring them up to the other side for the next repetition to work the opposite side *(b).*

Perform this movement slowly so that you feel the contraction in the correct area. It's easy to get caught up in the tempo of the exercise and begin swinging the body to complete each rep, but this makes the movement less effective. Two or three sets of 15 to 20 reps for each side will build thick Shawn Ray obliques to showcase those abs.

a

b

Serratus Magnus

The serratus muscles are located beneath and to the side of the lower pecs. They are clearly visible when the arms are raised overhead. They are short, thick muscles developed through any type of pullover exercise. Although not exactly part of the abdominal region, the serratus muscles add to the overall look of the six-pack.

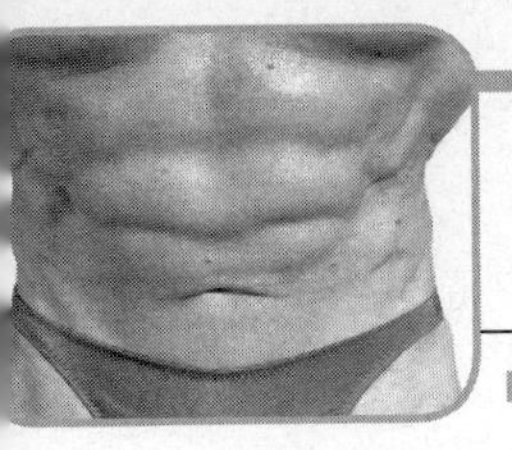

Dumbbell Pullovers

PRIMARY MUSCLES WORKED: Serratus • Latissimus Dorsi * Upper and Inner Pectorals

In addition to the upper and inner pecs, dumbbell pullovers expand the rib cage and develop the short and thick serratus muscles, which are located at the top of the rib cage and add to the finished look of the abdominal region. Combined with developed, well-defined abdominals and intercostal muscles, the serratus are an integral part of the finished physique. Dumbbell pullovers are one of the best exercises for this hard-to-develop muscle.

To perform the dumbbell pullover, lie across an exercise bench holding a single dumbbell with both hands *(a).* Keeping the hips low, take a deep breath and slowly lower the dumbbell until it reaches the level of the bench *(b).* Pause for a second, then bring the dumbbell back up until it is directly over the chest. Finish your chest workout with two or three sets of 10 to 12 reps of dumbbell pullovers.

a

b

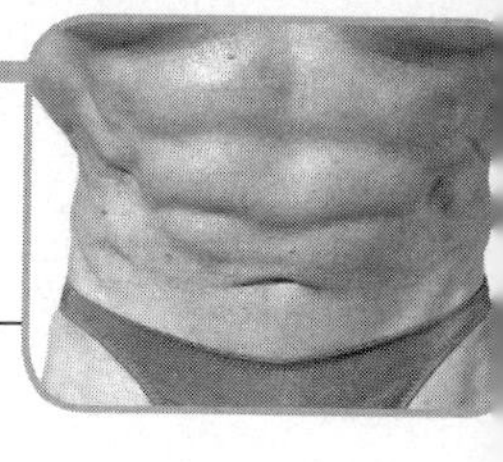

Straight-Arm Pull-Downs

PRIMARY MUSCLES WORKED: **Serratus • Latissimus Dorsi**

This is another great exercise to develop the serratus muscles. Many bodybuilders prefer to use this movement at the end of their lat routines for a final pump. It's also great for isolating the lats because it is one of the rare back exercises that doesn't involve the biceps muscles.

Stand in front of a lat pull-down machine and grab the bar with a grip slightly wider than shoulder width *(a)*. Bend the elbows slightly and pull the bar from the top position until it touches the thighs *(b)*. Flex the lats in the bottom position before returning the bar to the top for a good stretch. Two or three sets of 10 to 12 reps at the end of your back workout will pump up the lats and build the serratus muscles.

a

b

Now it's time to put these exercises together to fully develop the complete abdominal region. Whether you are a beginner, intermediate, or advanced bodybuilder, you must train the upper abs, lower abs, external obliques, and serratus muscles. See table 8.1 for sample routines.

TABLE 8.1 Sample Ab Routines

Exercise	Sets	Reps
Beginning routine		
Incline sit-ups (upper abs)*	3	30-40
Incline knee raises (lower abs)*	3	30-40
Dumbbell pullovers (serratus)	2 or 3	10-12
Intermediate routine: Workout 1**		
Crunches on bench (upper abs), supersetted with:	3	40-50
Hanging knee raises (lower abs)	3	20-30
Kneeling cable crunches (upper abs, obliques)	2 or 3	20-30
Dumbbell pullovers (serratus), after chest workout	2 or 3	10-12
Intermediate routine: Workout 2		
Incline sit-ups (upper abs), supersetted with:	3	40-50
Incline knee raises (lower abs)	3	30-40
Twisting hanging knee raises (obliques)	2 or 3	15-20
Straight-arm pull-downs (serratus)	2 or 3	10-12
Advanced routine: Workout 1***		
Incline sit-ups (upper abs), supersetted with:	3	40-50
Incline knee raises (lower abs)	3	30-40
Alternate crunches (obliques), supersetted with:	3	20-30
Vertical leg raises (lower abs)	3	20-30
Dumbbell pullovers (serratus), after lat workout	2 or 3	10-12
Advanced routine: Workout 2		
Crunches (upper abs), supersetted with:	3	40-50
Hanging knee raises (lower abs)	3	30-40
Kneeling cable crunches (upper abs, obliques), supersetted with:	3	15-20
Incline knee raises or reverse crunches (lower abs)	3	20-30
Straight-arm pull-downs (serratus)	2 or 3	10-12

*Superset the sit-ups and knee raises twice a week for the stated number of sets and reps.

**During the intermediate routine, add an ab exercise to develop the external obliques along with the upper and lower abs.

***The advanced routine includes two different supersets for the upper and lower abs. This totals 12 sets for the abdominal region twice a week.

You've mastered the exercises and techniques to develop mass—in both the fun to train and the stubborn muscle groups. You're eating right and balancing training with rest. Now it's time to enter a bodybuilding competition. The next part of this book details everything you need to know to step onto the contest stage with confidence.

PART III

Preparing for Competition

Getting ready to compete in a bodybuilding competition requires total commitment to training, nutrition, supplementation, and recuperation. It is more than just a full-time job, it is an all-day job. The third part of this book details the process of preparing for a bodybuilding competition and what to do on the day of competition. You will learn how to schedule your training and nutrition into a typical day so that you can achieve peak condition at just the right time. You will also discover exactly what bodybuilding judges look for in a winning physique. This section teaches you what it takes to win.

Chapter 9

Precontest Dieting

Bodybuilding is one of the most demanding competitive sports in the world. Not only must a competitive bodybuilder undertake years of intense resistance training to develop his physique, but he must also eat correctly all day to feed the muscles the nutrients they need for growth.

When it comes time to prepare for a competition, the demands on a bodybuilder are even more intense. Not only must the training in the gym continue to be heavy and hard, but also the caloric intake must be reduced in an attempt to eliminate subcutaneous fat. This decrease in body fat is absolutely necessary to compete in top condition.

The Importance of Getting Ripped

If you want to be successful in a bodybuilding competition, you must get as ripped as possible. Being "ripped" in bodybuilding refers to a very low body-fat percentage, which allows the muscles to show through the skin. It is only by being ripped that a bodybuilder can display the striations, muscularity, and vascularity that a bodybuilder needs to win. Although losing muscle mass as you prepare for competition is definitely not recommended, it is better to lose some muscle during the process of getting ripped than to retain all your muscle mass but remain too smooth. You have a much better chance of winning if you compete ripped and smaller than if you compete smooth and big.

I know this from personal experience. I have lost far more competitions by competing too smooth than by being too small. In fact, unless you compete at top national-level events or in the professional ranks, muscle mass is less a priority than conditioning for the majority of judges. At local-level competitions, the physiques are smaller and less developed than at the national level, so the deciding factor is usually the conditioning of the athletes as opposed to overall muscle mass.

However, sacrificing muscle tissue is not what precompetition dieting is all about. When done correctly, bodybuilders should not lose muscle mass as they prepare to compete. It takes years of hard work and dedication to build muscle, so no bodybuilder wants to diet incorrectly and lose valuable mass right before he displays his physique onstage.

Bodybuilding has been called the sport of illusion because of the role conditioning plays in how big a physique looks. For example, a ripped bodybuilder may appear much bigger onstage than he actually is. Proper proportions and symmetry also make a body appear much larger. However, competing in a ripped condition always makes the physique look much bigger. As my brother, Don, always told me as I prepared for a competition, "The more 'stuff' (definition and cuts) that pops out at the audience when a bodybuilder poses, the bigger and more impressive he will look when posing."

A bodybuilder dieting for a contest must keep in mind how important definition is for winning a competition. Eating a reduced calorie diet for months at a time is difficult for any bodybuilder, regardless of his experience and background. Going off the diet or eating more calories than are recommended is common. But realizing how critical it is to compete ripped is the motivation that keeps bodybuilders on the strictest diets so they can realize their goals.

You cannot control who your competition will be or how the judges will assess your physique at a competition. You can, however, control what type of condition you display at the contest. How your physique will look is completely up to you. Remember this during the sometimes long and difficult dieting process, and you will show up looking like a winner!

Losing Fat, Not Muscle

The key to achieving peak condition for a bodybuilding contest is to lose only fat while maintaining muscle mass during a dieting phase. This is a tricky process that requires the right diet and the right amount of exercise. Preparing for a contest without using steroids or other drugs makes it even more difficult because there is no room for mistakes.

Drugs such as anabolic steroids, growth hormone, and antiagonists such as clenbuterol help the competitive bodybuilder achieve peak condition by holding onto the muscle mass while decreasing the body fat. Natural bodybuilders who do not use these drugs must achieve this condition solely through diet and exercise. Therefore, the bodybuilders who use the drugs have it much easier than the natural bodybuilders.

The first rule in dieting for a bodybuilding competition is to lose the fat very slowly. A bodybuilder using drugs such as steroids can eat a diet that is very low in calories and carbohydrate without losing as much muscle mass as a natural bodybuilder. These drugs do an amazing job of helping you maintain muscle mass and strength even while you're on a low-calorie, low-carbohydrate diet.

Natural bodybuilders cannot risk losing muscle mass during precontest dieting, so they need to lose fat slowly. Whenever you drastically reduce body weight, the majority of the weight lost will probably be muscle and not fat. The human body always sacrifices muscle over fat when it comes to weight loss. This is because of a survival mechanism designed to hold on to the fat to prevent the possibility of starving in the absence of food. The only way to reverse this trend is to give the body a reason to hold on to the muscle (intense resistance training) and feed it in a way that makes it shed fat and not muscle.

When losing weight for competition, you do not want to lose more than one to one and a half pounds per week. More than this will most likely result in lost muscle tissue. To regulate weight loss, you need to know exactly how many calories you consume every day and adjust them until you're sure you're losing only body fat. You should know how many calories it takes to gain weight, maintain weight, and lose weight. This will require experimentation the first time you diet, but knowing how many calories you are eating before beginning a diet gives you a good reference point.

The number of calories in a precompetition diet is different for each person. It depends on the speed of your metabolism, the amount of muscle tissue you have, your daily activity level, your age, and your body type. A 170-pound, 22-year-old ectomorph who works construction needs a lot more calories than a 200-pound, 37-year-old mesomorph who works in an office.

Another method for losing fat while retaining muscle mass is giving yourself enough time to diet before the competition. When I competed in my first drug-tested bodybuilding contest, I gave myself just eight weeks to prepare. As the contest got closer, I saw that I would not be ready in time, so I resorted to drastic measures—five or six days a week of cardio, twice a day—to speed up the fat-loss process. Although I looked good enough for second place, my muscles were flat because of the excess cardio, and I did not hit my peak. When I returned to the same competition a year later, I dieted for 16 weeks to slowly lose the fat and maintain the muscle. This time, the dieting process worked perfectly. I was ready for the competition a week or two ahead of time. This extra time allowed me to eat more calories while I lost body fat, which meant my muscles were fuller and not flat for the competition.

Another way to retaining muscle mass while losing body fat is to make small changes to the diet. After you have established the correct number of calories, you will inevitably have to make changes in the diet as you progress through the precontest preparation. These small adjustments are part of the preparation process. If you stick to your original diet with no changes whatsoever, you probably will not hit your peak for the contest because the body changes throughout the dieting process. You may need to decrease the calories, increase the cardio, increase the calories, or decrease the cardio as the contest gets closer. It all depends on how your metabolism changes as your body begins to lose fat and possibly gain muscle. You must stay flexible.

In 1992, I competed in three competitions about a month apart from each other. The first contest was the Natural Illinois in which I had placed second the year before. I was looking forward to winning it all in 1992. The second was the Natural Mr. North America, and I needed to win at least my height class to qualify for the Natural Mr. Universe to be held in California three weeks later.

I dieted 16 weeks for the first competition followed by 4 more weeks for the second competition, then 3 more weeks before the last contest. This totaled 23 weeks of dieting. I was going to have to make adjustments in my diet as I prepared for these three contests because my body would be constantly changing during this process.

For the first contest, the Natural Illinois, I kept my calories pretty constant because I was dieting to lose body fat. Because I was fairly lean to begin with and had 16 weeks to lose the fat, I did not need to do cardio to get ready for this first competition. I hit my peak for the contest, showing up in hard condition but still full. I won my weight class but lost the overall to the lightweight competitor who was slightly harder than I was.

Here's what my diet looked like on Sunday, Sept. 13, 1992, approximately five weeks out from the contest:

Meal 1:	10 egg whites, 1 cup oatmeal, 1 cup pineapple juice, 1 slice dry whole-wheat toast
Meal 2:	2 servings protein powder, 6 ounces baby food, 1 banana (preworkout)
Meal 3:	Carbohydrate drink (postworkout)
Meal 4:	3.5 ounces flank steak, 2 ounces whole-wheat pasta, 2 ounces pasta sauce, 1 slice whole-wheat bread.
Meal 5:	7.5 ounces chicken breast, 6 ounces baked potato, 2.5 ounces oat bran cereal
Meal 6:	1 serving protein powder, 1 banana, 1/3 cup oat bran, 1 slice whole-wheat bread
Totals:	Calories 2,891, protein 212.7 grams, carbohydrate 447 grams, fat 28 grams
Breakdown:	Protein 29%, carbohydrate 62%, fat 9%

After the Natural Illinois contest I decided to increase my caloric intake. I had just dieted hard for 16 weeks, and my body needed a break. If I had continued to diet another four weeks, my body no doubt would hit a sticking point. In fact, for the first week after the contest I had at least one meal per day in which I ate whatever I wanted with no limitations.

After the first week, I went back on a strict diet but ate 300 to 400 more calories than before the first competition. Because I was lean and essentially fat-free, I was eating to keep the muscles full while maintaining my level of body fat.

Here's what my diet looked like on Wednesday, Nov. 18, 1992, three days before the Natural Mr. North America:

Meal 1:	10 egg whites, 1 cup oatmeal, 1 slice whole-wheat toast, 1 cup pineapple juice
Meal 2:	1 serving protein powder, 1/2 banana
Meal 3:	3.5 ounces turkey, 3 rice cakes
Meal 4:	1 serving protein powder, 1/2 banana, 3.5 ounces granola
Meal 5:	6 ounces chicken breast, 180 grams sweet potato
Meal 6:	6 ounces baby food (preworkout)
Meal 7:	Carbo Force drink containing 100 grams of carbohydrates and a Perfect Bar, which is a meal replacement bar containing protein and carbs.
Meal 8:	4 ounces flank steak, 1 cup brown rice, 3 ounces vegetable salad, 2 tablespoons low-fat Italian dressing
Meal 9:	1 serving protein powder, 1 banana, 1/3 cup oat bran, 3 rice cakes
Totals:	Calories 3,515, protein 241 grams, carbohydrate 544.8 grams, fat 41.3 grams
Breakdown:	Protein 27%, carbohydrate 62%, fat 11%

After this many weeks of dieting, my metabolism had increased to the point that I was eating nine small meals. Every time I ate a meal, my metabolism increased. I was so lean that I was in the ideal situation of feeding the muscles and starving the fat. I felt fuller than when I was dieting down for the Natural Illinois. Because I was already low in fat, my diet wasn't focused on simply losing the fat, but more on feeding the muscles to keep my metabolism revved up and my percentage of body fat low.

For the Natural North America in San Francisco, my weight was up to 200 pounds, about 4 more than I carried at the Natural Illinois. I felt I could have been a little tighter, but my muscles were much fuller with increased vascularity. When it was all over, I ended up with almost all the first-place trophies. I won the medium height class, the most muscular award, and the overall.

After the contest, I talked to a couple of the judges and some of the competitors who had competed in the ABA (American Bodybuilders Association) organization in the past. After they complimented me on my win, they warned me that the Natural Universe would be much tougher, and I would need to be harder if I wanted to win that contest.

When I got back home to Illinois, I was totally psyched up. If I did everything right, I was only three weeks away from achieving my lifetime goal! After eating basically whatever I wanted on Saturday night and all day Sunday, I went back on my diet Monday, but I lowered the calories to an average of 3,000 per day. I varied the calories by eating 2,800 the first day, 3,200 the second, and 3,000 the third. I wanted to make sure I was really ripped when I got onstage at the Universe.

Here's what I ate on Thursday, Dec. 10, 1992, two days before the contest:

Meal 1:	5.75 ounces chicken breast, 1 cup oatmeal, 1 slice whole-wheat bread, 1 cup pineapple juice
Meal 2:	1 serving protein powder, 65 grams banana
Meal 3:	3.25 ounces turkey, 3 rice cakes
Meal 4:	1 serving protein powder, 65 grams banana, 3.5 ounces granola
Meal 5:	6.5 ounces chicken breast, 240 grams baked potato
Meal 6:	2.5 ounces flank steak, 1 cup brown rice, 1 slice whole-wheat bread
Meal 7:	1 serving protein powder, 130 grams banana, 190 grams baked potato
Meal 8:	1 serving protein powder, 115 grams banana, 1/3 cup oat bran, 2 ounces granola
Totals:	Calories 3,128, protein 248 grams, carbohydrate 457.5 grams, fat 34 grams
Breakdown:	Protein 32%, carbohydrate 58%, fat 10%

One benefit of adding meals was that it let me increase my protein intake even though my overall calories were still around 3,000. I was still eating a lot carbohydrate, but during the last few days before competing, I decreased my sodium intake so my skin would get as tight as possible. I didn't eat egg whites for breakfast because they are loaded with sodium. I also decreased my water intake except for the protein drinks.

After three weeks of dieting with lower calories but still eating eight meals per day, I was noticeably harder. The skin on my lower abs, usually the last area to come in, was as tight as a drum. Surprisingly, my muscles were still very full. My pecs in particular, an area that tends to flatten quickly when dieting, were still full and thick. I felt very confident when I got on the plane to go to L.A. to compete in the Universe.

To my delight, I won it all at the Natural Mr. Universe in California! I took first place in the medium height class, won the most muscular trophy, and won the overall title. Onstage, my skin was tight, and I had great vascularity with fullness in all the muscle groups. I was as full as I was for the North America, but even tighter than I was for the Natural Illinois.

When it comes time to make precompetition changes, make small adjustments instead of drastic jumps. If you are eating 3,000 calories a day and are not losing fat fast enough, try dropping your calories to 2,800 and see what happens. If you are doing cardio three days a week for 30 minutes each session, don't jump to six days a week right off the bat. Try four days a week and note the changes. These small adjustments should allow the body to coax more fat loss without sacrificing muscle tissue. If you give yourself plenty of time to prepare before the contest, you can make small changes in your diet or training without the pressure of a competition only weeks away.

How to Develop a Fat-Loss Diet

The precompetition diet makes or breaks a bodybuilder. To win a bodybuilding contest, drug-free or not, a bodybuilder must be ripped and fat-free, and the diet determines conditioning on contest day. For a natural bodybuilder, nutrition is even more important because there are no drugs to help retain muscle mass, lose body fat, or shed excess water. A natural bodybuilder needs a perfect diet.

Caloric Intake

As a natural bodybuilder getting ready to compete, your first priority is to establish your caloric needs. You must know how many calories you need to eat to lose body fat slowly and consistently. A diet too low in calories sacrifices muscle tissue for energy and eventually slows metabolism. A diet too high in calories does not encourage fat loss fast enough and prevents you from reaching peak condition.

As discussed in the first section, write down everything that has to do with diet. Weigh your food portions and record the number of calories, protein, carbohydrate, and fat you consume each day. Several weeks before you begin your precontest diet, start recording your daily diet. If you don't follow this important first step, you won't know where to begin when the precontest diet starts.

In my case, I know that if I eat approximately 2,800 to 3,000 calories per day, I will slowly and consistently lose body fat. I've followed this diet for as long as 20 weeks without slowing my metabolism or losing appreciable muscle. It doesn't matter how heavy I am in the off-season or how many calories I am used to consuming, I need to reduce to an average of 3,000 calories per day, no higher and no lower, to lose fat and maintain muscle mass.

I mention caloric intake as the most important first step because dieting confuses many bodybuilders. They mistakenly believe that if they cut carbohydrate low enough or eat a lot of protein, or drink a lot of water, they will get ripped. Protein, carbohydrate, water, and other macronutrients are important, but the first consideration must be the number of calories consumed. In 1996, I was eating the perfect combination of protein, carbohydrate, and fat when I began my precontest diet, but my caloric intake was still too high, and I was not losing fat fast enough. I didn't start getting ripped until I lowered my calories to 3,000 per day.

If you've never dieted, you may have to experiment before you determine your optimal caloric intake. A good starting point is to record your daily diet in the off-season when you are gaining or even maintaining your weight. Then you will have a reference point when you begin dieting for your contest. If you know how many calories you need to maintain your body weight, begin by lowering that amount by 300 to 500 calories per day and go from there. It's also very important to monitor your condition and body weight daily to determine if you are losing too much muscle or not enough fat.

Protein

When putting together a precontest diet, protein requirement is the first area you should look at. Protein is important because it is the only macronutrient that repairs and rebuilds muscle tissue. Because maintaining muscle mass is one of your primary goals as a competitive bodybuilder, eat protein throughout the day to maintain a positive nitrogen balance to maintain and build muscle mass.

As discussed in chapter 4, intensely training bodybuilders should eat between 1.25 and 1.5 grams of protein for each pound of body weight. Using these guidelines, a 200-pound bodybuilder must eat between 250 to 300 grams of protein per day, or six meals with 42 to 50 grams of protein each. This equals approximately 1,100 calories per day (or 37 percent of a 3,000-calorie diet). It is important to know the number of calories from protein when your total number of calories is limited.

Some bodybuilders eat the same foods all day when dieting for a competition. However, all complete protein (meat, eggs, poultry, fish, chicken, and dairy products) contain different ratios of amino acids. Therefore, eating a variety of protein sources each day makes sure your body gets a varied source of amino acids. A bodybuilder dieting for a contest could eat egg whites for breakfast, chicken for lunch, turkey in the late afternoon, flank steak in the evening, and tuna fish before bed. Of course, he may also consume various protein drinks throughout the day for an additional source of protein. This is a much better plan than simply eating chicken six times a day.

To properly digest and assimilate protein, bodybuilders should eat six to nine small meals per day every two and a half to three hours. This keeps the body in a positive nitrogen balance and constantly feeds the muscle cells with high-quality protein and amino acids. It also prevents indigestion and eating more protein than the body can handle.

Fitting that many meals into a busy workday can be a challenge, but it can be done. Let's look at an example of a personal trainer who must meet with clients, do his own workout, and follow a diet that will help him reach peak condition.

Here is how he could schedule his meals:

5:00 a.m.	1 serving of whey protein in water with 1 tablespoon of glutamine
5:30 a.m.	Personal training appointment
7:00 a.m.	Breakfast
9:00 a.m.	Personal training appointment
9:30 a.m.	Protein drink
10:00 a.m.	Personal training appointment
11:30 a.m.	Preworkout drink

12:30 p.m.	Workout
2:00 p.m.	Postworkout drink
2:30 p.m.	Lunch
5:00 p.m.	Dinner
5:30 p.m.	Personal training appointment
7:30 p.m.	Protein drink and personal training appointment
8:30 p.m.	Personal training appointment

Despite having six appointments, the trainer was able to maintain his diet and eat every two and a half hours. He accomplished this by consuming protein drinks during appointments and moving his dinner earlier in the evening than usual. It takes some juggling, but if you're flexible, you can make it work.

Some bodybuilders believe that the more protein they eat, as much as 600 grams per day, the bigger their muscles will get. This is a ridiculous assumption. Unless you are taking steroids, which forces the body to use more protein by preventing the liver from eliminating it, your body can use only so much protein at a time before excreting it as waste. However, natural bodybuilders do not need excessive amounts of protein. In fact, too much protein forces a bodybuilder to cut back on his carbohydrate and fat intake so he doesn't exceed his caloric requirements. Because protein is an inefficient source of energy and only so much protein can be used to rebuild muscle tissue, it is clearly a waste of time to eat more than 1.5 grams of protein for each pound of body weight.

The best sources of protein are low-fat complete protein such as egg whites, chicken breast, extra-lean turkey breast, albacore tuna, salmon, haddock, flank steak, round steak, and protein powder. These foods provide the amino acids that rebuild muscle tissue, and they help you maintain muscle size during the dieting phase.

Protein powders offer another alternative. There are many protein powders on the market. Whey protein has a higher rating for protein efficiency than soy, milk, or egg protein powders. Recent research, however, shows that whey protein may be absorbed too quickly, which means blood sugar levels may drop soon after the whey protein is digested. This is bad news for a precontest bodybuilder who needs to keep his blood sugar levels steady throughout the day. New protein powders combine whey protein with the more slowly absorbed milk protein. The combination of these two complete protein sources, one fast and one slow, allows the protein to be absorbed and assimilated more effectively.

Carbohydrate

Carbohydrate is your body's primary source of energy. Carbohydrate is also the one macronutrient you must vary depending on if your goal is to lose or gain weight. Lately, many bodybuilders consider carbohydrate the evil ingredient that prevents them from getting ripped. Despite their recent bad press, they are essential in a bodybuilder's diet, precontest or off-season.

Complex carbohydrate is said to be "protein sparing," which means that if enough carbohydrate is available as an energy source, the body will not have to use protein for fuel. But if the body is low in carbohydrate, it may have to break down muscle tissue to steal amino acids for energy. You do not want to lose size and strength before you ever set foot onstage.

Many bodybuilders cut their carbohydrate intake, but increase their fat intake so that they'll have a source of energy and spare the protein for its muscle-building benefits. Because dietary fat is the most likely macronutrient to be absorbed and stored as body fat and because it contains twice the number of calories that protein or carbohydrate do (a gram of fat contains nine calories and a gram of protein or carbohydrate contains four calories per gram), it is a mistake to cut carbohydrate and increase fat. Besides, it is more difficult for the body to break down fatty acids than carbohydrate for energy. The key to utilizing carbohydrate in a precontest diet is moderation. If you follow several rules, you will become ripped and fat-free while eating carbohydrate.

The first rule is to cut out simple sugar. Eating too much simple sugar, especially on an empty stomach, causes the pancreas to release high levels of insulin to take care of the sugar and shuttle it off to the fat cells for storage. Fat mobilization is also put on hold any time the insulin level rises too high. For this reason, the insulin level must remain steady. If it drops too low and there is not enough carbohydrate in the system, the body may search for amino acids in the muscles to use as energy.

The second rule in eating carbohydrate in a precontest diet is to eat only complex, low-glycemic sources. Low-glycemic carbohydrate is absorbed slowly into the bloodstream. Foods to eat when attempting to lose body fat are oatmeal, brown rice, baked potatoes, sweet potatoes, whole-wheat pasta, oat bran, and vegetables.

Another good rule to follow is to eat some type of fiber with each meal. Many of the sources just listed also contain high amounts of fiber. Fiber slows the digestive rate, which limits the insulin reaction. Anything that helps to keep the blood sugar level steady (frequent meals throughout the day; complex, low-glycemic carbohydrate; high fiber) will help mobilize the fatty acids from the fat cells because this mobilization takes place only in an absence of insulin in the bloodstream.

The last rule to follow when eating carbohydrate in a precontest diet is to limit your portions with each meal. Small amounts of complex, low-glycemic carbohydrate that contain ample amounts of fiber will supply the glycogen you need for intense weight training sessions, without causing a large secretion of insulin.

It's also important to eat carbohydrate with protein because combining these macronutrients slows the insulin reaction. In fact, the whole glycemic index factor is skewed when combining carbohydrate with protein because it affects how the foods are digested.

Most bodybuilders can follow these rules and shed subcutaneous fat slowly and consistently. However, some individuals with very slow metabolisms, classified as endomorphs, cannot get cut unless they eat a low-fat, low-carbohydrate diet. These bodybuilders should eat more fibrous carbohydrate foods such as raw and steamed vegetables and fewer starchy sources such as oatmeal and baked potatoes. If you must eat starch, eat it in the morning or early afternoon. Fat cells are more sensitive to insulin output in the evening. Endomorphs should also eat slightly more protein to avoid the muscle catabolism that may occur with a low carbohydrate intake. If your metabolism is normal or slightly fast, you should include carbohydrate in your precontest diet.

Fat

The last macronutrient is fat. Because fat contains twice the number of calories as either protein or carbohydrate, you must keep it low during a precontest diet. All animal protein foods such as chicken, steak, turkey, and fish contain some fat. So, it's not difficult to get 10 percent of your calories from fat.

Essential fatty acids are important to many body functions and, unlike saturated or trans fatty acids, which can contribute to poor health, are beneficial to the heart and the cardiovascular systems. Essential fatty acids, or Omega-3 fatty acids, are found in vegetable oils and fatty fish.

An easy way to add essential fatty acids to your diet is to add flaxseed oil to your protein drinks. The extra fat also helps in fatty acid mobilization because it slows the digestion of the protein drink and inhibits some of the insulin reaction.

Omega-3s also increase the glutamine levels in the muscle cells. Glutamine is an extremely important amino acid that makes up 50 to 60 percent of the total amino acids in the muscle cells. This amino acid also helps to build the immune system, which is vital to the bodybuilder, especially when going through the stress of precontest training and nutrition.

A good rule of thumb is to eat fatty fish such as salmon for dinner at least three times per week when getting ready to compete. Actually, this is a good practice to follow all year because this fish contributes to good health and muscle growth. Eat lean red meat such as flank steak on the other days. Lean red meat is a good source of B vitamins and creatine. Too much red meat is high in fat, but four to five ounces is acceptable, especially in the context of a very low-fat diet.

Water

Water speeds the digestion and elimination of waste products, and it helps in the transportation and storage of many important nutrients such as protein, carbohydrate, and creatine. A dehydrated bodybuilder cannot grow or take advantage of the nutrients he consumes.

In the precontest period, water is even more important. It helps in eliminating waste products including the lactic acid produced by the intense weight training sessions. Drinking sufficient water, at least two gallons a day, will help your muscles recuperate more quickly, and they won't stay sore as long as usual, even when training intensely for a contest.

Also, water is the only liquid you can drink with zero calories. Coffee and tea contain high amounts of caffeine and should be consumed in moderation, if at all. Soda pop is obviously off-limits because it contains simple sugar and other chemicals. Even diet soda is loaded with sodium, which can affect the electrolyte balance. A hard-training athlete is better off with water. Needless to say, alcohol would not be included in a precontest diet for a bodybuilder getting ready to compete.

Water also helps to curb the appetite. Low-fat foods eaten in moderation will not fill the stomach for long. Even eating several meals a day spaced only three hours apart will not satisfy the hunger of a hard-training bodybuilder. Drinking lots of water in between meals, however, helps keep the appetite in check and prevents cheating or eating excessive calories by keeping the stomach full.

As with other aspects of the diet, timing is everything. Drinking too much water while you are eating interferes with the natural digestive process and the enzymes normally produced. Instead, drink lots of water between meals but start reducing the intake about 30 minutes before eating. Afterward, wait about an hour, then start drinking liberal amounts of water again.

I drink water purified by reverse osmosis. Tap water is likely to contain too many impurities for an athlete attempting to reach peak condition. Spring water is not closely regulated, so there is no guarantee that the water is as clean as the label indicates.

Precontest Diet

Now let's look at a typical precontest diet and break it down.

Meal 1: 11 egg whites (complete protein)
1 cup oatmeal (complex carbohydrate and fiber)
1 cup blueberries (carbohydrate plus some fiber)
1/2 cup pineapple juice (small amount of simple carbohydrate in the morning)

Meal 2: 2 servings protein powder (fast- and slow-acting complete protein)
1/2 banana (carbohydrate and potassium)
1 tablespoon flaxseed oil (essential fatty acid)

Meal 3: 4 ounces extra lean turkey breast (complete protein)
1/2 cup brown rice (complex carbohydrate and fiber)
1 cup fat-free vegetable soup or chili (complex carbohydrate and fiber)

Meal 4: 1 serving of meal replacement (complete protein source plus carbohydrate, essential fat, and vitamins)
1/2 banana (carbohydrate and potassium)
1 tablespoon flaxseed oil (essential fatty acid)

Meal 5: Postworkout meal
Carbohydrate drink (simple and complex carbohydrate)
2 servings whey protein powder (fast-acting protein)
1 or 2 servings creatine

Meal 6: 4 ounces flank steak or salmon (complete protein)
50 grams whole-wheat pasta (complex carbohydrate)
40 grams fat-free pasta sauce (small amount of carbohydrate)
vegetable salad (complex carbohydrate plus fiber)

Meal 7: 2 servings Profusion protein powder (fast- and slow-acting complete protein)
1/2 banana (carbohydrate and potassium)
1 serving oat bran (complex carbohydrate and fiber)

This precontest diet contains 3,186 calories with 307 grams of protein, 359 grams of carbohydrate, and 58 grams of fat. It breaks down to 39 percent protein, 45 percent carbohydrate, and 16 percent fat. The frequent meals help to keep the metabolism racing. This is important because when you reduce calories over a long period, your metabolism tends to slow to keep the body weight stable. Remember, the body always resists change. But by lowering the calories very slowly and increasing the number of meals, your metabolism will not slow, and the fat loss will continue.

The difference between a precontest diet and an off-season diet is the number of calories and amount of simple carbohydrate. Bodybuilders eat more calories in the off-season, as much as 1,000 more, and usually don't keep as tight a rein on their simple carbohydrate intake.

Precontest diets have changed over the years. In the 1980s, it was common for carbohydrate to make up the majority of a bodybuilder's calories. As time went on, however, bodybuilders began reducing their carbohydrate intake and increasing their protein. For my more recent natural bodybuilding competitions, I ate almost as much protein as I did carbohydrate. While this type of diet can only be followed for a limited time, it allowed me to enter my competition with the lowest amount of body fat possible.

Dietary fat intake has increased also. In the 1980s, extremely low fat intake was common. Now, we know that diets too low in fat (less than 10 percent of the total calories) can slow metabolism and prevent the body from reaching an ultraripped condition. For my last competition, I increased my fat intake to 15 percent by adding flaxseed oil to my protein drinks. Bodybuilders who eat a diet even lower in carbohydrate may increase the percentage of calories consumed from fat to 20 percent of total calories.

The following are the main points to remember during a precontest diet:

- Establish your caloric intake.
- Eat enough protein.
- Eat a variety of protein sources.
- Don't eliminate carbohydrate from your diet.
- Follow certain rules in eating carbohydrate.
- Include essential fat in your diet.
- Drink plenty of water daily.

The key to getting ripped while retaining muscle mass is to increase your metabolism. The faster your metabolism, the leaner you will be. A slow metabolism prevents the fat loss necessary to win a bodybuilding competition. A racing metabolism not only allows you to reduce fat levels to single digits, but it also allows you to retain your muscle mass. Two excellent methods of increasing your metabolism are to eat more meals and to add cardio to your training program.

• Eat frequent meals. Every time you consume a meal, your body must work to digest and metabolize those calories. The energy used in digestion stimulates metabolism. As part of your normal routine, you should be accustomed to eating six times a day. When you begin dieting, you will continue eating six meals a day but with reduced calories. In the beginning, this initial reduction in calories should be enough to stimulate fat loss. With only a slight reduction in calories, the body may eventually reach a plateau after it becomes accustomed to the new level of calories. Instead of lowering the calories even more, which may slow metabolism, your best option is to add meals while keeping the number of calories constant. Eating and digesting two extra meals will help stimulate metabolism. However, when eating more frequently, alternate protein drinks or smaller meals with normal-sized meals. Eating two larger meals back to back only two hours apart may interfere with digestion, which would not stimulate metabolism.

- Use cardio workouts to burn fat. Cardiovascular exercise such as walking, bike riding, and stair climbing stimulate metabolism by burning fat and creating a leaner body. First thing in the morning, late at night, and immediately after a weight training workout seem to be the best times for burning body fat while retaining muscle. Many bodybuilders overdo the cardio when training for a competition and trying to get as ripped as possible. The problem with this, however, is that it may sacrifice muscle with fat. Bodybuilders who use steroids and other anabolic or anticatabolic drugs can retain more muscle while doing lots of cardio exercise. But natural bodybuilders need to find the right balance of cardio exercise and fat loss if they want to retain muscle mass. The correct amount of cardio combined with a reduced-calorie diet can help a bodybuilder achieve single-digit body-fat percentages.

Eating the proper balance of the right foods is the first step to precontest preparation. The next chapter looks at workouts, including fat-burning cardio, that will let you step on stage ripped and ready to go.

Precontest Training

When a bodybuilder prepares for a contest, he or she faces the very difficult task of maintaining the size and strength developed over the off-season while simultaneously dieting to eliminate fat and water. This is the natural bodybuilder's greatest challenge—holding on to all or most muscle mass while getting ripped.

Steroids help you maintain muscle mass while surviving a low-calorie diet. They also keep strength sky-high even when subsisting on barely enough calories to feed a cat. Therefore, a lot of bodybuilders who use steroids to prepare for competition know much less about dieting and training than drug-free bodybuilders do. They don't need to know as much because the drugs do most of the work. Maintaining muscle mass and strength while dieting so strictly that you can't even remember your name—that's just not natural!

Heavy Training to Maintain Muscle

One of the most important points to remember when training for a competition is to continue to train as heavy as possible. Of course, when you reduce calories, at some point it becomes impossible to use the same heavy weights you used in the off-season, no matter how much you try. Inevitably you will have to lift slightly less. But you must not change the training philosophy of "big weights for big muscles." Training with light to moderate weights because you are getting ready for a contest does not work.

If you diet correctly, you should experience no major fluctuation in strength levels from the off-season to precontest training. If you normally bench press 315 for six reps in the off-season and drop to 225 for six reps while dieting, either you have lost too much weight in the form of muscle, or you are eating so few calories that you are using muscle tissue for energy. Whatever the case, something is drastically wrong. Training with light weights when preparing for a contest because you heard it will "burn the cuts in" will most likely cause you to lose size. Muscles only grow from the stimulation you subject them to. Therefore, if your chest muscles are accustomed to pushing 315 pounds in the bench press and you lighten the load by 90 pounds, the pectoral muscles will respond by decreasing in size and strength. A bodybuilder using steroids could probably get away with this type of training for a limited time because the drugs maintain muscle tissue even in the most extreme circumstances of limiting calories and performing "pump" workouts. However, a natural bodybuilder cannot afford to train this way.

When preparing for competition, your training weights will inevitably drop slightly. This is especially true toward the end of the diet, but you must fight it every step of the way. Attempt to go as heavy as you can every workout leading up to the contest. Your squats may drop from 425 pounds to 405 pounds, and your bench press may drop from 335 pounds to 315 pounds, but these are small decreases, and your muscles will barely notice them. Be sure to record all of your workouts. That way, if there is a big drop in weight, you can take immediate steps to discover the reason and adjust your training or diet. You can try training a little faster, taking less rest between sets, to make up for the slight decrease in workout weights. I did this in 1996 when training for the Natural Mr. Universe contest. That particular year, however, I was the heaviest I had ever been when I began dieting, 243 pounds, and didn't object to training faster to burn a few more calories and pump up my metabolism. Even with the faster pace, however, I still trained as heavy as possible. Remember, a weight training session should be anaerobic, and endurance training should be done on a treadmill, not a squat rack.

Training with shorter rest periods is a great way to increase training intensity. You can also use it occasionally in the off-season to give your joints a rest from training with heavy weights. However, precontest is not a good time to experiment with this because your weights will invariably drop. As a natural bodybuilder you will have enough trouble maintaining muscle mass while limiting calories without decreasing your normal resistance.

Training Frequency

One of the biggest mistakes natural bodybuilders make when preparing for a contest is to follow the same training routines that bodybuilders taking steroids do. They increase the volume of their workouts by adding sets, exercises, and even workouts under the assumption that the more time they spend in the gym, the more calories they will burn, and the more defined they will appear onstage.

A natural bodybuilder's goal when preparing for a contest is to hold on to their muscle mass while losing body fat. Increasing your training volume through additional sets, exercises, or workouts puts you at risk of asking your body to do more than it can handle. Because the main function of anabolic steroids is to aid in recuperation, a bodybuilder using drugs can actually overtrain and respond better because of the steroids.

A bodybuilder is not an endurance athlete. Endurance athletes like long distance runners eat a tremendous number of calories to fuel their incredibly long workouts, not to maintain the maximum amount of muscle mass on their bodies. In fact, they try to carry only enough mass, mostly in the legs, to produce an efficient stride. Anything else is extra weight that reduces their speed. Their goal is to train their cardiovascular and energy systems so that they can run as quickly as possible as long as possible. Excess muscle mass is counterproductive.

A bodybuilder, on the other hand, couldn't care less about his endurance or cardiovascular shape. He is only concerned with the amount of lean muscle mass on his physique. Why, then, do some bodybuilders use some of the training methods of a sport with opposing goals? If you want to compete with the maximum amount of muscle mass and the least amount of body fat, then train and diet for those goals and those goals only. Don't train to increase your endurance; that is not a goal of a competitive bodybuilder.

For these reasons, natural bodybuilders should train a maximum of five days per week when preparing for a competition. Of course, this is only for the weight training. The "off days" may be devoted to cardiovascular training. Advanced bodybuilders train each target area only once a week and intermediate bodybuilders probably train each target area twice a week.

Don't train more than two or three days in a row without taking a day off from weights. Training every day of the week, one target area per day, does not leave time for the body as a whole to recuperate. If you train chest on Monday, legs on Tuesday, deltoids and traps on Wednesday, back on Thursday, and arms on Friday before taking a day off from the gym, you run the risk of overtraining. Even though this routine allows six days of rest for each area of the body, it still subjects your body to six straight days of intense training. This is too much for a natural bodybuilder, especially if the workouts are hard and heavy as they should be.

A better routine for a natural bodybuilder getting ready for a contest should look something like this:

Monday	Chest, triceps, and calves
Tuesday	Legs and abs
Wednesday	Off day
Thursday	Shoulders and calves
Friday	Back, biceps, and abs
Saturday	Off day

This routine allows the body to recuperate after only two heavy workouts in the gym. Remember, you are already stressing your body by dieting. To subject the body to further stress by training every day increases your chances of becoming overtrained and losing valuable muscle tissue. Retaining your muscle tissue while simultaneously increasing the separation and hardness of the individual muscles should be your primary goal for precontest training.

Double-Split Training

Keeping this goal in mind, it makes no sense for a natural bodybuilder to train twice a day while preparing for competition. In double-split training the bodybuilder trains a large muscle group in the morning, then returns to the gym later to train one or two smaller muscle groups. The theory behind double-split training is that it allows a dieting bodybuilder with low energy to train one target area, go home to rest, eat a few meals, and return to the gym in the evening to train several smaller muscle groups.

At first glance, double split training provides two major benefits. It burns more calories because you raise the metabolism twice a day instead of once. And it allows you to train each target area intensely because you're resting and refueling between workouts for large muscle groups rather than training one muscle group intensely, then running out of energy for the subsequent muscles trained in the same session.

However, what proponents of this training philosophy forget is that you are training the system as a whole each time you're in the gym. Training twice a day will most likely lead to overtraining because your body has a limited amount of resources, especially if you are limiting calories. If you increase your calories thinking that you will burn them up in the gym, then you are making the mistake of following the training routine of an endurance athlete and not a bodybuilder. The best strategy is to train heavy and hard and get out of the gym until you are fully recuperated and ready to go back. This is the routine a bodybuilder attempting to increase his mass should follow, and this is the routine a bodybuilder attempting to maintain muscle mass while dieting to lose body fat should follow.

If you are eating correctly, you should have plenty of energy to train a major area and one or two smaller muscle groups in one 90-minute session. If it takes longer than that to train abs and legs, or chest, triceps and calves, then you are performing too many sets or taking too long between sets.

Double-split training is very popular among professional bodybuilders, and the reason for this is obvious. They are taking anabolic steroids and other drugs to help them recuperate. The supplemented muscles thrive on the extra work.

Basic Exercises for Precontest Training

Along with training heavy up to the day of the contest, as a natural bodybuilder you should also continue performing the basic exercises in your training routine. Just because you are getting ready to compete is no reason to drop the effective movements that helped develop the muscle mass in the first place. The basic exercises help you retain muscle mass as you diet. If you stop doing the basics, you risk losing size as the contest gets nearer. Include the following basic exercises in your precontest workouts:

- Chest: Barbell bench press, incline dumbbell press, dumbbell bench press, incline barbell press, dumbbell pullovers
- Back: Wide-grip chins to the front, barbell rows, one-arm dumbbell rows, seated cable rows, deadlifts, partial deadlifts
- Thighs: Squats, leg press, hack squats, stiff-leg deadlifts
- Deltoids: Seated barbell press, seated dumbbell press, upright rows, high pulls, barbell shrugs, dumbbell shrugs
- Triceps: Lying triceps extensions, seated triceps extensions, close-grip bench press, dips
- Biceps: Barbell curls, incline curls, seated dumbbell curls

The basic exercises work several muscle groups across several joints, which means you can use heavy weights, providing more potential for building and retaining muscle mass.

Isolation Exercises

Contest training is also the time to add exercises that isolate and peak-contract individual muscles. This is important for developing separation and delineation between the various muscles. Without this refinement, a bodybuilder, no matter how massive or symmetrical, will look more like a lump of clay than a perfectly sculpted work of art.

Perform isolation exercises with lighter weights and at a slower tempo than you perform basic exercises. Basic exercises must be executed explosively so that you can use the heaviest weights possible and stimulate the greatest number of muscle fibers. However, this process neglects many smaller, individual muscles. That is why you should add the following isolation exercises to your precontest training program.

Chest Cable exercises produce the ultimate peak contraction of the pecs. Barbells and dumbbells are great for handling big weights and building mass and power into the chest muscles, but cables isolate and target areas of the pectoral region that basic exercises neglect. Crossing the hands in front of the body during cable crossovers allows a greater peak contraction. This technique develops the hard-to-reach inner pecs and carves striations into them. You can manipulate the cables to work the upper, inner pecs; the middle, inner pecs; or the lower pecs. Three sets of 10 to 12 slow, peak-contracted reps at the end of a chest workout do the trick.

Cable crossovers.

Back The large back area is composed of many different muscles, both big and small. Well-developed small muscles in the upper back such as the infraspinatus, teres major, and rhomboids can add incredible detail to any pose from the rear. Although these muscles are trained to some degree during wide-grip chins, barbell rows, one-arm dumbbell rows, T-bar rows, and seated cable rows, the more powerful lats and traps do most of the work.

To stimulate these small, "cookie-cutter" muscles, add one or two extra exercises at the end of each back training session. To perform one-arm cable rows, grab a handle of a low pulley cable attached to moderate weight. Row the handle in the same manner as a one-arm dumbbell row, but bring the elbow higher to peak-contract the upper back muscles.

One-arm cable rows.

To perform a modified version of bent-over barbell rows, lie face down on an elevated, flat exercise bench. Do barbell rows with a reduced weight and bring the elbows slightly higher than normal. Try to peak-contract the rear delts and hold the top position for a couple of seconds before slowly lowering the weight.

Barbell rows on bench.

Speaking of rear delts, you can also use bent-over laterals in your back routine supersetted with barbell rows. This stimulates the small, upper-back muscles with a basic, mass-building exercise. In each of these isolation movements for the upper back, the elbow is back and up so it stays in line with the rear delts and upper back. This is in contrast to pulling the bar into the solar plexus to stress the belly of the lat muscle.

Chins and pull-downs are also great exercises for peak-contracting the upper-back muscles. Although these exercises are excellent for building width into the upper lats, they also bring out detail and separation in the upper back. Chins and pull-downs behind the neck are inferior to front chins and pull-downs to the front for building width, but they peak-contract the detail muscles of the upper back more effectively because the elbows are pulled to the rear.

Behind the neck pull-downs.

Delts Cables are the best way to bring out detail in the deltoid muscles. Exercises such as cable side laterals, cable bent-over laterals, and cable upright rows keep tension on the area of the muscle being worked in a way that barbells and dumbbells cannot. Use these exercises after you have bombed the delts with heavy barbell and dumbbell exercises. The deltoids will burn with the tension provided by the cables after being pumped with the basic exercises.

Cable side lateral raises.

Thighs Like in the back, the smaller, detailed muscles of the thighs are surrounded by larger, stronger muscles that dominate most of the work of heavy, basic exercises such as squats and leg presses. Isolation exercises stimulate and define these smaller muscles so they can stand out on their own.

Leg extensions are the primary movement used to separate the heads of the quadriceps muscle. Perform this exercise slowly, peak contracting the muscles hard. You can use heavy weights if you perform the exercise with proper form.

Sissy squats also separate the upper quadriceps muscle. Hold a plate against your chest and keep your upper body straight as you bend the knees and shift your weight forward onto the balls of the feet. Attempt to squat low enough to touch the glutes to the heels, providing a maximal stretch in the quadriceps. This exaggerated movement and extreme stretch in the upper thigh creates separation. Performing this exercise after heavy squats and leg presses makes you anything but a sissy.

Sissy squats.

The machine thigh adductor isolates, delineates, and develops the longest muscle in the body, the sartorius muscle in the inner thigh, by working it through its full range of motion. Although any of the quadriceps exercises, particularly those in which the feet are pointed out, works the sartorius muscle, this exercise isolates this muscle.

Machine thigh adductor.

An alternative to the thigh adductor exercise on the machine is the cable inner thigh adductor. Perform this exercise with the help of an ankle attachment that hooks onto the cable. Hold on to something for balance, stand on one leg, and pull the leg attached to the cable in front of and across your body. You will feel this exercise immediately in the sartorius muscle of the inner thigh.

Cable inner thigh adductor.

Standing cable extension.

Another great exercise for quadriceps separation is the standing cable extension. Using the same ankle attachment, stand on one leg and raise the leg attached to the cable so that the thigh is parallel to the floor. Holding on to a secure bar for balance, extend the leg, performing a leg extension movement. This exercise emphasizes the muscles of the upper thigh.

Lunges are also good for developing separation in the quads. These can be done with dumbbells or with a barbell across the shoulders. Lunges also hit the hamstrings and glutes. As with the other quads separation exercises, lunges are more effective when the quads are already fatigued from the basic exercises. Lunges also help develop the striations in this muscle group that are now the standard for being ripped.

Triceps Developing separation in the three heads of the triceps can make the muscle appear much larger than it really is. Check out Arnold's triceps development in his prime. Although not nearly as thick and developed as his incredible biceps were, his triceps appeared to be in proportion because they were separated and defined. Many exercises can help you develop triceps separation.

One-arm dumbbell triceps extension.

One of the best exercises is the one-arm dumbbell triceps extension, which requires more concentration and a slower tempo than working both arms simultaneously. Although this movement is not as effective for developing mass and thickness as seated triceps extensions or lying triceps extensions with a barbell, it is great for carving in delineation between the heads of the muscle.

Lying dumbbell triceps extensions bring out the outer head of the triceps. Lying triceps extensions with a barbell develop mass, but doing the exercise with dumbbells and positioning the hands so that the palms face each other stresses the outer head. This head of the triceps plays a significant role in the overall look of the arm.

Bench dips are another great exercise to develop the triceps, especially at contest time. This simple exercise adds fullness to the long inner head, which is crucial when posing the arms from the rear. To perform bench dips correctly, stand between two benches with your back to one. With your arms behind you, support yourself with your hands on the bench behind you and place your feet on the bench in front of you. Dip your hips as deep as you can between the benches, then push back up to the starting position with the power of your triceps. Some bodybuilders like to pile 45-pound plates on their laps (ouch!). But I prefer using just my body weight at the end of my workout for the ultimate pump.

Biceps Precontest, focus on exercises that showcase the brachialis muscle and stress the biceps peak. The brachialis muscle is the little knot of muscle on the outside of the arm that lies between the biceps and triceps. When fully developed, it adds depth and size and is very important in any pose that shows the outside of the arm.

Concentration curls develop the all-important peak on the biceps. Many bodybuilders do this exercise seated on a bench with the elbow tucked into the thigh, but you can also stand in a bent-over position with your arm hanging in front of you. This is more difficult because it requires more discipline and, of course, concentration to keep the arm straight while slowly squeezing the biceps. However, it places more stress on the outside head of the biceps, which is responsible for an impressively peaked arm.

When performed correctly and consistently, concentration curls can add a peak to any arm, even those with genetically short biceps. Look at early photos of Franco Columbu and note how much better his short biceps look later in his career thanks to the peak he developed through concentration curls.

Concentration curls.

Hammer curls are one of the primary exercises for developing the brachialis muscle because the pronated grip minimizes the contribution of the biceps and allows the brachialis to participate. Grab a dumbbell in each hand with the palms facing each other and curl one arm, maintaining the wrist position. Curl the forearm across the body toward the opposite shoulder. This stresses the brachialis even more than a traditional hammer curl.

Reverse barbell curls are another primary brachialis exercise. Grab a barbell with the palms facing down and curl the barbell up slowly, feeling the forearms and brachialis muscles working. You can also do reverse curls on a preacher bench. Heavy weights are not a priority.

Dumbbell preacher curls are a good alternative to barbell preacher curls. Working one arm at a time encourages more concentration and builds more of a peak to the biceps than the barbell equivalent. Barbell preacher curls build size, especially in the lower part of the muscle. But if you want to develop size and a great peak, use dumbbells when getting ready to compete.

Abdominals Although diet plays a big part in how much definition you display, the abdominal region is usually the center point of the physique when it comes to being in shape. Basic ab exercises such as sit-ups and leg raises work the overall abdominal region, but other movements develop the detail and refinement necessary for maximal definition.

Twisting crunches are a great exercise for the intercostals, the muscles that surround the abdominals and lie directly over the rib cage. These long, thick muscles add to the overall look of impressive abs. Regular crunches focus on the upper abdominals, but performing crunches with a twist (bringing the right elbow toward the left knee, for example) directly affects the intercostals. Perform this exercise slowly and deliberately to feel the intercostals working.

Hanging leg raises are a superior movement for building and refining the lower abdominal muscles. It takes concentration to keep the upper body steady while slowing raising the legs parallel to the floor before lowering them to the starting position. There is no better exercise to develop the lower abs. You can also perform this movement with the knees bent for similar results. As an added benefit, this exercise helps carve in separation between the heads of the quadriceps muscle.

Seated knee raises are another good movement for developing the lower abdominal muscles. Because this exercise is easier to perform than some of the other lower-ab exercises, do seated knee raises toward the end of your abdominal routine. Sit at the end of a flat exercise bench leaning back and holding on to the bench behind your hips. Raise the knees toward the chest while tensing the lower abs. This exercise also helps to add separation into the thighs.

Off-Season and Precontest Routines

Adding isolation movements to a precontest training regimen is not as easy as it sounds. Recall the importance of basic exercises to maintaining muscle mass while dieting. If you do the basic exercises plus the isolation movements, you will have too many sets in your training routine and risk overtraining. And your ability to recuperate will be hampered somewhat by your reduced caloric intake.

So how do you add isolation movements and continue training with basic exercises? To give you an idea of how to structure your training routine, take a look at the difference between my off-season and precontest routines (table 10.1).

TABLE 10.1 Off-season and Precontest Routines

Off-season		Precontest	
Chest workout 1		**Chest workout 1**	
Exercise	*Sets*	*Exercise*	*Sets*
Bench press	5	Bench press	4
Incline dumbbell press	3	Incline dumbbell press	4
Flat flys	3	Flat flys	3
Pullovers	3	Pullovers	3
Chest workout 2		**Chest workout 2**	
Incline bench press	4	Incline barbell press	4
Dumbbell bench press	3	Dumbbell bench press	4
Incline flys	3	Incline flys	3
Dips	2	Cable crossovers	3
Triceps workout 1		**Triceps workout 1**	
Push-downs	3	Push-downs	4
Decline lying extension	3	Lying triceps extension	3
Parallel dips	3	Parallel dips	3
		Lying dumbbell extension	3
Triceps workout 2		**Triceps workout 2**	
Push-downs	3	Push-downs	3
Seated triceps extension	3	Seated triceps extension	4
Bench dips	3	Bench dips	3
		One-arm seated dumbbell extension	3
Abs workout 1		**Abs workout 1**	
Incline sit-ups	3	Incline sit-ups	3
Incline knee raises	3	Incline knee raises	3
		Alternate crunches	3
		Lying leg raises	3

(continued)

TABLE 10.1 ***(continued)***

Off-season		Precontest	
Abs workout 2		**Abs workout 2**	
Hanging leg raises	3	Hanging leg raises	3
Weighted crunches	3	Weighted crunches	3
		Kneeling cable crunches	3
		Seated knee raises	3
Legs workout 1		**Legs workout 1**	
Squats	5	Squats	4
Leg extension	4	Leg press	4
Leg press	3	Machine thigh adductor	3
Leg curls	4	Leg curls	4
Dumbbell leg curls	3	Alternate leg curls	4
Legs workout 2		**Legs workout 2**	
Leg extension	3	Leg extension	4
Squats	5	Squats	4
Hack squats	3	Hack squats	4
Leg curls	4	Lunges	3
Alternate leg curls	3	Leg curls	4
Stiff-leg deadlifts	3	Stiff-leg deadlifts	4
Delts workout 1		**Delts workout 1**	
Seated military press	4	Arnold press	4
Side laterals	4	Side laterals	4
Upright rows	3	Cable upright rows	4
Bent-over laterals	3	Bent-over laterals	3
Barbell shrugs	4	Barbell shrugs	4
		Seated cable rows to neck	3
Delts workout 2		**Delts workout 2**	
Seated dumbbell press	4	Seated dumbbell press	4
Seated side laterals	4	Seated side laterals	4
High pulls	3	Cable side laterals	3
Lying side laterals	3	High pulls	3
Dumbbell shrugs	3	Lying side laterals	3
		Dumbbell shrugs	3

Off-season		Precontest	
Back workout 1		**Back workout 1**	
Close-grip pull-downs	3	Close-grip pull-downs	3
Chins to the front	4	Chins to the front	4
Barbell rows	4	Barbell rows	4
Seated cable rows	3	One-arm cable rows	3
Deadlifts	3	Seated cable rows	3
Back workout 2		**Back workout 2**	
Front lat pull-downs	4	Front lat pull-downs	4
T-bar rows	4	T-bar rows	4
One-arm dumbbell rows	3	Lying barbell rows	3
Close-grip chins	3	One-arm dumbbell rows	3
Partial deadlifts	3	Close-grip chins	3
		Hyperextensions or partial deadlifts	3
Biceps workout 1		**Biceps workout 1**	
Incline curls	3	Incline curls	3
Barbell curls	3	Barbell curls	3
		Concentration curls	3
Biceps workout 2		**Biceps workout 2**	
Dumbbell curls	3	Seated dumbbell curls	3
Preacher curls	3	One-arm dumbbell preacher curls	3
		Alternate hammer curls	3
Calves workout 1		**Calves workout 1**	
Calf raises	4	Seated calf raises	4
Standing calf raises	4	Standing calf raises	4
Calves workout 2		**Calves workout 2**	
Standing calf raises	4	Standing calf raises	4
Leg press calf raises	4	Donkey calf raises	4

The table lists two different routines for each target area, which I alternate each week so that the muscles do not become accustomed to any one routine. My normal breakdown of the target areas is: Day 1—chest, triceps, and calves, day 2—abs and thighs, day 3—rest, day 4—delts and calves, day 5—abs, back, and biceps, days 6 and 7—rest.

The only difference in my chest routines is replacing dips with cable crossovers in the second precontest workout. Pecs are a difficult muscle group for me and tend to flatten out during dieting. For this reason, I keep the workouts heavy and basic, almost identical to my off-season training.

The cable crossovers and isometric posing help bring out the striations. My precontest diet does the rest. However, if you are fortunate and your pecs grow quickly and easily, you might want to add more cable movements in place of the basic barbell and dumbbell exercises.

I add two new exercises to my triceps routine when getting ready for a contest. As with all the target areas, I perform the heavy, basic exercises first to maintain the size and thickness developed in the off-season.

With the first routine, I superset lying dumbbell extensions with parallel dips to develop the outside head of the triceps, which is very visible when the body fat is low. With the second routine, I superset one-arm seated dumbbell extensions with bench dips to help develop the separation between the three heads of the triceps muscle. I superset both of these exercises with the dipping exercises because I am not using additional weight with these movements, and it's not as exhausting as if I were supersetting two heavy movements.

For abs, it's important to add exercises to develop the total abdominal region so that the intercostals, obliques, and serratus muscles are sharp and defined. I always perform at least four ab exercises twice per week when getting ready for a contest.

The first workout always includes incline sit-ups supersetted with incline knee raises to develop the upper and lower abs. Precontest, I add alternate crunches to target the intercostals and superset them with lying leg raises, which help to further develop the lower abs and induce separation of the heads of the quadriceps.

For the second ab workout, I usually superset hanging leg raises with weighted crunches. These are basic exercises that focus on the upper and lower abdominals. When getting ready to compete, I add kneeling cable crunches, which hit the upper abs and intercostals and superset them with seated knee raises, another good exercise for the lower abs and quad separation.

Thighs are a little more complicated. The thigh muscles are very big and strong and can take a lot of work before they become overtrained. However, too many exercises or too many sets can and will lead to overtraining, so the workouts must be carefully thought out.

My standard thigh workout includes leg extensions to warm up the quadriceps and knees followed by heavy squats and leg presses to add thickness and size. Hamstrings are next, and I work them with leg curls and dumbbell leg curls.

This workout stays the same for precontest training except for the addition of exercises that will add refinement and separation by working the smaller detail muscles in the quadriceps. After the leg extensions and squats, I usually superset leg presses with an isolation exercise such as sissy squats or the machine thigh adductors. For hamstrings, I may substitute dumbbell leg curls with alternate leg curls on the machine.

Your choice of leg exercises depends on what you need. If your thighs are naturally thick and massive, you may want to eliminate either squats or leg presses and substitute for them an isolation exercise such as lunges or leg extensions. My legs are naturally thin, so I continue training them heavy with exercises such as squats and leg presses, even before a contest.

My second leg workout is similar to the first. I substitute hack squats for leg presses and add stiff-leg deadlifts to the hamstring workout. Precontest, I superset the lunges with hack squats for three sets to stimulate more separation in the quadriceps. If I don't feel up to supersetting that day, I may forgo the lunges and instead add three or four more sets of leg extensions after hack squats to achieve the same goal.

For deltoids, I substitute cable exercises for some free-weight exercises to put continuous tension on the muscle and add striations and hardness. Instead of the standard military press, I perform the Arnold press first in the exercise rotation. This movement puts more stress on the side head of the delts, which is important when getting contest ready.

I continue the assault on the medial head by doing side laterals. I usually perform drop sets on the last set or two of side laterals to blast this part of the deltoid. I may complete six to eight reps with the 55-pound dumbbells, then drop to the 40-pound dumbbells for another four to six reps.

Instead of upright rows with a barbell, I do the exercise with cables for a better pump and burn. I end the deltoid workout with the bent-over laterals I do in the off-season. For traps, I superset barbell shrugs with seated cable rows to the neck using a rope attachment. This exercise adds more detail and thickness to the upper, inner trap region.

For the second deltoid workout, I begin with seated dumbbell presses for four sets and follow this basic exercise with seated side laterals. Precontest, I add three sets of cable side laterals to further pump up the side delts and add striations and hardness. I also perform high pulls during precontest training but do a drop set the last set or two. Then, I finish with lying side laterals for the rear delts and dumbbell shrugs for the traps.

For the first back routine in the off-season program, I start with close-grip pull-downs for the lower lats then follow with chins to the front for the width of the lats. For thickness, I perform barbell rows and seated cable rows before finishing up with deadlifts. Precontest, I add one-arm cable rows and superset them with the seated cable rows.

For the second routine in the off-season, I start with lat pull-downs to the front and follow them with T-bar rows, one-arm dumbbell rows, and close-grip chins. I finish off with partial deadlifts in the rack for the low back and overall back thickness. Precontest, I superset barbell rows lying on an elevated flat bench with one-arm dumbbell rows. Instead of partial deadlifts, I may do hyperextensions or three sets of both exercises if I feel up to it.

The biceps is a small muscle and doesn't require many sets. For the first workout of incline curls and barbell curls, I add three sets of dumbbell concentration curls for the peak and development of the brachialis muscle.

For the second workout, I usually begin with heavy seated dumbbell curls and follow that exercise with preacher curls with a barbell. Precontest, I usually switch to preacher curls with dumbbells. I follow that with alternate hammer curls for the separation of the brachialis and the biceps.

For my calves, the workout doesn't change much because maintaining size is the primary goal for both off-season and precontest. The first routine includes seated calf raises for the soleus muscle and standing calf raises for the larger gastrocnemius muscle. For the second routine, I substitute donkey calf raises for leg press calf raises.

Posing Practice

In addition to isolation exercises, another way to add separation and detail to your physique is posing. The muscles attain a more refined and finished look by combining training with posing than with training alone. Posing is difficult work, especially if you've never done it before. If you plan to enter your first competition, start practicing your poses at least 12 weeks before the event.

Begin by practicing the mandatory poses. These include front double biceps, front lat spread, side chest, side triceps, rear double biceps, rear lat spread, front abdominal and thigh, and most muscular. In addition, you can practice your favorite poses that look good on your physique. Practicing the individual poses makes the muscles harder and more dense. Flexing and tensing the muscle groups is a form of isometric exercise. Natural bodybuilder Chris Faildo from Hawaii credits his extreme muscularity and hardness to the intense flexing he practices several times a day when preparing for a competition. The muscles also seem to grow into the poses when you practice them regularly. I discovered this as a teenager. I didn't look very good in many of the mandatory poses when I began competing, but the more I practiced, the more natural my body began to look in them. This applies to all poses.

But, above all, practicing the poses and flexing the muscles hard every day will help you attain the hard, defined look that usually wins first place in bodybuilding competitions. After each workout, take an extra 10 minutes to flex and squeeze the muscle group you just finished training. Attempt to hold each pose for 20 to 30 seconds to bring out the denseness in the muscle groups.

Besides posing at the gym after training, practice each evening before going to bed. The more you can do, the better your physique will look onstage. Plus the more you practice posing, the easier it will look when you finally make it to the stage. During a bodybuilding competition it's always obvious who practiced posing and who neglected it. The competitors who put in the work at home look like polished professionals onstage. Those who failed to practice make the posing look painful and embarrassing. They also don't look as hard and refined as they could have.

Cardio Training

Cardiovascular, or aerobic, training is important to a bodybuilder preparing to compete. Weight training is anaerobic; it uses primarily carbohydrate for fuel and doesn't tap into stored body fat. Although the precontest diet encourages fat loss, many bodybuilders try to speed the process by adding aerobic exercise.

Cardiovascular exercise, if performed correctly, uses stored body fat to fuel the movement. Many bodybuilders find they can eat more calories and stay bigger if they do more cardio to lose body fat. Unfortunately for drug-free bodybuilders, there are limits. Just as adding more sets and exercises is not the answer to becoming more ripped, adding more and more cardio exercise eventually leads to overtraining and causes the body to sacrifice muscle tissue for energy.

Remember, you are training hard and heavy while simultaneously reducing your calorie intake. If you add an excessive amount of cardiovascular training on top of this, you will most likely lose muscle tissue. The primary goal of a natural bodybuilder preparing to compete is to maintain as much muscle tissue as possible while losing body fat.

When it comes to cardio training for a competition, follow the advice of Chris Aceto. He says to do as little as possible to reach your goal of getting ripped and defined. It doesn't make sense to randomly perform cardio every day when three days of aerobics per week works just as well. In fact, doing cardio every other day instead of every day may even be better because you have less chance of losing muscle tissue.

Whenever I've performed too much cardio, as I did when preparing for the Natural Illinois contest in 1991, I have sacrificed valuable muscle tissue and competed looking flat and depleted. On the other hand, there have been some contests, like the 1992 Natural Mr. Universe and the 1998 Natural Olympia, when I did no cardio training and competed in the best shape of my life. Clearly, cardio training is not the be all and end all of contest preparation.

Off-season, don't do cardio training; you're working to get bigger and don't want to expend valuable calories on aerobic exercise. Plus, if you do cardio three times a week during the off-season, you will need to do it every day when getting ready for a contest. If you don't perform cardio during most of the year, then three days per week may be all you need when getting ready to compete.

If you are training four days per week in the gym, you can use your three rest days for aerobic exercise. Three days per week should be sufficient. If you find you need to do more than this, it probably means you're running behind schedule and need to lose fat fast.

Bodybuilders who use steroids or beta-agonists such as clenbuterol do not have to worry as much about losing muscle tissue during cardiovascular exercise. These drugs prevent the body from going into a catabolic state by limiting the secretion of cortisol. Cortisol is usually released when the body is under too much stress or is being overtrained. If you limit your caloric intake, train heavy and hard with weights, and then add aerobic training to your regimen every day, your chances of putting the body into a catabolic state are very good.

Of course, everyone is different, so you'll have to try the various recommendations to see what works for you. Some bodybuilders, for instance, have very slow metabolisms and must do cardio training daily to get ripped. These competitors should be very careful about losing muscle tissue.

To get the most out of aerobic training, you must perform it at the right time. First thing in the morning before breakfast or late at night several hours after your last meal is the best time because your body is running on empty at this point. As a result, the body will have to use stored body fat for energy. If you can't exercise at these times, the next best time is immediately after a weight training session. At this point, you will have depleted most of the stored glycogen in the muscle cells, and your body will also have to tap into stored body fat to power through the aerobic workout. The point of cardio is to force your body to use stored body fat for energy. You don't want to use the stored glycogen in the muscles because this carbohydrate supply is limited from dieting. If you use up this glycogen and there are no other sources of energy, the body will have to tap into the muscle tissue and steal amino acids to fuel the workout. This is a very inefficient source of energy, and it leads to lost muscle tissue.

The most common forms of cardiovascular training are walking (outside or on the treadmill), riding a stationary bike, and climbing on a stair-stepping machine. Most bodybuilders avoid more intense forms of aerobic training such as running or aerobics classes. They don't want to risk losing muscle tissue by performing such intense regimens. This type of training is too similar to the anaerobic weight training going on in the gym.

Each form of cardio training provides benefits and drawbacks, and you will have to try them to see what works for you. The stationary bike, stair-climbing machine, or running can put too much stress on your quads and flatten them. However, Mr. Legs himself, Tom Platz, used to run when getting ready for a contest. But, in addition to losing body fat, he also lost muscle size in his legs and upper body. Some personal trainers recommend running for their clients who are too heavy and want to lose size (both muscle and fat). But it's probably a good idea to stay away from running and other intense forms of cardio if you want to retain your muscle mass.

If you have naturally thick quads and want to make that area more lean and defined, you may be able to use the stair climber or bike for your aerobic training. However, even if your legs are genetically superior, you might be better off burning body fat through less intense exercise and save the muscle mass for the stage.

Cardiovascular training for losing body fat and retaining muscle tissue should last a relatively long time, but should not be too intense. If I do aerobic exercise in the morning, I try to go 50 to 60 minutes at a moderately fast pace. My favorite form of cardio is walking outside or on the treadmill. Although I live in Chicago and the weather can get pretty nasty in the winter, I still prefer walking outside for burning body fat. And if it's really cold, I have to walk fast just to keep warm!

Sometimes I do my cardiovascular training immediately after a weight training session. Because most of the glycogen stored in the muscle cells has been depleted, my workout doesn't have to be as long as it would be in the morning. After 25 to 30 minutes of walking on the treadmill, I have gotten the same benefit I would have from 50 to 60 minutes without a preceding workout.

Do not do cardiovascular training on the days you train big muscle groups such as thighs and back. This can only lead to overtraining. If your chest workout is combined with triceps and calves, that workout is also too demanding for cardio work. You can, however, combine aerobic training with the delts and calf workout on occasion. Although this workout is intense, both of these muscle groups are small, and you should have energy left when the weight training session is completed.

I am always skeptical when I hear drug-free bodybuilders talk about how they perform two or three cardiovascular sessions per day to get ripped. Because the body has only a limited supply of energy and recovery ability, doing more and more cardio will not necessarily translate into a big and ripped physique. When looking for energy to complete these workouts, the body will always start with muscle tissue before body fat. Doing cardio every day or several times per day will almost certainly force the body into a catabolic condition, making it impossible to retain all your muscle tissue while losing all your body fat.

If you are losing fat according to schedule and have plenty of time before stepping onstage, you may not even need aerobic training to get ripped. I didn't spend much time on cardio when I competed in the Natural Mr. Universe in 1992 or the Natural Olympia in 1998, and I was in my best condition for both of these competitions. I achieved this through precontest diet only and no aerobic training.

If and when you decide to incorporate cardiovascular training into your precontest regimen, begin slowly. Start with three days per week first thing in the morning on an empty stomach. This aerobic exercise, combined with the intense weight training and the reduced caloric intake, may be all the stimulus you need to slowly lose body fat.

Sometimes it is better to do more cardio in the beginning stages of the contest diet. After dieting for several months, metabolism has a tendency to increase, and continued aerobic training may be counterproductive. That's why it is good to keep records of your training, diet, body-fat percentage, and body weight. If everything shows that the metabolism is increasing and you are losing body fat at a faster rate, you may need to cut out the cardiovascular workouts altogether to prevent loss of muscle tissue.

The following are guidelines for precontest training. Follow them to develop a lean, hard, well-defined physique right at contest time.

- Train only four or five days per week. To retain the most muscle mass while preparing to compete, avoid spending every day in the gym. Reducing your caloric intake makes it difficult to recover if you are also training hard and heavy with the weights every day. To prevent overtraining, never train more than two or three days in a row without a day off. Even though you may be training a different area of the body, the body as a whole needs a day off to recuperate.

- Avoid double-split training. Forget about training twice a day (double-split training). Just as training every day is too much for the body to recover from, training twice a day leads to loss of muscle tissue because this type of training is too demanding for a drug-free body eating fewer calories than usual. Only bodybuilders using steroids could possibly hope to recover from hard training twice a day.

- Continue training heavy and hard. When getting contest ready, don't change your training strategy to easy and light. To maintain muscle, continue the type of training you did to attain it. Although your training weights may drop slightly when you reduce your calories, attempt to train as heavy as you can with good form. This is the only way to hold on to your muscle mass while dieting to lose body fat.

- Use the basic exercises. When training for a bodybuilding contest, don't forget about the basic exercises. Although isolation exercises are important for bringing out refinement and separation among the muscle groups, it's the basic exercises that maintain the muscle mass that is crucial to winning a bodybuilding contest.

- Add isolation movements. Precontest training is the time to add isolation exercises to the training routine. These exercises, when added to the basic exercises, help to striate, define, and separate the individual muscles so they stand out in bold relief when posing onstage. Perform the isolation exercises after the heavy, basic exercises. These movements polish the mass and refine the total package of the physique.

• Practice posing to bring out muscle hardness. Flexing and tensing individual muscle groups makes the physique dense and hard. You cannot attain this look through weight training and diet alone. The isometric tension involved in squeezing and flexing the muscles daily striates and refines the muscle mass.

• Use cardiovascular training as needed. To attain the lowest level of body fat, aerobic exercise may be included in the precontest training schedule. Cardio training, when used correctly, uses stored body fat for energy and helps to achieve a ripped look more quickly and easily. Be careful not to overdo cardio, however. You might sacrifice muscle tissue along with the body fat.

Proper precontest diet and training provide the physique you want for competition. Chapter 11 shows you how to develop a posing routine that will show off your physique to its advantage.

Posing Routines

Although posing the muscles is a great way to develop the hardness and muscularity necessary for winning a bodybuilding contest, a creative posing routine that accentuates your physique's strengths while minimizing its weaknesses will help you win competitions. You will perform a short and powerful routine to impress the judges during the prejudging. Later, in the evening show, you will showcase your creativity through a longer routine set to music. Unless you are in the running for the overall title, this routine is for fun and to wow the audience.

Posing is truly an art form, and when you witness someone who has mastered it, it can be moving and beautiful. On the other hand, a poorly executed posing routine with no passion or creativity can be embarrassing and even painful to watch.

Individualizing Your Routine

Because a great posing routine is the product of the bodybuilder's imagination and personal style, it is difficult to tell someone how to master this art form by following a series of steps. However, you can follow general guidelines to develop a posing routine that fits your personality and physique.

Realizing my genetic potential at age 33, the year I won the Natural Mr. Universe for the second time.

When I was a teenage bodybuilder and looking for someone to emulate, I searched through the magazines for a bodybuilder with a structure similar to mine. I really admired Franco Columbu's thickness and mass, and Frank Zane at his peak looked like a Michelangelo statue, but I knew that these bodybuilders had a different type of physique than I did. Surprisingly, the greatest bodybuilder in the world, Arnold Schwarzenegger, was the one I most resembled. Arnold had great, highly peaked biceps, and he was wide across the shoulders with a big rib cage. His thighs were a little thin compared to his upper body, but he looked great when he hit wide, sweeping poses like the front double biceps or the three-quarter back shot. When I started copying his poses, I found that I looked best in these positions, not the poses hit by Columbu and Zane.

When I reached my twenties and was competing in state and regional competitions, I started to look for other top national and professional bodybuilders who had physiques similar to mine. I admired Rich Gaspari, who was the best bodybuilder in the world in the '80s next to Mr. Olympia Lee Haney. Rich was my age, my height, and even began training at the same age that I had. However, Rich's physique was totally different from mine. He had narrow shoulders, a relatively wide waist, and short legs compared to his longer torso. I had wide shoulders, long legs, and a relatively short torso. My physique looked more like Mike Quinn, 1987 National Physique Committee (NPC) champion and a top pro bodybuilder in the '80s, and Phil Williams, the 1985 NPC Nationals winner. I watched videos and studied photos of these two bodybuilders for ideas for new poses for my routine.

The first place to begin is with the poses themselves. Choosing the correct poses is essential in eventually developing a great routine. Correct poses are those that fit your physique. A bodybuilder who is very thick and blocky, for example, is better suited to crunching, muscular poses than wide, open poses. Conversely, a bodybuilder who is wide with good symmetry should choose poses that accentuate that strength. None of the poses are bad, just right or wrong for the physique displaying them. Poses that accentuate your individual strengths will score higher with the judges and the audience.

If you are looking for poses to copy for your posing routine, look for a bodybuilder with the same type of physique as yours. For example, if you have a thick, muscular body, look at pictures of bodybuilders such as Franco Columbu and Nassar El Sonbaty. If you have a symmetrical physique, look at photos of bodybuilders such as Frank Zane and Milos Sarcev. If you are lucky enough to have a physique that combines good width and symmetry with impressive thickness and mass, then study the poses of Lee Haney and Ronnie Coleman.

Your posing routine is your opportunity to show the judges your physique to its best advantage. The mandatory poses do their best to reveal your weaknesses and flaws. The individual posing routine is your chance to show the judges what you want them to see and hide what you don't want them to see.

If you have weak arm development, don't do a lot of poses that show off your arms. This should be common sense, but it is amazing how many competitive bodybuilders do a pose because it looks good on one of their favorite bodybuilders. They are not taking into consideration how it looks on their own physique.

The best posers hide their weak points from the judges. Arnold had a wide waist, so he chose a lot of twisting poses that made his shoulders look wider and his waist smaller. Franco Columbu had a short, stocky physique, so he hit poses that showed off his muscularity and thickness. Even when doing the front double biceps, Franco crunched down on his abs to accentuate his definition and thickness rather than sucking in his waist in a vacuum position that would have revealed his lack of shoulder width.

These bodybuilders became champions because they analyzed their physiques and discovered which poses best suited them. No physique is perfect, not even that of a Mr. Olympia champion. The key is to show the judges the physique you want them to see. This takes hours of practice in front of the mirror.

Once you have chosen a series of poses, you need to put them together into a cohesive routine. Developing a posing routine is like learning a new dance like the tango or salsa. You don't start off stringing the new steps together, flowing gracefully through with no mistakes. Instead you learn one new step at a time and master it before moving on to the next. Following is a routine that I developed.

Front Double Biceps

Three-quarter Back

Twisting Back Biceps

Rear Double Biceps

Rear Lat Spread

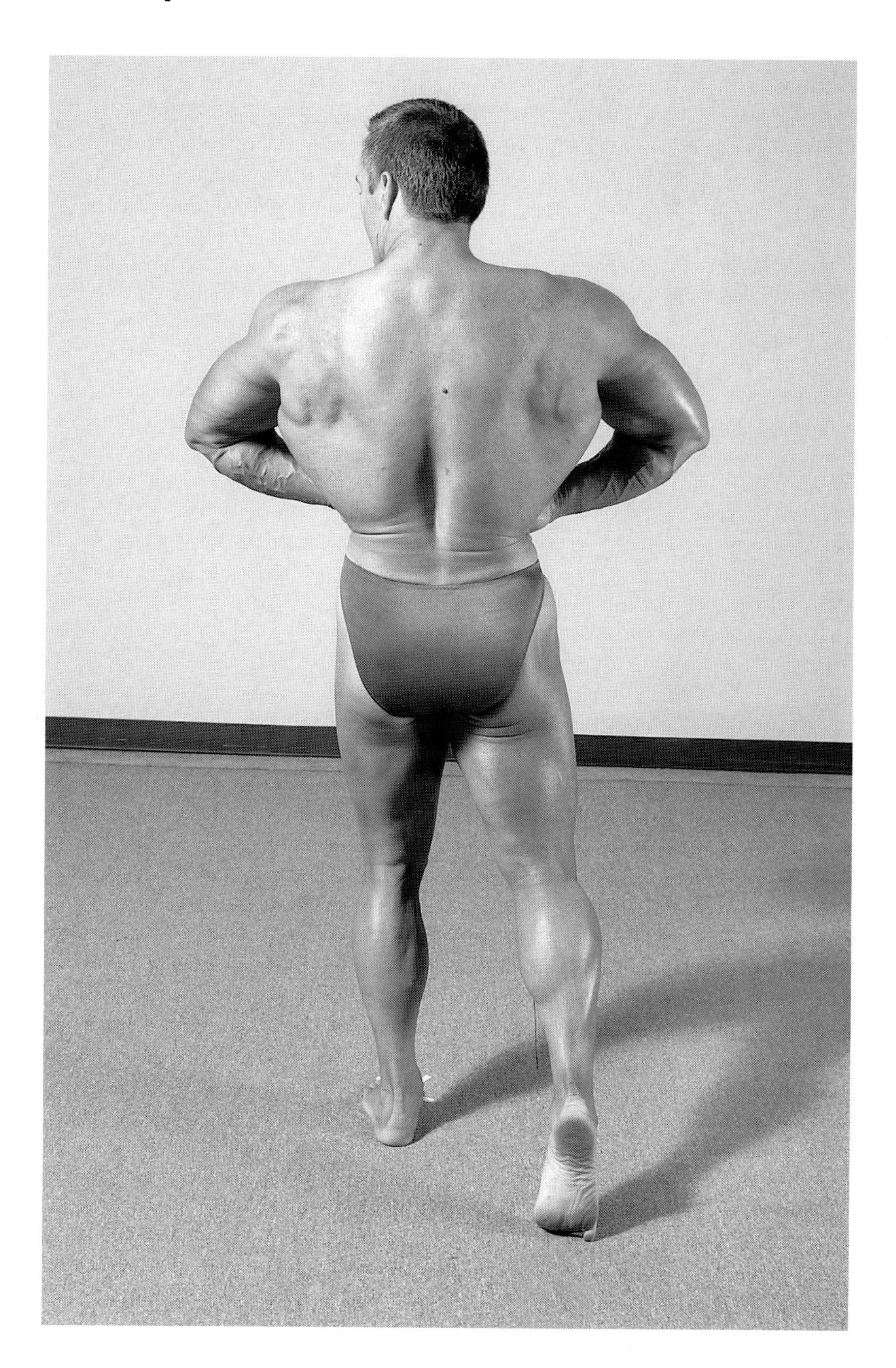

Hands-on-Hips Most Muscular

Side Double Arm

Left-side Chest

Front Overhead Abdominal

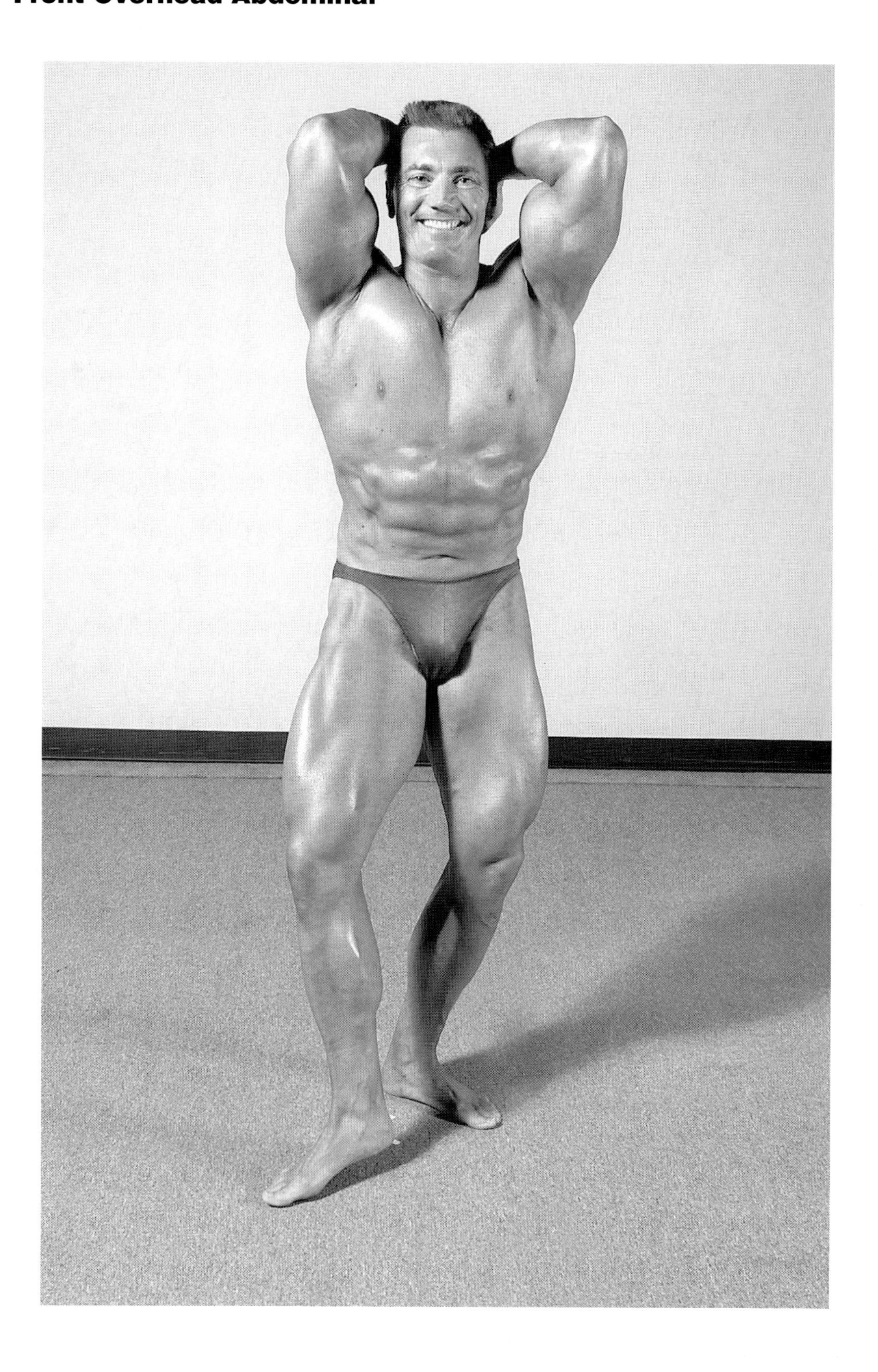

Most Muscular

Developing a Posing Routine

A good posing routine should show all four sides of the body in a variety of poses. A combination of kneeling, twisting, and straight-on poses appears much more imaginative than a series of static, straight-on poses lacking style. Each pose should flow gracefully to the next and appear effortless. It is the transitions between poses that provide the grace and style.

To develop a posing routine, select 10 to 20 poses that accentuate your physique and hide your weak points. Make sure you've included poses for all four sides of the body. If you can, include kneeling and lunging poses to show more variety. If your physique is not advanced enough to include 20 poses, pick out the best 10 or 15 so you won't have to include poses that are less flattering. The judges look at a lot of physiques during prejudging, and even if you hit just 10 poses, you want each to be so great that the judges are impressed when you walk off the stage. As your physique advances, you will be able to add poses to your routine.

After you have selected your poses you must put them into some type of order. This is where your creativity and imagination take over. The first thing to remember is not to hit too many poses in the same position. For example, if you begin your routine facing the front, don't hit more than two or three poses in this position before showing a different side of your physique. Otherwise, the judges will get bored, and your routine will look stiff and unimaginative.

One option is to develop your posing routine in a circle. Begin facing the front, move to the left side, show the back, move to the right side, and finish by facing the front again. Better yet, show all four sides in a more random order while constantly changing positions. Begin with two poses from the back, then show the left side followed by a couple of poses on the right side, then move into three poses to the front before returning to the back. This shows more variety and looks more spontaneous.

After selecting the poses and their order, it is time to work on the transitions. You can learn a lot about the transitions between poses by watching other bodybuilders pose, either at a competition or on videotape. Arnold and Franco even went so far as to take ballet classes to learn the proper transitions between the poses. You can see this at the beginning of the film *Pumping Iron.* Or watch the posing routines of master posers Ed Corney, Mohammed Makkawy, Flex Wheeler, and Shawn Ray to see how important the transitions between poses are in creating a smooth, graceful routine. How your physique looks during the transitions is as important as the actual poses. Remember that the judges watch you the entire time you are onstage.

To use the transition between poses to your advantage, create wide, sweeping arcs with your arms as you move from pose to pose instead of dropping your arms after hitting a pose and moving to the next one. Work to make the whole routine as beautiful and dramatic as possible. Remember, it's not just the poses that are important in a posing routine, but also how you arrive at each pose.

Some bodybuilders are extremely flexible or have expertise in other areas such as the martial arts or dance. If you have a special skill and want to include it in your posing routine, by all means incorporate those moves. It will add creativity to your routine and may make your presentation that much better than your competitors. Flex Wheeler does the splits every time he performs his posing routine, Darrem Charles break dances, and Tito Raymond often does a back flip at the end.

Showing off your athletic ability helps make you look like a better bodybuilder and a better performer.

The posing routine in prejudging lasts 60 seconds. Therefore, it should be short and to the point. Hit your best poses, then get off the stage.

The evening routine is usually 90 seconds long, which gives you time to use longer transitions and include other components such as dance steps or martial arts movements. It is also set to music, which makes this a totally different type of routine. Your choice of music is important. Don't pick a song just because it is one of your favorites. If this type of music doesn't suit your physique, it is not a good choice. A thick, rugged bodybuilder should not choose a soft, romantic song to pose to. (Lee Haney refers to it as "twinkle toes music.") Instead, he should choose a hard-rock song or something more powerful like the theme music from movies such as *Conan the Barbarian* or *Excalibur.*

Now it's time to coordinate your poses and music to create an entertaining and effective routine. As you're working, you may have to change the order of the poses to fit the music. Just make sure that the poses are well suited to your physique. Don't be tempted to add inappropriate poses just to fill space in the music. The music should fit your poses, not the other way around.

It's also a good idea to get input from knowledgeable people. Talk to bodybuilders who have been competing for awhile to learn the correct way to hit a pose. Find a competitive bodybuilder who is a good poser and ask for his advice. I always asked my brother, Don, for advice when making up a routine. Although Don is not a competitive bodybuilder, he is an accomplished graphic artist and understands the aesthetics of what makes a body look artistic and impressive. Bodybuilding is an artistic endeavor, after all.

After you have put together your posing routines, you must practice them over and over until you can do them in your sleep. When the contest day finally arrives, you will have a lot on your mind, and you don't want the added stress of trying to remember your routines. Practice the routines at least three times a day during the two weeks before the competition. Begin putting the routines together at least eight weeks before the contest.

It's more fun to practice posing when you are in great condition. In fact, you may find that you can add new poses as your body becomes more ripped. It's amazing how different the body looks as you get into shape. Frequent posing will also motivate you to stay on your diet. Looking at your body this often will reveal how ready you really are for the competition.

You've trained, dieted, and developed your posing routines. The work is nearly done, but there's still one critical week before your competition. Chapter 12 outlines in detail your final week preparations—what you must do and, maybe more important, what you should avoid.

Final Week Refinements

Now we come to the final week before competing. This week is crucial. Just when it seems like all the work is finished, it is time to put on the finishing touches. Failing to do this leaves you open for loss. I can tell you through experience that there is no worse feeling than to prepare for a contest all year only to blow it in the last week or even the last few days. Many bodybuilders look great as they head into competition, then do something stupid trying to get an edge and lose it all. Others are close but not quite there and decide to do nothing. They also end up losing because they lacked that final 5 percent hardness that makes the difference between winning and losing. There are many different contest diet techniques for the final days before competition. Some are essential to reaching peak condition, and others are a disaster waiting to happen.

Carbohydrate Depleting and Loading

Carbohydrate depleting and loading was very popular in the 1980s but isn't as widely practiced today. Perhaps the recent trend toward eating less carbohydrate has something to do with its declining popularity.

Critics of this program say that carbohydrate loading was originally developed for athletes who needed all the glycogen they could get to make it through grueling endurance events. Bodybuilders have no need for extra carbohydrate because they don't need lots of glycogen to make it through the prejudging at a contest. As tough as it may be to tense every muscle in the body simultaneously over and over again, the glycogen depletion doesn't compare to that of running a marathon.

The philosophy behind carbohydrate depletion and loading is to deplete the body of muscle glycogen in the first three to four days of the week of the contest, then load up on carbohydrate in the final two or three days. The depletion phase results in flat and small-looking muscles. After the loading phase, however, the depleted muscle cells suck up the extra glycogen resulting in full, skin-expanding muscles that shock the audience and judges.

Carbohydrate depletion and loading can work if the body is not overly depleted in the depletion phase, if the body does not receive too much carbohydrate in the loading phase, and if water intake is limited during the final few days when the extra carbohydrate is being consumed. As you can see, there are a lot of ifs in the equation. The question is: Is this strategy worth the risk?

In my opinion, the answer is no. To get it right, carbohydrate depletion and loading takes a lot of experimentation, and if you mess up, you may blow a whole year of preparation in only a few days. If everything works according to plan, however, how much of a difference will your physique really show? Not enough to warrant the risk, based on my experience. Let's examine what's wrong with this precontest procedure.

First is the depletion phase. Dieting itself, with its lower caloric intake and fine line between losing body fat and losing muscle mass, already depletes the body. By the time the final week arrives, you should be as lean as you can hope to be for the contest. To deplete the body by lowering your carbohydrate intake puts you at serious risk for losing muscle mass you won't be able to regain before going onstage. Why risk losing valuable muscle tissue at this point when you have already been dieting for the last three to four months?

The depletion phase is a necessary part of the carbohydrate depletion and loading scheme, but it is physically and psychologically undesirable this close to the big event. Physically, you risk losing muscle tissue, which will make you appear flat and small when you step onstage. Psychologically, you risk psyching yourself out by watching your physique disappear before your eyes only days before entering the contest.

Next is the carbohydrate loading phase. If everything works perfectly, the body overcompensates for the lack of carbohydrate during the depletion phase by storing carbohydrate directly into the muscle cells during the loading phase. This process fills the muscles with glycogen, causing them to appear full and pumped. The problem is that carbohydrate stores four grams of water for each gram consumed. If you ingest too much carbohydrate, your body will hold the excess water under the skin and over the muscles, which blurs any definition that otherwise might show.

The major difference between the carbohydrate depletion and loading technique used by professional and natural bodybuilders is that professionals use diuretics during their final hours before getting onstage. If they eat too much carbohydrate and end up retaining excess water, they pop diuretics to lose the water and show up onstage big, full, and ripped. If you're using drugs to get that rock-hard look, you don't have to worry about making a mistake. Drug-free bodybuilders, however, don't have that luxury and must do everything exactly right.

I used carbohydrate depleting and loading several times during the 1980s, and I missed my peak every time. I usually showed up holding water and appearing too smooth. I did everything you're supposed to do: I counted every gram of carbohydrate while depleting and then did the same thing during the loading phase. I wrote down and accounted for everything from Sunday until getting onstage on Saturday, but all my hard work and preparation led to disappointment because I showed up onstage in less than peak condition.

This combination of size and conditioning allowed me to win the first Natural Olympia competition in 1998.

While preparing for a contest in 1989 everything was going perfectly as I slowly lost body fat and held on to all my hard-earned muscle mass. A week out from the contest, everyone at the gym thought I was going to sweep the event because of my added mass and fullness combined with ever increasing definition and muscularity.

In order to obtain that final, winning look, I depleted and loaded carbohydrate during the last week. I was shocked when I learned, after prejudging, that I was not going to win and was in the running for third. Although I had hardened up by the evening finals, it was too late and the decision was in. I ended up in fourth place, and, after viewing photos from the prejudging, I could clearly see why. I was holding way too much water. I looked very smooth and out of shape.

One week later, I entered the National Physique Committee (NPC) Junior Nationals. I decided not to mess with the carbohydrate loading and depletion this time and simply went back to my regular precontest diet. Aside from cutting back on fluids the last few days before the event, I didn't alter my diet, including carbohydrate consumption. As a result, I competed eight pounds lighter and made a miraculous transformation in only one week. I had the same physique that I had had the previous week, I had just lost the excess water and was able to reveal the muscularity hidden beneath all that fluid.

For the 1998 Natural Olympia win, I cut back my carbohydrate consumption at the beginning of the last week and was planning to increase carbohydrate consumption at the end of the week. But thankfully, I was not able to because I was in a foreign country (Greece) and was unable to obtain the food I needed. As a result, I showed up in the best shape of my life. Had I increased my carbohydrate consumption as originally planned, I probably would have held water and risked losing the contest.

In contrast to the carbohydrate depletion and loading technique, Chris Aceto, a top nutrition expert for many amateur and professional bodybuilders, advises drug-free bodybuilders to "carb down" during the last week of competition. He advises eating a moderately high amount of carbohydrate during the beginning of the week and tapering off as the week progresses toward the competition. The high carbohydrate level at the beginning of the week prevents the muscles from flattening. And the low level right before competition prevents water retention.

Sodium Loading and Depleting

Another contest preparation technique is sodium loading and depleting. Similar to the carbohydrate technique, this method tries to trick the body into shedding more sodium than usual. This leaves the body in a dry condition, with no excess water under the skin, which is a great condition for a competitive bodybuilder to be in.

Similar to carbohydrate loading and depletion, you must count every gram of sodium you take in during the loading and depleting phases. Although this technique looks good on paper, applying it in the real world often doesn't work. Again, there is too much room for error. The problem with this technique is timing. If you don't deplete the sodium in time, you will walk onstage holding water. But if you get rid of the sodium too far ahead of time, your body will respond by holding on to the remaining sodium, which results in the same same water-logged condition.

The problem with sodium loading is that you are also supposed to drink lots of water during this phase, which leads to even more water retention. Sodium holds water outside the muscle cell instead of inside, which makes you look smooth and fat. When you cut back your water intake the last few days before competing, some of the excess sodium may remain in the body because you're not taking in enough fluid to flush it out.

Intentionally loading the body with sodium only days before competing creates too big a risk that you won't eliminate the excess water in time. However, you can cut out foods with sodium two or three days before competing. Wait until the last 48 to 60 hours before the contest to cut sodium so your body will not have enough time to respond by holding on to excess sodium that will retain water. Instead you'll achieve the dry and hard look necessary for winning first place.

Small changes in the amount of carbohydrate or sodium in your diet in the week leading up to competition will not hurt. But making big changes in an attempt to perform a miracle on your physique will rarely give you the results you expect and may even ruin the condition that you have worked so hard for. Do not change your carbohydrate intake if your diet is working and you are in peak condition. You can increase carbohydrate slightly in the last two days, if you also decrease your water intake. Don't load sodium early in the week. Keep doing what works, then in the last three days before competition eliminate foods that contain high amounts of sodium.

I have entered several competitions where I didn't manipulate my sodium intake and, although my body fat was very low, I still lacked the hard look that would have given me victory. However, the two competitions where I attained my hardest condition were the 1992 Natural Mr. Universe and the 1998 Natural Olympia. For both of these contests, I began cutting my sodium intake on the Wednesday before the Saturday event. Up until that time, I was still eating egg whites for breakfast and dressing on my salads. Three days before the contest, I cut those foods and replaced the egg whites with chicken breasts. Nothing I ate during those last three days contained high amounts of sodium.

Before I began depleting sodium, I didn't intentionally increase my sodium intake, I just kept things the same. I ate the same diet that last week that I had during the precontest dieting phase. Cutting out sodium the last three days was enough of a change that my body responded by eliminating any excess water it may have been holding.

Water Intake

The last precontest diet technique concerns water intake. Bodybuilders typically drink gallons of water every day when preparing to compete. Although water accounts for a big percentage of muscle cell volume, too much water, just as too much carbohydrate, can spill over into the subcutaneous space between the muscle and the skin to create a smooth appearance. This spillover occurs when sodium holds water outside the muscle cell and underneath the skin. Decreasing water intake in the last two days before competing makes the skin tighter and gives the bodybuilder the "Saran Wrap skin" that wins competitions.

Opinions vary on whether to drink or not drink water as the contest draws near. Berry De Mey, the great Dutch professional bodybuilder, forced himself to drink two to three gallons of water the day before competing. He believed that this high volume of water acted as a natural diuretic and eliminated the excess water his body may have been retaining.

In the 1980s, the bodybuilders from Hamarz Gym (where I trained) completely stopped drinking water three days before competing. I did this a few times back then. However, this is an extreme practice and can be very dangerous. I definitely don't recommend dehydrating the body and would never do it again. Besides, if you diet correctly, there is no reason to follow this risky dehydration technique.

Some bodybuilders use a hydration technique in the last week of preparation that is similar to carbohydrate and sodium loading. During the first part of the week you drink twice as much water as usual, then cutt back drastically in the last two or three days before the contest. The theory, of course, is that the body keeps eliminating water at the same rate it was forced to eliminate it in the first part of the week, resulting in a dry, hard physique by the time of the contest.

However, just like the carbohydrate and sodium depletion and loading theories, this constitutes too big a change from the norm and opens up the body to error. Drinking twice the amount of water normally consumed is too dangerous because you run the risk that you won't eliminate the excess fluid in time.

Cut back on fluids in the last two days before the contest. If you cut back before this, your body will respond by holding on to the water in the body. Two days seems to be the ideal amount of time to tighten the skin and eliminate subcutaneous water. Totally dehydrating yourself is too dangerous and may flatten the muscles and dull your vascularity. You want to be dry, but you also want to be full and pumped.

Follow your precompetition water intake until Thursday evening (if prejudging is scheduled for Saturday morning). At this point, begin cutting back. On Friday, you can sip water throughout the day but limit it to no more than a cup of water per meal. This is pretty tough when you have been swallowing gallons of water per day, but it is this sudden change that will eliminate excess fluid under the skin.

Continue this fluid deprivation until prejudging is over. You will be as dry as can be and craving water. You can drink enough water to satisfy your thirst, but not as much as you normally do. Hold back until the evening show is finished. The little bit of water you allow yourself to drink after the prejudging normally will pass immediately through the body if you continue to stay away from the sodium.

You must approach sodium and fluid deprivation carefully because eliminating either of these substances too far before the contest will cause the body to hold on to either the sodium or the water. If you time it right, however, you should be able to eliminate all excess water and leave the body in a dry, hard condition.

Final Week Schedule

Putting it all together, here is how you should approach sodium, carbohydrate, and water in the last week of dieting:

- Sunday, Monday, Tuesday: Eat the normal precontest diet; drink the normal amount of water (two and a half to three gallons).
- Wednesday: Begin cutting back on sodium. Substitute turkey or chicken breasts for egg whites, and eliminate salad dressing and other condiments that contain high amounts of sodium. Continue drinking the same amount of water to help flush out sodium. Continue eating the same amount of carbohydrate.
- Thursday: Continue eliminating sodium. Begin cutting back on water intake after 5 p.m. Sip a cup of water with each meal. Avoid or cut back on water between meals. If you feel you are flat, eat more low-glycemic carbohydrate and cut back on protein.
- Friday: Continue eliminating sodium and cutting back on water intake. Don't eat too much carbohydrate, but eat a higher percentage of carbohydrate than protein.
- Saturday: Eat a low-sodium breakfast containing protein and complex carbohydrate. Sip water throughout the day up until going onstage.

The key to getting ready during the week before competing is not doing anything that will mess up the hard work you have put in to get in condition. Cut back on the sodium and water to tighten the skin, and slightly increase carbohydrate intake to fill out the muscles and increase the vascularity. If you've done everything right, you should be in awesome condition the week before the show and should only need to fine-tune your contest-ready physique. By week's end you will be ready to compete. The next chapter walks you step-by-step through the day of the competition.

Prejudging, Finals, and Posedown Tactics

Finally, it's here: contest day! This is the day you've been training for these last few months, perhaps even the whole year. If you're like me, you probably won't sleep that well before competition day. Remember how hard it was to sleep the night before Christmas when you were a kid? That's usually how I feel the night before competing. But knowing what to expect and how to take care of the details can help you stay relaxed and confident.

Preparing for the Big Day

Before breakfast, prepare food to take with you to the contest. This won't be anything exciting, just some dry chicken or turkey breasts along with dry sweet potatoes or dry brown rice. You'll eat these protein and complex carbohydrate minimeals every couple of hours to keep your blood sugar level steady. Some bodybuilders go crazy on the last day and eat loads of simple carbohydrate so they can fill out and get a great pump when they get ready backstage, but you might want to play it safe and not risk losing the dry, hard look you've worked so hard for. There will be plenty of time to eat after the contest is over.

Besides the risk of losing that ripped look on contest day by eating lots of simple carbohydrate, there is also the uncertainty of when you will finally get onstage. Many competitions include lots of different divisions (men's open, women's open, men's novice, women's novice, mixed pairs, teenage, masters, and more). If you are entering a competition similar to this, there is a chance you will sit around all day waiting to get onstage. If you eat foods containing high amounts of simple sugar, you risk creating a yo-yo effect in your blood sugar level. This could seriously affect your ability to pump up when it comes time to get ready. Therefore, stick with your regular diet on the day of the competition.

After getting your food ready, eat breakfast before heading to the competition. A good precontest breakfast is dry chicken breasts and oatmeal with a banana or blueberries on top. Don't drink anything, but you may sip water after the meal. Another breakfast option is to mix a couple of servings of low-sodium protein powder into your oatmeal. The point is to get some low-glycemic food into you to get your very important day started.

When you are done with breakfast, pack your gym bag. Include a couple pairs of posing trunks (just in case something happens to the pair you plan to wear), a big towel and a small towel (for pumping up), oil or Pam cooking spray, two identical cassette tapes of your posing music (just in case the first one is lost or destroyed), and some simple carbohydrate food to eat right before going onstage.

Wear your posing trunks to the contest with loose workout shorts over them and a T-shirt. Over this wear sweat pants and a tracksuit top or an extra-large sweatshirt. Basically, just wear whatever feels comfortable but I would recommend wearing clothing that hides your physique so you are keeping your competition wondering what you look like underneath the clothes. Black is my favorite color for a bodybuilding prejudging because it gives the illusion that I am much smaller than I actually am. This helps in the psyching out process that is usually a part of any bodybuilding contest.

Arriving at the Contest Site

It is important to arrive at the contest site early. You want to avoid the added stress of missing the check-in or having to sign up late. If you arrive early and things are running behind (as they usually are), just stay cool and find a place to sit and relax and wait for the check-in process to begin. I like to remain as inconspicuous as possible before the real action begins.

Psyching out and psyching up usually accompany the prejudging at any bodybuilding event. Many competitors are very uptight during a competition. Bodybuilding is a unique sport because it is directly concerned with what the human physique looks like rather than what the body can do. For this reason, competitive bodybuilders tend to be very serious and not as relaxed as some other athletes in other sports may be. Most people, after all, are somewhat self-conscious about their bodies, and bodybuilders are no different. They compete in an event where they will display their bodies for evaluation, so it's no wonder they are uptight.

Some bodybuilding competitors dress to show off their physiques while walking around during the check-in. They do this, of course, to pump up their own egos and, hopefully, psych out their opponents. This can be a double-edged sword, however. Many competitors and even some judges look down on this display. As a result, this competitor might be taken less seriously than he had hoped. It's always better to dress conservatively and save the physique display for the stage.

At the check-in and during the pumping-up process, it's very important to keep in mind that the only thing that counts is how you look onstage. It is easy to let yourself get psyched out if you concentrate on how impressive everyone else looks. Backstage, when everyone is pumped and oiled up, almost everyone looks great.

After you've checked in, you will most likely have to sit around and wait for the time to pump up before going onstage. This waiting period could be several hours depending on how many competitors there are and where your event is scheduled in the lineup. As with the check-in process, the best course of action is to find a nice place to relax and wait until it is your time to perform. Eat one of your small meals every two and a half to three hours to keep your blood sugar level steady. Sip some water if you need to, but stay dry for the most part.

I remember competing in the National Physique Committee (NPC) Southern States contest in 1987 and being blown away by how huge everyone looked in the lobby during check-in. At only 5 feet, 8 inches and 208 pounds, I was competing with some real monsters, and it was hard not to feel inadequate. Things only got worse when we went backstage to pump up. The heavyweight class was filled with huge guys, bodybuilders who were much taller and bigger than I was. I remember having a hard time pumping up because I kept bumping into all the huge bodies crammed into the backstage area.

I solved the problem by retreating to a smaller dressing room and pumping up there with my brother Don. After getting properly pumped and oiled, I went back to the bigger dressing room where all the heavyweights congregated. I smiled to myself because I couldn't help but notice that a lot of the bodybuilders in the room were now looking at me, wondering where I had come from. They didn't recognize me as the bodybuilder in the black tracksuit. I ended up taking second place, beating all of the huge bodybuilders (except one) who looked so intimidating earlier.

What I learned from that contest is that it is always better to concentrate on your own physique than to worry about your opponent's. It's easy to psych yourself out if you look at your competitors when they are pumped and oiled up backstage. But it's up to the judges to determine who has the better physique. That's not your job. Your job is to present your physique to the best of your ability to the judges, the audience, and, yes, your competitors. If you have done your homework and are well prepared, eventually everyone will take notice.

Arnold Schwarzenegger, however, believed in the opposite approach. Arnold said that you should concentrate on your physique during the year but when it comes time to compete, it's time to concentrate on your opponents' physiques. Arnold actively engaged in psychological warfare with his competition, letting them know that he was going to win and there was nothing they could do to defeat him.

If you have this type of personality and want to try this game, be prepared for the same reaction from your opponents. You could end up with egg on your face if your "psyched out" opponent ends up defeating you when the results are announced. In my opinion, it's better to let your physique do the talking.

No matter what approach you use, however, it is important to display utter confidence throughout the day of the competition. From the moment you arrive at the auditorium, you need to act like a winner. This includes checking in, pumping up, and finally getting onstage. Walk with your head high and think like a winner. Believe me when I say that your opponents and the judges will take notice.

The head judge will most likely announce when it is time for your class to go backstage to begin getting ready. Prejudging is usually conducted in three rounds, and, depending on the size of the classes, you will probably have to go backstage during the second round of the class before yours. It's best to stay in the auditorium so you will know when you need to go backstage. The lineup could change suddenly if the promoter or judges decide to switch things around.

Many bodybuilders eat simple sugar before going backstage to pump up. This provides a quick rush to the muscles so you can get a greater pump before going onstage. Some bodybuilders eat candy bars or drink soda, but many of these foods contain sodium, and, if you have been cutting back on sodium the last few days, your body may respond by holding water later in the day. The best foods before pumping up are fruit preserves or baby food. Check the label to make sure they are low in sodium. Also avoid foods that contain fat or sodium because they slow the digestive rate. You want pure sugar that will quickly get into the bloodstream to increase vascularity and get into the muscles immediately.

Pumping Up

When you get the word to go backstage for prejudging, proceed with the other competitors and begin pumping up. Some bodybuilders get caught up in the excitement backstage and begin doing a full workout. This is not necessary and will probably wear you out before you even walk onstage. Remember, the winner is not the one who pumps up the hardest backstage, just the one who looks the best onstage.

Keep your warm-up suit on while pumping up and gradually take off clothes as the time to go onstage gets closer. You don't want to reveal too much too soon; you want to keep your opponents guessing how your physique looks. You can even try to find a private area to pump up in to keep your physique hidden from your opponents until it is time to go onstage. When I competed in the 1992 Natural Mr. Illinois, I pumped up in the foyer of the women's bathroom, a place none of my opponents thought of going. My strategy worked because everyone in my class was wondering where I was, and when I walked backstage at the last minute, all pumped up and ready to go, I shocked many of them. This was a big psychological edge for me.

To begin pumping up, start with push-ups for the chest and barbell rows for the lats. You can also do light barbell military presses for the delts and barbell curls for the biceps. Perform all of these exercises with very light weights for about 15 to 20 reps. After you get a good pump going, take off your warm-up jacket and continue pumping up with your T-shirt and sweatpants on. Eventually, the sweat pants will come off. About five minutes before lining up, take off the T-shirt and shorts and begin oiling up.

I usually avoid conversation with the other bodybuilders and keep to myself. If you have a friend who can help you pump up, this can provide a psychological edge. This person can help you focus on getting ready for the contest and avoid focusing on your opponents. It also gives the impression that you are someone special because you have people helping you to get ready. It creates an atmosphere of a winner.

The last thing you want to do before lining up is apply your oil. Oil gives your muscles the sheen they need under the bright stage lights. Well in advance of contest day, experiment to determine which type of oil looks best on your physique. Some bodybuilders use standard baby oil, but this can create too much shine if you apply too much. I've always used peanut oil. The sheen isn't as harsh as standard baby oil. When using the tanning preparation, Dream Tan, I can't rub any type of oil on my body, so I spray Pam cooking oil on the muscles instead.

When you line up to go out onstage, remember to walk tall and display an air of confidence to the audience and judges. This should not be hard to do after all the hard work you have put into getting ready. Stand with the muscles tensed and hard, but keep smiling and look relaxed and confident.

Prejudging

The prejudging at a bodybuilding competition is, essentially, the whole contest. Although it is not as popular as the evening finals, this is where the judges decide the outcome of the competition. If you do not give your best effort at the prejudging to look the best you can, you will probably place poorly.

Except for the professional competitions held by the International Federation of Bodybuilding (IFBB), which judge during the prejudging and the evening finals, all of the assessments at a bodybuilding competition are conducted at the prejudging. The evening finals are merely a showcase for the competitors to perform their posing routines for the audience before the judges announce the final places and give out the awards. The only exception is when deciding the overall winner. After all the individual class winners have been announced at the evening finals, the judges compare each class winner against the others to decide who has the best physique in the contest.

Because the prejudging is so crucial to how you place in a competition, it is critical that you understand exactly what the judges will ask you to do and how you can look your best during the judging process. The more you compete, the better you will perform onstage. There is no better teacher than experience. However, knowing what to expect and being prepared before you step onstage will go a long way toward helping you to present your physique at its best.

Round One: Standing Relaxed

The first round of the prejudging is the relaxed round. The judges compare you to the other competitors when you are standing relaxed to the front, from the side, facing the rear, and then from the other side. They look for a combination of size, symmetry, proportion, and definition in your physique compared to your opponents.

The first position is standing to the front. Keep your lats flared, your abs hard and tight, your quads flexed, and your shoulders high and squared. Try to look as relaxed and natural as possible in this position. Your posing practice at home will pay off when you finally get in front of the judges on contest day.

The next position in the relaxed round is standing relaxed from the side. In this position, flex the arm that is facing the judges, keep your chest high, and flex the abs and intercostals hard. You would be surprised how many bodybuilders fail

Standing relaxed to the front.

Standing relaxed to the side.

to practice this position and end up losing ground with the judges right at the beginning of the judging.

The next position is standing relaxed from the rear. Keep the lats and lower back flexed with the arms flared out to the sides. It is also important to flex your glutes, hamstrings, and calves. This is one of the hardest positions to hold because so many muscle groups are on display.

The next position is standing relaxed from the other side. Just like the second position, flex the arm facing the judges, keep the abs and intercostals flexed, hold the chest high. Another trick is to push the leg farthest from the judges into the leg closest to the judges. This makes the leg facing the audience look bigger than it actually is because you are pushing the hamstring with your other leg.

Before you return to the starting position facing the judges, make sure your quads are flexed and your abs are tight. Be careful not to show yourself to the judges until you are ready. You are only in front of them for a limited time, and

Standing relaxed from the rear.

they must move quickly to make their decisions. Therefore, you need to be prepared every second you are onstage.

At this point, round one is finished, and you and your class will be led offstage. The second round consists of each bodybuilder coming back onstage individually to perform his own posing routine for the judges. If you were one of the first bodybuilders in line for round one, you need to be ready to go back onstage soon, so be careful that you don't wander too far away. If you're not ready when they call you, you may not be disqualified, but it will make you look bad in front of the judges. If you were one of the last bodybuilders to line up in round one, you have time to pump up a little bit more or apply more oil if you need it.

Round Two: Individual Posing Routine

In round two each bodybuilder performs his or her individual posing routine for the judges. The time limit for each routine is usually 60 seconds. Many bodybuilders use the same routine that they plan to perform in the evening. The evening posing routine is usually 90 seconds and uses music you have selected. If you use the same routine during the prejudging, but without music and 30 seconds shorter, it will not be the same. For this reason, you need two different posing routines, one for the prejudging and one for the evening show.

For your posing routine for the prejudging, choose 10 to 12 of your best poses and put them together into a graceful, flowing routine. Because the third round of the prejudging consists of the mandatory poses, try to choose other poses for this round, unless, of course, some of the mandatory poses are your best options. For example, the front double biceps and rear lat spread are two of my favorite poses, so I always include them in my individual routine even though they are mandatory.

When you come out to perform your individual posing routine, begin with one of your best poses, continue the routine, finish with your best pose, acknowledge the audience and judges, and walk off the stage. If you've done it right, you should finish the routine before the 60-second time limit elapses.

Round Three: Mandatory Poses and Comparisons

The final round of the prejudging is the comparison of the mandatory poses. The head judge will ask the lineup to strike the mandatory poses together. This is when the judges make their final comparisons before handing in their score sheets. This is the most competitive part of the prejudging because the judges are comparing you directly to your competition.

Every competitor is required to do a number of mandatory poses so that the judges can compare the bodybuilders in the lineup. These poses show every part of the body from the front, both sides, and the rear. The mandatory poses expose any weak areas or structural flaws. Mastery of the mandatory poses is essential to winning bodybuilding competitions.

The first mandatory pose is the front double biceps. Perform this pose facing the audience with your feet shoulder-width apart. Raise your arms to shoulder level and flex the biceps. As with the rest of the prejudging, remember to keep your quads flexed, you abs flexed or sucked in, and your lats spread during the pose.

Practice this pose frequently before competing. You may want to stand with your legs bowed out or maybe with one leg straight and the other slightly bent. Same with the arms—you may look better with the arms straight out, or you may look better with the elbows raised slightly above parallel. You must experiment with all of the mandatory poses to determine which position looks best on your body.

The front double biceps pose shows the judges more than just your arms. They look for the differential between the width of your shoulders and your waist. They also look to see that your biceps are in proportion to your triceps and that your pecs are in proportion to your lats. They check out your legs to see if they are in proportion to your upper body. Finally, they look at the overall definition of your body. This pose opens up the body from the front and makes it difficult to hide weaknesses.

Front double biceps.

The next mandatory pose is the front lat spread. Keeping the legs flexed, grab the sides of the waist with each hand and the elbows pulled back. As you bring the elbows forward, spread the lats and flex the pectoral muscles. Hold the chest high and the waist sucked in as you spread the lats. Don't bring the elbows too far forward. They should be in line with the upper body in the finished position. Keep the legs bowed out in this pose. The front lat spread is a straight-on pose, unlike the front double biceps, where you can tilt or twist the body to add more symmetry and grace. Keep the chest up and the shoulders wide as you spread your lats to show the judges your width.

In this pose, the judges look to see if the overall width of the upper body is in proportion to the legs. They look at the thickness and definition of the pecs in comparison to the width of the lats. Finally, as with all the mandatory poses, they look for the overall definition and hardness of the body.

Front lat spread.

The next mandatory pose is from the side. The side chest pose showcases the thickness of the pectoral muscles, the arms, and the shoulders. If your left side faces the judges, grab your left wrist with your right hand and pull your right forearm under your rib cage while simultaneously bending and flexing your left arm and crunching the pectoral muscles. Your left leg should be bent and flexed to show the hamstring and calf muscles.

There are two methods for performing the side chest pose. You can lift the rib cage, showing the depth of the upper body, or you can flex the abs and the intercostals, creating more of a crunching pose. If you have thick, full pecs and a big rib cage, the first pose suits your physique the best. If, on the other hand, you have excellent abs and intercostals and are not blessed with a wide, deep rib cage, the second method may be better for you. Try both versions to see which one suits you. With both methods, make sure that the arm not facing the judges (the right arm, in this example) pushes the pectoral muscle to press your pecs together.

Flex the calf of the leg facing the judges by lifting the heel of the left foot and pushing the ball of your foot onto the stage. Push your left leg against the right leg (the leg not facing the judges) as you flex the calf. This displays your left hamstring muscle.

Side pose, lifting ribcage.

Side pose, flexing abs.

In the side chest pose, the judges look for the size and thickness of the pectorals, biceps, and deltoids. They also look for the proportion of the hamstrings compared to the quadriceps muscles, something they cannot determine when looking at the body from the front. The judges also check to see if the calf muscles are in proportion to the upper leg. Some bodybuilders look great in the first two front mandatory poses because they have impressive width, but they do not look as good from the side if they lack thickness.

The next mandatory pose is from the rear. The rear double biceps is extremely important because it showcases the entire back side of the physique including the arms, back, hamstrings, and calves. Many bodybuilding contests are decided by this pose because it shows the muscle groups that many bodybuilders neglect: hamstrings, calves, and the back. It also reveals the condition of the competitor because it highlights the glutes, hamstrings, and low back—areas that are usually the last to lose body fat.

Rear double biceps.

To begin the pose, put one foot back and flex the calf, hamstrings, and glutes. Make sure to tense the other leg also. Raise the arms above the head and slowly bring them down into a double biceps pose. Unlike the front double biceps, keep the elbows pulled back to flex the muscles of the upper back properly. Squeeze the upper back muscles by bringing the elbows way back and then bringing them back in line with the shoulders. Bringing the elbows back highlights the thickness of the upper back muscles; bringing the elbows forward shows the width and definition of the back.

Keep the arms parallel to the floor in the finished position of the rear double biceps. Tense the biceps hard and don't forget to keep flexing the hamstrings, glutes, and calves. This pose takes a lot of practice because there are many muscle groups to keep tight at one time. When practicing this pose at home, use a mirror so you can see the back. Make sure your arm position displays the back muscles to their best advantage. Practice this position so many times that when you hit the pose onstage, you will automatically do it correctly.

With the rear double biceps pose, the judges look to see if the development of the physique from the rear is equal to that from the front. It's amazing how different some bodybuilders look from the rear compared to the front. Sometimes they look like they have two different physiques.

The judges look primarily at the back muscles. They check out the width and thickness of the lats, as well as the muscularity of the upper back and traps. They take note of the development of the deltoids and the arms from the rear, as well as the hamstrings, glutes, and calves. The judges also check the bodybuilder's condition by looking at the hardness and definition of the low back, the hamstrings, the upper back, and the arms.

The next mandatory pose from the back is the rear lat spread. This pose highlights the width of the latissimus dorsi muscles. Many bodybuilders have a difficult time mastering this pose, but the ones who do it well always inspire applause and admiration from the judges and audience.

To properly execute the rear lat spread, begin with the same leg position as the rear double biceps pose. Put one foot back and flex the calf while simultaneously tensing the hamstrings. Grab the sides of the waist with the hands while bringing the elbows to the rear. Slowly bring the elbows forward while spreading the lat muscles. Bring the elbows as far forward as they can go to fully demonstrate the width of the back.

With the rear lat spread pose, the judges look for proportion between the width of the lats and the waist. They also look for the development and hardness of the calves, hamstrings, and glutes. Learning to do this pose properly is important because there will almost certainly be other bodybuilders onstage who cannot, and you will look all the better if you are one of the few who can.

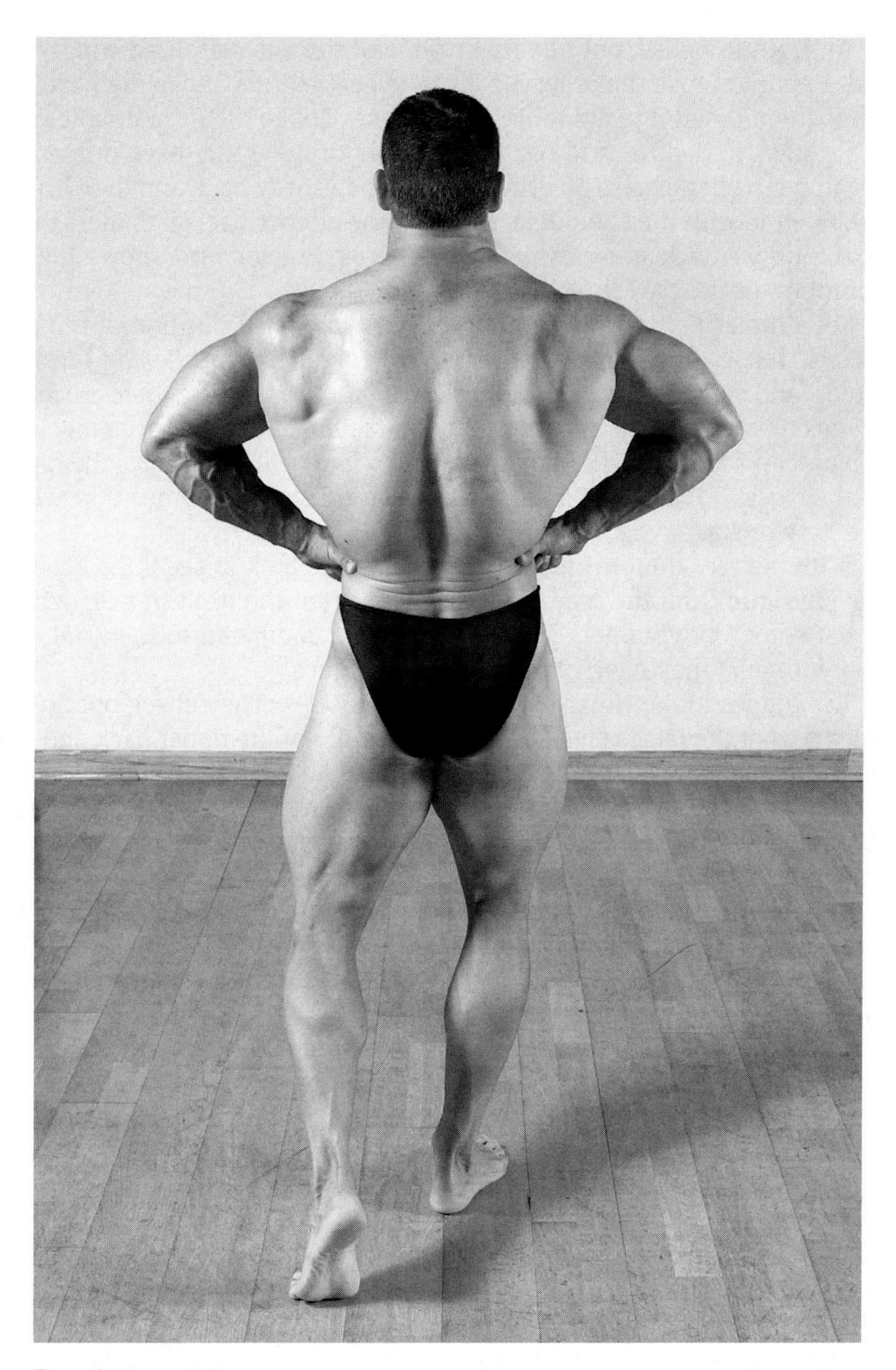

Rear lat spread.

After the rear lat spread, make a quarter turn to the right for the side triceps pose, which highlights the development and shape of the triceps muscle. This position displays the thickness of the muscles in the same way the side chest pose does. The judges look for complete development of the physique; that includes thickness and width. Practice this pose often at home to show your physique to its best advantage when you finally get onstage. Sometimes just a slight twist at the waist makes this pose look more impressive.

Side triceps pose.

To properly execute the side triceps pose, cock the leg facing the judges to show the hamstring and calf muscles. If your right side faces the judges, grab your right hand with your left arm behind your back. Lock your right arm and flex the triceps muscle hard. Flex the intercostals and abs and twist slightly to show them to the judges. Keep the shoulders high; don't dip them down. Keep the abs and intercostals tight; the judges look at the whole picture.

With the side triceps pose, the judges look at the development and shape of the upper arms, specifically the triceps. They also look at the size and condition of the deltoids, chest, quadriceps, hamstrings, and calves. They check out the abs and intercostals for sharpness and definition, and the balance between the legs and the upper body.

After the side triceps pose, face the front for the abdominal and thigh pose. More than any other mandatory pose, this one shows the judges the condition you have achieved for the contest. Because it is one of the last mandatory poses, many judges make their final decisions based on it. The abdominals are a ripped bodybuilder's trademark, and this pose highlights the abs more than any other.

To properly display the physique in the abdominal and thigh pose, begin with the legs. Extend your best leg forward and flex the quadriceps muscles. Some bodybuilders look better in this pose by locking the leg in front, while others keep the knee slightly bent, displaying more of the inner thigh by cocking the knee out to the side.

Once the legs are in position, place your hands behind the head with the elbows facing the ceiling. Crunch down hard on the abdominals to highlight the abs, intercostals, and serratus muscles. Keep the legs flexed and keep the lats as wide as possible by holding the shoulders up. The crunching nature of the pose causes

Overhead abdominal.

some bodybuilders to slouch forward. Although this flexes the abs, it spoils the overall look of the body. Keep the upper body straight and don't slouch.

With the abdominal and thigh pose, the judges look at the overall condition of the body, which they judge by looking at the abs. They also look for the development and separation of the quadriceps muscles. They judge the proportion of the shoulders and the waist and the development and width of the lats. Mostly, the judges look at the definition and condition of the body as a whole.

The last mandatory pose is the most muscular. The most common form is the hands-on-hips most muscular. To properly perform this pose, place your best leg forward and tense the quadriceps while placing both hands on the hips right below the pelvis. Bring your elbows slightly forward and tense the pecs, delts, arms, and abs to display the size and muscularity of the upper-body muscles. This pose shows the condition of the body because the front of the body is on display for the judges to analyze.

Hands-on-hips most muscular.

Crab most muscular.

The judges may also ask for a crab most muscular. This is most bodybuilders' favorite pose and an audience pleaser. To perform this pose, place your best leg forward and tense the quadriceps muscles. Bring your arms in front of you with your fists clenched (as if you were punching your hands together), bend your upper body slightly forward, and flex the pecs, arms, and traps. This pose showcases the thickness and muscularity of the upper body, particularly the pecs, arms, delts, and traps.

In both most muscular poses, the judges look for the thickness of the upper-body muscles. The hands-on-hips most muscular shows the abdominals more than the crab most muscular, but both poses help the judges determine your condition. They also look to see that the upper body is in proportion to the legs, and they check to see if the pecs, delts, arms, or traps are out of proportion to each other.

When doing the mandatory poses with the rest of your class, be sure to listen to the instructions from the head judge. Sometimes the head judge calls the poses out of sequence during the comparison poses, especially near the end of the prejudging. Watch the other competitors and hit your pose when they hit theirs. You don't want to hit your pose too soon, giving your opponents the opportunity to hit their poses a few seconds later and make a greater impact. Give yourself enough time to hit the pose correctly to show off your physique to its best advantage and hit it at the same time as your competition.

After the mandatory poses are completed, the judges often move competitors to make side-by-side comparisons. This is common in classes with a lot of competitors. If there are 10 or more bodybuilders in a class, the judges may ask five bodybuilders to step forward to do the mandatory poses together while the other bodybuilders stay in the back. After they are done with these five, they will ask the other bodybuilders to step forward to do the same comparisons. Even though the final placements are not announced until the evening show, you should have a good idea of where you will place based on whom you are compared to during the prejudging.

At very large competitions like the NPC Nationals or NPC USA Championships, the judges determine the top 15 bodybuilders after the individual posing routines. Only these top 15 are allowed to continue on to the third round. The other bodybuilders go home.

Of those 15 bodybuilders, the first five called to the front for comparisons in the mandatory poses are most likely the top five in the class. The next group will be judged from 6th thru 10th, and the final group will be judged from 11th to 15th.

If you are in a large class and are not one of the top-five bodybuilders called forward, don't show too much disappointment. If you pose with enthusiasm and energy when you are called to the front, the judges will notice, and some may change their scores after seeing your physique. Of course, your physique is the deciding factor, and if you don't have one of the top-five physiques that day, then that's just the way it goes. There will always be another competition. But the point is never to show defeat to the judges, no matter what happens. Keep your attitude upbeat and positive, and the judges will remember you, even if you don't make the top five this time.

However, don't be afraid to show appropriate emotion and passion during this round of the prejudging. This is your last chance in front of the judges to show them what you've got. This is also the only time of the prejudging when you compete directly against your rivals. If you have a better muscle group than the bodybuilder next to you, don't be afraid to flaunt it and show it off to your advantage. This is my favorite part of the competition. Bodybuilding is not a contact sport, so this part of the competition is as physical as it gets (not including the posedown).

After the head judge dismisses your class, wave your hand to the judges and audience and walk off the stage. The most difficult part of the competition is over. Go backstage, put your warm-up suit on, and leave.

Between the Prejudging and the Night Show

After the prejudging, you should have a good idea of where you will place. It's also a good idea to bring along friends who are knowledgeable about the sport. They can watch the show from the audience and give you input afterward. But remember that it is difficult to find friends who will be honest with you. They might tell you that you will win easily when, in fact, you're destined for fifth place. Only the judges know for sure, but someone with an eye for bodybuilding should be able to approximate where you stand.

I was fortunate to have my brother Don at the prejudging for many of my competitions. He had a good eye for physiques and was brutally honest when telling me where I would end up. Because he was almost always right on the button, it was hard to take when he told me I wouldn't win. But when he thought I would win, I was confident I would go home with the first place trophy.

The course you take before the evening show is determined by what happened at prejudging and where you think you will place. If it's all over, go eat at a restaurant and relax until you have to go back for the evening show. If you are a top contender, however, stay on your diet and do whatever you can to get better before you go back onstage. If you need to get fuller, eat more. If you need to get harder, take a sauna, run with a sweat suit on, cut your water intake, or pose continuously until the muscles begin to harden. If you need to get darker, apply several more coats of tanning agent. If you have no idea where you will place in the contest, take the cautious route and stay committed to your diet until the show is over. There's no sense blowing months of preparation by going to a restaurant and pigging out prematurely. You never really know what's going to happen at night until it happens. No matter where you think you'll place, go through your posing routine a few times before evening show. This keeps the muscles pumped and gives you confidence.

Standing Out in the Finals

The finals, or evening show, of a bodybuilding competition is for the bodybuilding audience more than the prejudging is. By the time the evening show arrives, all of the judging (except for the final comparisons for the overall winner) is finished. Sometimes a promoter warns the competitors at the end of the prejudging to stay on their diets because the judging was really close. However, judges rarely, if ever, change their votes during the evening show. Promoters make this announcement because they want to prevent the competitors from pigging out and looking terrible at the night show. They want the competitors to be in top shape so they can put on a good show for the audience. The truth is that the judging is all over.

By the time you arrive for the evening finals, you should have applied more tanning solution if your "tan" has faded since the prejudging. You want to be dark enough for the stage lights. You may also choose to change your posing trunks for the night show. A different color gives you a new look and may provide an edge that will make an impact on the judges if you end up in the final posedown for the overall title.

Usually the competitors are required to attend a meeting before the evening show to make sure everyone is there for the finals. The promoter and emcee need to know if anyone has dropped so they don't announce a competitor who isn't there. At this time the promoter announces any changes to the lineup. It is not unusual to change the order of the contest if a fitness competition is being held along with the bodybuilding contest. Therefore, you need to pay attention to where your particular contest is in the schedule.

Be prepared for a long wait. Depending on how many contests are scheduled and where your contest is in the lineup, you could wait several hours before going onstage. You might not get onstage for your posing routine until well past 10 p.m.

Continue with your regular diet through the finals. Eat right before you leave for the night show, and bring something like dry turkey or chicken breasts and a dry sweet potato in case you feel you need more food before you pose. About 15 minutes before you get ready to pump up, eat a simple sugar like a couple of teaspoons of fruit preserves.

Watch the evening show from the audience so you will know when you need to go backstage to begin getting ready. If the promoter did not announce a change, your contest should be exactly where it was in the lineup during the prejudging. When you arrive backstage, be prepared for a more hyped-up atmosphere than you encountered during the prejudging. Most of the competitors will have family and friends attending the evening show who were not there during the day. Also, many of the competitors will have a good idea of where they will place. Even those who didn't fare well will be psyched up to go out and give their best for the appreciative audience. The nervousness is out of their systems and they are ready to show everyone what they have.

The evening show is more relaxed. The work of the prejudging is over; all that is left is to go out and pose for the audience. If you are in great shape (or if you have a lot of friends and family in the audience) expect a much louder reception from the audience at the evening show. This is what you have worked so hard for, so enjoy it. Have fun and let the audience and the judges see that you are having fun.

Strategy and Tactics for Posedown

All the competitors in your class will be backstage after everyone has finished their routines. The emcee will announce the top-five competitors in the class, and the expeditor will make sure that the correct competitors go back onstage. Most promoters bring the top five onstage in order for a posedown. Sometimes, however, a promoter skips the posedown and announces the top-five places while the competitors are standing offstage.

The posedown is one of the most exciting parts of a bodybuilding contest. In a nonphysical sport such as bodybuilding, this is as physical and competitive as it gets. In the posedown, all five finalists hit their best poses to show off their physiques. Often bodybuilders move around the stage or step in front of other competitors. One may even challenge another competitor, following him around and copying him pose for pose.

There are different viewpoints on how you should conduct yourself during a posedown. Bodybuilders such as Frank Zane and Chris Dickerson believe it is a mistake to follow other competitors around the stage, challenging them to different poses. They believe the best strategy is to stay in one place, hit your own poses, and let the other bodybuilders come to you. Other bodybuilders, such as Mike Quinn, believe in moving around the stage openly challenging other bodybuilders. The audience loves this and often cheers for their favorites.

I follow Zane and Dickerson's advice. I do my own poses and don't follow anyone else around the stage. However, I do move around and let other bodybuilders follow me. This gives the audience and judges the impression that you are the leader and the other competitors are following your lead. If another bodybuilder attempts to copy the poses I am doing, I may match him and make a show of it for the audience, or I may start posing faster in an attempt to screw him up. This is a strategy that Arnold Schwarzenegger used against Lou Ferrigno at the 1975 Mr. Olympia posedown.

Sometimes, the pushing and shoving at a posedown can get out of hand. This can be dangerous because you have a bunch of depleted, hungry bodybuilders who may feel edgy and aggressive. I've never seen a fistfight, but it's always a possibility. I once pushed a competitor who kept shoving his arm into my face. I quickly regained my composure after I pushed him away, but I almost lost it for a second. However, most of the jostling is in good fun, and the audience gets into it. As a competitor, it's good to act aggressive and have fun, but always keep the reaction of the other competitor in mind before you start pushing someone around onstage.

No matter how long a posedown lasts, never stop posing while you are onstage. You don't want to look like a quitter or someone who isn't hungry for the title. Although this part of the finals is not judged, the judges are still watching you. Even if you don't win your class that evening, there will be other contests, and if the same judges are doing the honors, you want them to remember you favorably. Act like a winner every second you are onstage.

After the posedown, the emcee announces the final placings, beginning with fifth place. If you have made it this far, congratulations! No matter what place you end up with, act like a true sportsman onstage. Again, the judges and audience are watching your every move. If you place lower than you think you should have, you will be the bigger man or woman if you act with dignity and grace. Even if the judging was flawed, you will only make things worse by acting up onstage, throwing a tantrum, or being a bad sport.

Bodybuilding judging is subjective. Sometimes, as a competitor, you may feel that there is a conspiracy against you, but believe me, there isn't. Chances are, you were not quite as good as you or your friends thought you were. Another possibility is that you did not present your physique as well as some of the other competitors did. Often, bodybuilders could have placed higher if they had been darker, posed better, or used more (or less) oil. There will be other contests, so don't ruin your reputation by creating a bad image onstage when your place is announced.

There is also the possibility, of course, that you will win the contest! For a natural competitive bodybuilder, there is no better feeling than winning a contest against your peers through training intensely, eating correctly, and presenting yourself well. When you get to the winner's platform, you will vividly recall the difficult workouts, the deprivation of the diet, and the conquest of your weak areas that brought you to this point. You did it, not the steroids, the diuretics, or the growth hormone, only you! This is what the sport of bodybuilding is all about, and you should be proud to be a winner.

Index

Note: Information contained in photographs, tables, or figures are indicated by an italicized *ph, t* or *f*.

About the Author

John Hansen has been a natural bodybuilder for more than 27 years. He has competed in more than 35 bodybuilding competitions and won numerous drug-tested international titles, including Natural Mr. Universe (professional division) and Natural Olympia (professional division). He has won first-place titles in many other competitions including Natural Mr. North America, Natural Illinois Bodybuilding Championships, Illinois State Bodybuilding Championships, and Mid-America Bodybuilding Championships.

Since 2000 Hansen has been a regular contributor and columnist for *Ironman* magazine, in which he advises readers on every aspect of drug-free training and nutrition.

Hansen lives in Westmont, Illinois.